Who's in the Driving Seat?

THE DRIVING INSTRUCTOR'S GUIDE TO
CLIENT-CENTRED LEARNING

Ged Wilmot & Claire Wilmot

Active Driving Solutions Ltd.
1 Falcon House, Falcon Business Centre, Victoria Street, Chadderton, Oldham, OL9 0HB, UK

www.activedrivingsolutions.com

This edition first published 2018 by Active Driving Solutions Ltd.

Copyright © 2018 Ged Wilmot & Claire Wilmot

All rights reserved. No part of this publication may be reproduced, stored in a retrieval system, or transmitted, in any form or by any means (electronic, mechanical, photocopying, photographing, recording or otherwise) except as permitted by the UK Copyright, Designs and Patents Act 1988, without the prior permission of the publisher.

Permissions may be sought from the publisher at the above address.

The right of Ged Wilmot & Claire Wilmot to be identified as the authors of this work has been asserted by them in accordance with the UK Copyright, Designs and Patents Act 1988.

This book is sold subject to the condition that it shall not, by way of trade or otherwise, be lent, resold, hired out, or otherwise circulated without the publisher's prior consent in any form of binding or cover other than in which it is published and without a similar condition being imposed on the subsequent purchaser.

Disclaimer:

Although the authors and publisher have made every effort to ensure that the information in this book was correct at the time of printing, the authors and publisher do not assume and hereby disclaim any liability to any party for any loss, damage, or disruption caused by errors or omissions, whether such errors or omissions result from negligence, accident, or any other cause.

The advice and strategies found within this book may not be suitable for every situation. This work is sold with the understanding that the authors and publisher cannot be held responsible for the results accrued from the advice in this book.

Cover design by Ged Wilmot
Cover photo by Barry Mellor - www.barrymellorphotography.co.uk

ISBN-13: 978-1979038102

ISBN-10: 1979038104

This book is dedicated to all the fantastic driving instructors around the world who are committed to doing their very best to keep our roads safe.

CONTENTS

Preface .... **xiii**

    Why we wrote this book xiv
    Ged's story xvi
    Claire's story xxi

Acknowledgements .... **xxv**

Introduction .... **xxvii**

    What is this book about? xxvii
    Who is it for? xxvii
    A note on terminology xxviii
    How to use this book xxviii
    Your FREE online bonus content xxviii
    Will I learn anything new? xxix
    Chapter and appendix summaries xxx

Chapter 1: Why Drivers Crash **1**

    Why do drivers crash? 2
    Root cause 1: Attitude and beliefs 4
    Root cause 2: Driver distraction 8
    Root cause 3: Physiology 14
    Root cause 4: Perceptual limits 20
    Root cause 5: Inexperience 24
    Root cause 6: Absolving responsibility 25
    Pre-driver-age education has failed us 26
    Road safety campaigns and public information films 27
    The National Driver Offender Retraining Scheme 28
    Adapting our current teaching methods 28
    Points for reflection 30

Chapter 2: Coaching 31

What is coaching? 32
The origins of coaching 35
Defining coaching..36
The coaching spectrum 37
Why coaching?..38
How coaching can help develop safer driving for life................42
Nine fundamental principles of coaching 43
Raising awareness..51
The "Learning Ladder"...55
Self-reflection 61
Developing responsibility 63
Is coaching always the answer? 68
Instruction: Instructor-led 68
Coaching: Learner-led 70
When coaching doesn't work..71
Remaining non-directive is unrealistic 71
Sticking to the learner's agenda isn't always the best strategy 72
Don't be afraid to break out of the comfort zone 73
Beware of the fun factor 75
Your feedback is vital..76
Points for reflection 78

Chapter 3: An Introduction To Client-Centred Learning 79

The origins of client-centred learning......................................80
Is client-centred learning the same as coaching?......................80
The DVSA's definition of client-centred learning 83
Instructor-centred teaching vs client-centred learning.............84
A blended approach 87
How to decide which approach to use 88
The client-centred ADI..94
Points for reflection 96

Chapter 4: The 5 Key Skills Of A Client-Centred Instructor..... 97

How we communicate 98
Key skill 1: Rapport 99
Key skill 2: Active listening 106
Key skill 3: Asking questions 112
Key skill 4: Feedback 123
Key skill 5: Intuition 132
Points for reflection 134

Chapter 5: What Does A Client-Centred Lesson Look Like? ...135

The active learning agreement 136
The structure of a client-centred lesson 139
Step 1: Identify development goals 140
Step 2: Prepare 146
Step 3: Responsibility agreement 147
Step 4: Practice and self-evaluation 148
Step 5: Reflection and debrief 150
Reflective logs 150
Points for reflection 160

Chapter 6: Learning Styles 161

Theories and models 162
We're all unique 163
Learning preferences are contextual 163
Be aware of your own learning preferences 165
Seek feedback 165
Visual aids 166
Storytelling 170
Discussions 172
Demonstrations 173
Talk through 174

Experiential learning 176
Role reversal 178
Commentary driving... 179
The GROW model... 182
Mind mapping 187
The role model technique 192
Befriending thinking.. 193
Perceptual positions... 194
Gibbs' reflective cycle 196
Scaling 197
Points for reflection 204

Chapter 7: Addressing Limiting Beliefs.............................. 205

What is a "belief"? 206
Performance-interfering thoughts (PITs)................................207
Faulty thinking patterns..209
The ABC model 211
The Belief Window.. 214
The impact of our beliefs 215
Performance-enhancing thoughts (PETs)............................... 216
Cognitive behavioural coaching 217
Useful coaching techniques to dispute limiting beliefs............220
Become curious...223
And if all else fails 223
Points for reflection 224

Chapter 8: Dealing With Negative Attitudes 225

What are attitudes and how are they expressed? 226
The Belief Window and driver attitude...................................227
Where do our attitudes come from?..229
Paying attention to our learner drivers' attitudes....................230
How to deal with negative driver attitudes 234
React calmly..236

> Be a role model 237
> React towards the issue, not the person 237
> Understand where the belief stems from 238
> Rationalise the behaviour of the other person 239
> Explore the potential consequences of road rage 242
> Don't treat everyone else like they're an idiot 244
> Look for positive examples of good driving/riding 244
> Reframe the situation 246
> Act "as if" 248
> It all comes down to choice 250
> Who am I? 250
> Points for reflection 251

Your Next Steps… 253

Keep In Touch 255

Appendix A: Useful Coaching Scenarios 257

> Passengers 257
> Children 264
> Music 268
> Mobile devices 272
> Route planning 277
> Different road types 279
> Time of day 282
> All-weather driving 284
> Emotional and physical state 286
> Extra skills 289

Appendix B: Goals For Driver Education Matrix 293

About the Authors 295

References 299

PREFACE

"The greatest risk for a young lady is being a passenger in a car being driven by a young man."[1]

Why we wrote this book

Lots and lots of people are dying on our roads every year. Yes, we know that's not the most uplifting start to the book, but in a nutshell, this is our WHY. We both came into the driver training industry at the age of just 22 with a bold desire to make a difference. By that age, we'd already seen our fair share of bad driving. We'd read all the stories about teenagers crashing their cars and killing their girlfriends, boyfriends and best mates. We even knew people who'd been involved in fatal crashes. So, perhaps rather naïvely, part of our "drive" to become driving instructors was that we wanted to help stem the tide of death on the roads.

Have we succeeded? Well, we'd like to think that we've made a difference, yes, no matter how small that difference is. You're making a difference, too. You work every day to help people learn a new skill. You help people gain confidence and independence. You assist in creating safe and responsible drivers. And we'd like to thank you for that because the people you teach are sharing the road with our loved ones.

On 16 March 1935, Mr Ronald Beere was the very first person to pass the driving test (scan this QR code or visit **http://gedclai.re/ronald** to see his story). That same year, there were 2.4 million vehicles on the road and 7,343 road deaths.[2] Comparing that to 2016, where we had 37.3 million vehicles and 1,792 road deaths, we can see that although we have more than 15 times more traffic, road deaths have dropped by more than 75%.[3,4] While this is an incredible achievement, 1,792 road deaths per year are still 1,792 too many. That's almost five people every day, each of whom is someone's mum, dad, brother, sister, son, daughter or best friend.

Every time we see another fatal news story online or on the television, it breaks our hearts. Surely there *must* be more we can do to help stop the carnage on the roads? Vehicle safety and engineering are improving year on year, enforcement has been tightened up, but in many ways, education doesn't seem to advance at the same pace. Driving instructors play a vital part in the road safety puzzle, which is exactly where you fit in.

Some have asked us what inspired us to write this book for driving instructors, so we'll now share our individual experiences which brought us to this point.

Ged's story

About 20 years ago, I was teaching a 17-year-old called Carl — not his real name — to drive. Carl was one of those lads who always wore a baseball cap on back-to-front; his tracksuit bottoms were tucked into his socks, and he had a pair of Rockport boots on his feet. A variety of gold chains adorned his neck, he had LOVE and HATE tattooed on the knuckles of his hands, and a huge, fake Rolex watch hung off his arm. If you remember fashions back as far as the end of the last century, then I'm sure you have a pretty good image of Carl in your mind!

I didn't enjoy teaching Carl. In fact, I hated it, not because of what he wore, but because of his attitude. To put it mildly, this guy was an absolute nightmare. Every Monday morning, I'd look at my diary and see his name on the page; immediately my mood would slump, and I'd dread the day ahead. On the rare days when Carl was already up, and his dad wasn't screaming at him to get out of bed, he'd come out of his house, slam the front door behind him and swagger over to my car. He'd casually nod at his mates as he sauntered over, and they'd often egg him on to wheel-spin my car away from his house, or something similarly stupid.

As Carl sat down in the driving seat, he'd routinely scoff at its upright position and wind it back until it was practically horizontal. After debating how precarious his driving position was and negotiating something we were both reasonably happy with, he'd start the engine and rev it a couple of times to show his mates what a rebel he was. Sometimes, in an effort to impress them, Carl would try to set off like an Exocet missile to look ultra-cool. On better days, he'd stall the car, and his mates would fall about laughing. I was never entirely sure how 'cool' Carl thought he could appear when driving a bright yellow Nissan Micra with L-plates, but he certainly tried anyway.

Carl had serious attitude issues. He seemingly had no concept of danger whatsoever. He treated driving like a game, and I was always nagging away at him: "Slow down, Carl"; "Too fast"; "Start braking"; "No, that gap's not big enough for us to get through"; "Wait … Wait … I said WAIT!" The last straw was when, during a mock driving test, he tried to "beat" an oncoming car when turning right at a set of traffic lights. I remember watching him staring up at the red light, gas and biting point at the ready, thumb poised on the handbrake button, ready to shoot off and beat the car opposite. By this stage, I could read Carl like a book. As the lights turned to red and amber, Carl dropped the handbrake and went for it, just as I anticipated. I stopped the car with my dual controls before he could swerve across the path of the oncoming car. He flipped. "WHAT THE HELL DID YOU DO THAT FOR?! For ****'s sake! I could have easily made that. You're doin' my ******* head in, mate!"

After asking Carl to pull over, switch off the engine and hand over my car keys, I gave him a lecture about the dangers of his driving. I explained how his poor attitude and desire to take risks could not only result in him crashing and killing himself but someone else, too. It was evident from his body language that I wasn't getting the message through to him, so I decided to end his lessons right there and then. I couldn't cope with him any longer. He walked home.

Later that day, I had a phone call from Carl's dad, begging me to continue teaching him. Apparently, I was Carl's third instructor, and the only one he'd ever got on with. I tried to explain my concerns about Carl's dangerous attitude and behaviour to his dad, but he didn't really seem bothered. I wasn't surprised by this, since I'd also seen Carl's dad's driving. It was obvious where Carl got his attitudes and beliefs from. I told him that if Carl wanted me to carry on teaching him, he'd need to call me himself. I wanted to help Carl, but I needed to know that he was prepared to listen.

A couple of hours later, I got that phone call. Carl grunted what could loosely be described as an apology, and, after a few more stern words, I agreed to see him through to his driving test. He was on his best behaviour from that day onwards. Carl failed his first driving test for — guess what — not making progress! He passed on his second attempt. When we arrived back at his house, he grunted, "Cheers" and got out of the car to tell his mates the great news.

As I drove away from Carl's house, I felt a range of emotions. On the one hand, I felt an enormous sense of relief — no more Carl on Monday mornings! On the other hand, I felt scared when I wondered what he'd be like on the road without me nagging away at him to slow down every few seconds. I was convinced it was only a matter of time before he got a speeding ticket or crashed his car.

Sadly, I was right.

About six months later, I opened the local newspaper to see Carl's face staring back at me. He'd knocked down a four-year-old girl close to his home. She was in a critical condition in intensive care. Her parents were at her bedside praying for their little girl to live.

Carl had been driving while under the influence of alcohol and without insurance. The Serious Collision Investigation Unit estimated that his vehicle had been travelling at least 10-20mph above the speed limit when the crash happened.

I was devastated. I cried. I felt responsible. My mind raced: "Did I teach Carl correctly?"; "What more could I have done?"; "Why wouldn't he listen to me?"; "If someone better than me had taught him to drive, this probably wouldn't have happened."

I felt like giving up, but I didn't.

I'm glad I didn't quit. Over the following months and years, I slowly began to accept that Carl's crash wasn't all my fault and that, in fact, I'd taught him as best as I could with the skills and resources I had available to me at the time.

Since then, I've used the experience to make me a better instructor and shared the story with my trainee instructors so that they can learn from it, too. I'll always feel partly to blame for what happened because I didn't succeed in changing his bad attitude or behaviour. I don't think my rants and lectures at the roadside made the blindest bit of difference, but back then I had no other tools in my toolbox.

I'm confident that I could do a much better job now. I have many more methods and techniques at my disposal today. I've taken some truly transformational courses, read some amazing books and listened to some inspirational speakers. They've all taught me a great deal about how people learn, where beliefs come from and how to promote change. I now feel confident that if I taught another Carl, I would do a much better job.

Carl's story inspired me to start writing this book. I never want another ADI to have to go through what I went through. More importantly, I don't want any more parents to have to sit at their child's bedside praying for their life. Fortunately for Carl, the little girl survived, but many other children involved in similar crashes don't make it.

Is our industry's movement towards a more client-centred approach going to solve all these problems? No. But do I believe that it could make a difference and save lives? Most definitely.

Coaching and client-centred approaches are not a "magic bullet", but I believe that they're empowering to both learners and instructors, and are a substantial improvement on techniques we've used in the past.

In the coming chapters, we'll provide you with tools and techniques to help you and your learners get the most out of your lessons. I know it's an old cliché, but we're not here to just get people through their driving test, we're here to help our learners become *safe drivers for life*.[5] I don't believe that traditional teaching methods do this effectively enough. I've seen transformational change in the people I've worked with, using the techniques in this book. I've seen ADIs who have come to life when they find out how to coach and become more client-centred. I've seen their learners thrive, too.

In addition to having provided ADI coaching workshops to ADIs across the UK and Northern Ireland, Claire and I regularly offer one-to-one sessions to ADIs, helping them to understand the benefits of coaching and client-centred approaches. The feedback we get is consistently positive, so, simply put, we know this works. As we believe that time and money shouldn't get in the way of becoming the best ADI you can be, Claire and I decided to write this book for the PDIs and ADIs who, for whatever reason, can't attend our one-to-one sessions.

I sincerely hope that this book becomes an essential addition to your collection. Whether you're a trainee driving instructor or someone with years of experience under your belt, I'd like to think that this book will help spark ideas that will help you become an even more amazing driving instructor than you already are.

Ged

Claire's story

As a parent, I was stunned when I once heard a presenter at a conference tell the audience that "The biggest killer of young women is the young man who was driving the car when she died." He was referring to the frequency at which teenage girls are killed when passengers in a car powered by a teenage boy — often their boyfriend. I know it will be only a few years until our daughter will be travelling as a passenger in a car with other teenagers.

So how can Ged and I minimise the risks of one of our children becoming a statistic? It will probably be highly embarrassing if we offer driving assessments to any of their friends that come to pick them up! Black box technology could help make our children more mindful of their own driving. Encouraging them to use driving apps that block calls and messages might prevent the worst happening. Is all this enough? Probably not.

Road safety education started from as early as two years old with both of our children, when we used coaching methods to help them learn how to cross the road safely. I vividly remember standing at the pavement edge with our daughter, waiting to cross the only road we needed to cross to get to her nursery school. "You tell me when there are no cars, Faith." We stood there on a quiet road for what felt like 40 minutes! After several gentle reminders to tell me when there were no cars, she looked and said, "No cars, Mummy."

We continued our roadside routine every day. The time we spent stood at the side of a near-empty road gradually decreased as time went on. I never decided for her, and I always tried to make sure she didn't see me check if it was safe too. She rarely misjudged. I was amazed at how good she got at looking out for vehicles, even ones turning in at the end of the road, just in sight.

Both our children not only became aware of how big a gap they needed to cross, but also learned to watch for drivers and look for signs that they were allowing them to cross, and how important it was to get eye contact with the driver. They became responsible for their safety when crossing the road, and I trusted them, too.

Our son, Charlie, was just six years old when he walked home from school, *alone*, whilst I'd managed to get distracted chatting with some of the other mums in the school playground. Although we only lived a couple of minutes' walk away from the school, I went into full-blown 'panic mode' when I realised he was no longer in the school grounds. I looked everywhere and called his name, then crossed the road and ran home to see if he was there. As I reached the driveway, I could see him waiting patiently by the front door. I was *so* relieved to see him. I asked him why he'd walked home without me, but I couldn't be angry with him when he looked up at me with pride and said, "But I looked properly, Mummy, and I made sure it was safe."

If I'd ever needed evidence that coaching raises awareness and increases responsibility, this was it.

Every day, on the school run, everyone seems to be in a rush. I watch other parents and children. Often, the parents hold the hand of their child, look both ways and guide their child across the road, the child not looking, but trusting that their mummy or daddy has made sure it's safe. Sometimes, children dart off, and parents shout for their child to stop before they run out into the road. The parents are the risk managers, not the children. But what if the children became the risk managers?

If they can be this responsible for themselves at such a young age, surely, they can be responsible at 17 behind the wheel of a car? The thought of ever losing either of our children in a car crash fills me with fear and dread, and spurs me on to try to reduce the chances of it ever happening. I firmly believe that using coaching techniques throughout our children's lives, up to and beyond 17 years of age, is one way we can make a difference. It's one of the main reasons we wrote this book.

I hope you find this book useful in your quest to become a better driving instructor. In the process, I'm certain you'll find the techniques not only helpful for the in-car teaching environment but also your everyday life as a friend, partner or parent. You're only here on this planet for a relatively short amount of time, so make the most of it, be kind and help others. Choose to make a difference.

Claire

ACKNOWLEDGEMENTS

To our wonderful children, Faith and Charlie. Thank you for all your understanding over the last few years. You've been so patient while Mummy and Daddy have locked themselves away in the office writing this book. Now it's finished, we promise to stop replying, "In a minute!" whenever you want us for something. You are our world.

To Claire's parents, thanks for giving us time to work on the book, your support with childcare has been invaluable and very much appreciated!

To Ged's parents, thanks for making Ged the man he is today. Ged's dad, who passed away in 2010, always wanted to publish a book. He spent years writing a novel, but the onset of dementia cruelly took away his ability to complete it. We feel blessed to have had the opportunity to have completed ours — we know he would have been very proud.

Thanks to the late, great Sir John Whitmore, whose work has been a real inspiration to us both. It was a great privilege to meet John in person and learn from him. We shared several early-morning phone conversations where we brainstormed how to bring coaching to the fore in the driver training industry. His legacy lives on in all those that worked with him.

To our lovely friends, Janine and Sarah, thank you for taking the time to read our book in its raw format with probably double the words than in this edited and improved version! Big thanks to Phil Hirst and Lou Walsh, who helped fine-tune our final edit. All of your constructive feedback has been enormously helpful.

To our editor, Dani Brushfield-Smith, who helped us bring our book to fruition. We're so grateful you were able to come to our rescue after we were so badly let down by someone else we trusted with it.

Thank you to Baz Mellor for the book cover photography and to Amy Bradley and Jamey Du Plessis for your wonderful illustrations. To Andy Gibney of 3P Publishing, who helped with our back cover blurb — we really appreciate your help.

Huge gratitude goes to Professor Jonathan Passmore, from whom we learned lots about coaching and how to apply it to driver training. His course, presented at the University of East London, provided us with lots of tools to use in driver training, many of which feature in *Chapter 7: Addressing Limiting Beliefs*. Thanks also to Dr Lisa Dorn of Cranfield University for supplying us with helpful information and resources.

To Jacqui Malpass, a brilliant book writing coach, we appreciate you sharing some great tips with us on how to better structure our book to help engage the reader more effectively.

Thank you to the amazing Tamara Monosoff, who inspired us with so many elements of this book, especially all the interactive features like the QR codes and personal chapter introduction videos.

Thank you to Lou Walsh, for sharing her experiences and techniques on mind mapping in *Chapter 6: Learning Styles*.

To our amazing life and business coaches, Kate Trafford and Jay Allen: Kate, thank you so much for all your encouraging support and guidance, especially when the enormity of this project seemed to be insurmountable; and Jay, thanks for kicking our arses when we needed it. In the time it's taken us to add the final touches to our book, you have written two books in their entirety. Your dedication and ability to "get **** done" is a real inspiration!

And last, but by no means least, thank you to our dear friend and fellow driving instructor, Kathy Higgins. Without that evening in the Metal Box Club in Liverpool, where you introduced us to each other, there would be no Ged and Claire!

INTRODUCTION

What is this book about?

This book explains the principles of coaching and client-centred learning — why they work, how you can quickly adopt them, and the benefits they will bring to your learners and to your business. By the end of this book, you'll have the knowledge, skills and confidence to use coaching and client-centred techniques in your work as a driving instructor.

Who is it for?

The book is primarily for Potential Driving Instructors (PDIs) and Approved Driving Instructors (ADIs) who work with learner drivers. Whether you're just starting out on your training to become an instructor, or you already have years of experience under your belt, you'll find this book very relevant.

Driving instructor trainers will also find this book extremely beneficial in preparing their PDIs for the Test of Instructional Ability (Part 3), as well as improving the skills of qualified ADIs in time for their Standards Checks. Now that both tests have been brought in line with the National Standard for Driver and Rider Training, it's essential that PDIs and ADIs fully understand the concepts of coaching and client-centred learning.

Even if you don't work with learner drivers, trainee instructors or qualified instructors, there are still plenty of useful insights for you, too. We've both been DVSA Approved Fleet Driver Trainers and have used these skills in full licence holder refresher courses and advanced driver training courses, as well as with new and experienced company car and van drivers. Many of the approaches explored in this book also apply to a classroom environment.

A note on terminology

For consistency, we use the term "learner" throughout this book, as opposed to "pupil" or "student". The "learner" is simply the person who is learning, whether that person be a novice or experienced driver.

We generally reserve the term "client" for when referring to the person being coached in other professional coaching fields. The term "client-centred learning" is used by the DVSA and is the term widely recognised by the driver training industry. The "client" is the "learner".

How to use this book

This book has been written so that it can either be read from start to finish, or in individual sections. You can find a summary of each chapter and appendix at the end of this introduction. You'll find this book useful as a reference tool, dipping in when you need to refresh or reflect on your skills.

At the end of each chapter are some 'points for reflection', marked with this rear view mirror icon. Take some time to read through the questions posed and consider how you can take action on the things you have learned.

Your FREE online bonus content

This book is interactive! In some sections of the book, we've provided links to chapter introduction videos, additional information, articles, videos and downloads relating to the section you are reading. To access these resources, either enter the URL into your web browser or scan the QR code with your mobile device.

Alternatively, you can access all of the online bonus content and resources, listed by chapter, at **whosinthedrivingseat.com**

"What on earth is a QR code?"

This strange black pattern on the right is a QR code. QR stands for 'Quick Response'. Visit **http://gedclai.re/qrcode** to watch a 1-minute YouTube video about QR codes. The main advantage of scanning a QR code is that it is quicker than manually typing a web address (URL) into your browser. But if you'd rather visit the web address instead, that's fine – we have provided short URLs along with the QR codes, so they're quick to access either way.

"How do I scan the QR codes?"

If you have an iPhone or iPad with iOS 11 or above, your device will scan QR codes without needing any additional software. Simply open up your camera app and point the camera at the QR code. A popup will appear at the top of your screen. Tap the popup and the relevant page will open in your web browser.

If you have an Android device, you will need to install a free QR code reader app in order to scan the QR codes. We have provided a simple guide and a link to lots of suitable apps at **http://gedclai.re/qrcode**

"Will I learn anything new?"

If you have no idea about coaching or client-centred learning, then yes, you'll learn lots of new things. Be prepared to write notes or highlight sections of the book that you find interesting and would like to try out. It might even surprise you just how much you already use some of the techniques, even though you've never been "taught" them before.

If you're already familiar with coaching and client-centred learning, then we hope this book will complement what you already do in your lessons and that you pick up some extra tips along the way.

Chapter & appendix summaries

Chapter 1: Why Drivers Crash

We start by examining the problem this book aims to solve — drivers crashing and people being seriously injured or killed on our roads. We explore six root causes of crashes and, in particular, why those aged 17-25 are most at risk. Some of the causes may be obvious to you, some not so obvious. By the end of the chapter, you'll understand the challenges we face and get an idea into how we, as driving instructors, have a pivotal role to play in ensuring our drivers really do go on to become "safe drivers for life".

Chapter 2: Coaching

The "coaching" buzzword has been around our industry for some time now, but there does seem to be a lot of confusion amongst PDIs and ADIs about what exactly coaching is and how it fits in to our work as driving instructors. In this chapter, we take an in-depth look at coaching and its nine fundamental principles, along with the key elements that will ensure your learners get the most out of their lessons. We're also honest about where coaching can fall short.

Chapter 3: An Introduction to Client-Centred Learning

What is client-centred learning? Is it the same as coaching? Is a "client-centred" approach synonymous with one that is "client-led"? Is it okay to instruct? In this chapter, we answer those questions and outline the key factors which will determine which approach to use at any given moment. We also explain how we can use the best traits of our own role models to help us become better, more effective driving instructors.

Chapter 4: The 5 Key Skills of a Client-Centred Instructor

As the chapter title suggests, in this section we break down the five key skills that will set you on the path to becoming not just a fantastic client-centred driving instructor, but a better parent/partner/friend, too. It's essential that we continue to develop and fine tune these skills if we are to maintain a good level of communication with everyone around us.

Chapter 5: What Does a Client-Centred Lesson Look Like?

This chapter starts with outlining the importance of having an active learning agreement and managing your customers' learning expectations. Don't overlook this essential element! We then break down the structure of a driving lesson into its component parts, sharing lots of tips, tools and techniques which will help you fully understand how to ensure your lessons remain client-centred from beginning to end.

Chapter 6: Learning Styles

In this chapter, we look at how every learner is unique and how, therefore, they all learn differently. We also examine the importance of knowing your own learning preferences and how these can influence your approach to teaching. You'll finish this chapter with some great new ideas of how you can adapt your approach to suit each of your learners.

Chapter 7: Addressing Limiting Beliefs

"Get out of your PIT and get a PET!" As driving instructors, we're often bombarded with our learner drivers' limiting beliefs (or "Performance Interfering Thoughts"). We look at how these limiting beliefs can affect our learners' actions, as well as giving you some great techniques that can help tackle them quickly and easily, enabling your learners to focus on generating some "Performance Enhancing Thoughts" instead.

Chapter 8: Dealing with Negative Attitudes

One of the biggest challenges we have as driving instructors is dealing with our learners' negative attitudes towards rules and regulations, safe driving practice and, of course, other road users. In this chapter, we look at what negative attitudes are and how they are formed, as well as how we can challenge them effectively.

Appendix A: Useful Coaching Scenarios

Once you've mastered the theory behind coaching and client-centred learning, it's important that you actually put it into practice. Without implementing what you have learned, nothing changes. So we've devoted this whole section to giving you some specific exercises (both practical and theoretical) which you can integrate into your lessons straight away. Many of the examples are based around the higher levels of the Goals for Driver Development (GDE) Matrix — essential areas often neglected in driver training programmes.

Appendix B: Goals for Driver Development (GDE) Matrix

The GDE Matrix is discussed in *Chapter 2: Coaching*. In Appendix B, we provide you with our own simplified interpretation of the five hierarchical levels of driver behaviour and the essential elements of driver training.

CHAPTER 1

WHY DRIVERS CRASH

Did you know that an average of almost five people die on our roads every day?[6] It's a frightening statistic, especially when you factor in that a significant proportion of those involved in road traffic collisions are young drivers.[7]

Watch Video Message: Ged & Claire Introduce Chapter 1

http://gedclai.re/chapter1

Why do drivers crash?

The latest statistics from the UK's Department for Transport (DFT) show that roughly 20 per cent of all road fatalities occur in incidents involving at least one young car driver.[6] As the vast majority of driving instructors' work is with young people aged between 17 and 24 years old, it makes sense to take some time to look specifically at young drivers and explore why they're more likely to be involved in crashes than other age groups.

First, let's look at the top crash factors for all drivers in general. The list below features the ten most frequently reported contributory factors in UK road accidents* (across all age groups), according to the DFT's 2017 data.[8]

1. Driver/rider failed to look properly
2. Driver/rider failed to judge other person's path or speed
3. Driver/rider careless, reckless or in a hurry
4. Poor turn or manoeuvre
5. Loss of control
6. Pedestrian failed to look properly
7. Slippery road (due to weather)
8. Sudden braking
9. Travelling too fast for conditions
10. Following too close

---

* Personally, we dislike like the term 'accident', as it suggests that nobody is at fault, which is rarely the case. To refer to a road traffic collision as an 'accident' in which someone is bereaved or seriously injured can be offensive and upsetting. We prefer the term 'crash', 'collision' or 'incident', and only use the word 'accident' here and in other sections of the book when making reference to official terminology.

Why Drivers Crash

Although it's great to have access to this kind of data, the list isn't as useful as it could be, because it doesn't tell us the most important thing we need to know about these crashes — the *root* cause — the *WHY*.

- **Why** did the driver fail to look properly?
- **Why** did the driver lose control?
- **Why** was the driver careless or reckless?
- **Why** was the driver following too closely?
- **Why** was the driver going too fast for the conditions?

So why do drivers do these things? And what can we do, as instructors, to help our learners avoid crashing for the same reasons once they pass their driving tests? Our shared experience has taught us that crashes rarely occur from a weakness in knowledge or even a lack of car control; we believe that crashes result from a complex mix of personal factors. It's never as simple as not looking properly or braking suddenly.

Humans are very complex beings. We all have unique personalities and are shaped by our individual experiences and the people around us. We all make personal choices when it comes to our actions, and we act differently in different situations. Our personal factors have an enormous influence over our decisions.

As more scientific evidence comes to light and our understanding of human beings evolves, we should, in turn, look to improve the way we work. It's no longer enough to only teach our learners how to control the vehicle and to pass a driving test. We have a responsibility to address the personal factors that each learner driver brings with them to their lessons so that we can prepare them for a lifetime of safe driving. An ADI's worst nightmare is hearing that one of their former students has been involved in a serious or fatal car crash. But it happens. A lot.

In this section, we'll look at these six root causes:

1. Attitude and beliefs
2. Driver distraction

3. Physiology
4. Perceptual limits
5. Inexperience
6. Absolving responsibility

As you read through the following sections, ask yourself how many of these personal factors you currently explore with your learners. Then, for those which you don't cover (or may not cover sufficiently), give some thought to how you could integrate them into your driver training programme.

Root cause 1: Attitude and beliefs

An individual's attitude and beliefs can be the cause of risky driving behaviour.

- The driver lost control because **she was reading a text message** from her mum.
- The driver was carelessly driving because **he was trying to impress his mates** on his way home from college.
- The driver was driving too fast because **he gets a thrill** from driving at high speed.
- The driver was following too closely because **he was running late** for work.

Attitudes, including our attitudes to risk, are formed from a very early age. We usually decide what's acceptable and unacceptable based on the beliefs and actions of our adult role models and peers. If Mum, Dad or a close friend drives fast, drives home after a few wines at the pub or routinely shouts abuse at other road users, these behaviours aren't out of the ordinary; we *believe* they're "normal".

Some drivers may have an "unusual" attitude to risk, stemming from the need for a thrill or adrenaline rush from physical activities. Behind the wheel, this can lead to driving too fast, dangerously and anti-socially.

Three other factors also shape our attitudes: our optimism bias, the pleasure principle and the confidence feedback loop.

Optimism bias

Optimism bias is a cognitive illusion; it's our tendency to overestimate our likelihood of experiencing positive events in our lives and underestimate our risk of experiencing negative events. Eighty per cent of us have an optimism bias; in other words, the clear majority of us are more optimistic than realistic.[9] And the interesting part is that we don't even realise it!

If you ask a group of people to consider the level of their driving abilities compared with the rest of the population, most of the group will rate themselves as being above average. Ask them to rate their chances of having a crash within the next 12 months and, again, most drivers believe that *other* people are at a higher risk of being involved in a road traffic collision than they are. Both of these beliefs are, of course, statistically impossible; we can't *all* be better than everyone else.

Optimism bias has many benefits in that it enables us to set ourselves challenging goals and believe we can achieve them. Optimism can even improve our health.[10] However, unrealistic optimism or over-confidence can lead to risky behaviour and poor decision-making.

- Drivers who follow vehicles too closely or routinely break the speed limit say things such as **"I've got good reactions; I could easily stop in time if I needed to."**
- A driver who texts while driving might believe that they're great at multitasking: **"Glancing down to text is no more dangerous than changing the radio station."**
- Someone who takes a bend at high speed believes that their car can handle it and that nothing's likely to be around the corner, **"Because I know this road like the back of my hand, and it's always clear."**

- People drink and drive because they believe, **"One or two drinks won't affect me."**

The optimism bias can have grave consequences for us as drivers because we tend to think "it won't happen to me." We somehow believe that we have the unique ability to stay safe, irrespective of the choices we make.

The pleasure principle

Most unsafe driving behaviours can be rewarding, too. Our actions are directly motivated by our desire for pleasure and to avoid pain. Often, it's our desire for immediate pleasure that matters more than the promise of future gratification.

- "I don't wear my seat belt because it creases my shirt. Besides, seat belts are so uncomfortable." **Reward for not wearing a seat belt: driving comfort and a nicely pressed shirt.**
- "I can multitask when driving to work. Calling my clients while driving means I save time at the office." **Reward for using a mobile phone while driving: productivity.**
- "Driving a few miles per hour above the speed limit means I get home earlier, so I have more time to spend with the kids before they go to bed." **Reward for speeding: shorter journey times and longer family time.**
- "I feel more relaxed and confident behind the wheel when I've had a spliff." **Reward for driving under the influence of drugs: feelings of relaxation and increased confidence.**

These beliefs and behaviours become reinforced through the confidence feedback loop and continue to be strengthened until something horrendous happens to break the cycle.

The confidence feedback loop

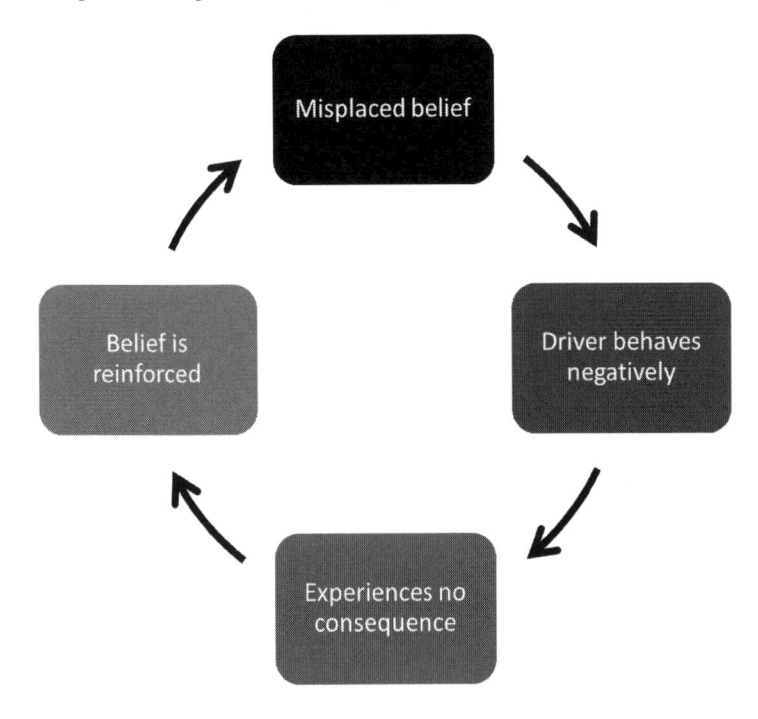

```
        Misplaced belief
         ↗           ↘
Belief is          Driver behaves
reinforced           negatively
         ↖           ↙
        Experiences no
          consequence
```

If left unchallenged, our optimism bias and beliefs, driven by the pleasure principle, will lead to a dangerous feedback loop. Our misplaced belief that "it won't happen to me" becomes alarmingly robust when combined with the feelings of confidence we gain from our risky behaviours going unpunished.

Consider the many unsafe driving habits that we commonly see on the roads every day: driving without wearing a seat belt, driving under the influence, speeding, following vehicles too closely, texting while driving, and so on. By getting away with it repeatedly, the driver's confidence grows, and the behaviour continues — until a crash, or a major near-crash finally shakes their confidence, and they recognise the danger of that behaviour. Only then is the driver's belief likely to change.

We explore how to address the issue of driver attitude in *Chapter 8: Dealing with Negative Attitudes.*

Root cause 2: Driver distraction

Distractions are all around us. Some distractions *inside* the car include:

- passengers (including children)
- texting
- talking
- food and drink
- smoking
- grooming
- reading (including maps)
- satnavs
- reaching for an object
- DVD players/music/other audio
- in-vehicle gadgets and controls

We also have distractions *outside* the car, of course, such as billboards and posters, objects, shop displays, flashing LED signs, video screens, interesting people, and so on.

Drivers have always been subject to some forms of distraction. In "the olden days", drivers still had to deal with passengers and the radio, and many drivers still ate and drank while at the wheel. There was even concern about the possible hypnotic effect of windscreen wipers when they were first introduced![11]

As years have passed, more technology has crept into our cars. Thus, drivers are now subjected to a myriad of internal and external distractions, all competing for their attention.

As accident databases are mostly created from post-accident reports, it's hard to estimate how many times driver distraction is the root cause of a crash. Not every driver will realise or admit that they were inattentive or distracted when the incident occurred. However, to offer some context to the importance of this root cause, a recent study of teen drivers by the AAA Foundation for Traffic Safety found that:

> *"Drivers were seen engaging in some type of potentially distracting behaviour leading up to 58% of all crashes examined. The two most frequently seen driver behaviours were attending to passengers (14.9%) and cell phone use (11.9%)."*[12]

Our emotional state, although not a physical distraction, can also distract us from the driving task. From the euphoric state of excitement, happiness and amusement at one end of the scale, to the dark despair of sadness, depression, grief and anger at the other end of the scale, all emotions present a challenging distraction to any driver, regardless of experience. Emotions are tough to switch off and can cause our minds to wander, and our driving style to alter.

The multitasking myth

Do you consider yourself to be a good multitasker? We must admit that we thought ourselves as adept multitaskers until we read the work of leading neuroscientist, Earl Miller:

> *"[Our brains are] not wired to multitask well ... When people think they're multitasking, they're just switching from one task to another very rapidly. And every time they do, there's a cognitive cost in doing so."*[13]

The fact is, our attention is a limited-capacity resource; we can do a limited number of things at any one time but focus on only *one* thing at a time. When we try to switch between different tasks our brains produce more cortisol (the stress hormone) and adrenaline (the fight-or-flight hormone), and this can overstimulate the brain. By multitasking, we burn up essential brain fuel that should be reserved for our concentration. And when we're driving, we need to maintain maximum focus.

Every time we're distracted by a phone call, text message or other notification, our minds pay attention to the distraction. Even if we choose not to look at our phone, needing to make that decision in the first place distracts us from the task at hand; whether it be wondering who's trying to contact us, or worrying about the consequences of not answering.

This distraction also applies to the conversation within the car. Even when two passengers are conversing among themselves, your focus of attention is likely to be bouncing back and forth between driving and their conversation. Scan the QR code, or visit **http://gedclai.re/multitaskingmyth** to see a short video explaining multitasking in relation to driving.

Children

As parents of two young children, we know first-hand how distracting it can be to drive with youngsters in the car. Singing, screaming, fighting, chatting, crying — if you're a parent, you'll know what we mean. In addition to the repeated whines of "Are we nearly there yet?" every five minutes, parents are subjected to requests to answer life's most challenging questions, play games, dispense food and drink — and then clean it up when it drops on the floor or spills on the seats. All *very* distracting!

In fact, researchers at Monash University Accident Research Centre in Australia found that children are 12 times more distracting to a driver than a conversation on the phone.[14] The study found that during a 16-minute trip, the average parent takes their eyes off the road for three minutes and 22 seconds. Behaviours included looking at a child in the rear seat, looking at a child through the rear-view mirror, helping a child and playing with a child.

Other passengers

Passengers of all ages can be distracting, but young travellers, who may not understand the complexity of the driving task, can be particularly distracting. And we're not only referring to young children.

Young drivers with similarly aged passengers are far more likely to crash than if they drive alone or with an older passenger. Research by the AAA Foundation has found that the fatality risks to 16- or 17-year-old drivers increase by 44% when carrying one passenger aged under 21, doubles when carrying two passengers under 21 years old and quadruples when carrying three or more passengers under 21 years old.[15]

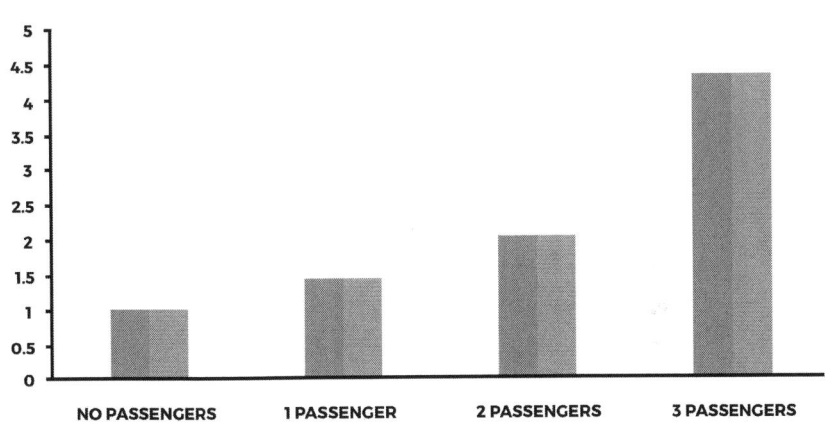

Relative risks of driver death per mile driven in relation to combination of passengers in the vehicle

NUMBER OF PASSENGERS UNDER 21 YEARS OLD

Technology

On a global scale, we're all now more reliant on technology than ever before. It's in our homes, in our cars and even in our pockets. We have satnavs and heads-up displays in our cars, along with voice-activation and Bluetooth technology. We have internet-enabled devices within easy reach, 24 hours a day. Wearable technology is becoming really popular too, with the recent popularity growth in smartwatches, smartglasses and fitness trackers.

Smartphones have been around for over a decade now. Every year, they've become an ever more integral part of our lives, and for the younger generation especially. A survey conducted by Deloitte in 2017 found that:

> *"Seventeen per cent of 16-24 year olds look at their smartphones at least 100 times daily; 12 per cent of 16-19 year olds claim 200 views or more daily."*[16]

So, what happens when these young people get into the driving seat? They certainly won't find it easy to leave their phone alone, particularly on a long journey, which is why we are all too familiar with news reports and social media stories of people having crashes while they're distracted. Just look around you whilst waiting at traffic lights — how many drivers do you see looking down at their phones?

A study of 1,691 moderate-to-severe crashes involving teen drivers found that the average eyes-off-road time for drivers who were operating or looking at their phone was 4.1 seconds.[17] 4.1 seconds. Just think about that. Close your eyes for just over four seconds and imagine driving your car for that long with your eyes closed. At 30mph, that means the driver is travelling 55 metres (60 yards) with their eyes off the road, 5 metres longer than the length of an Olympic-size swimming pool. At 50mph, it's 92 metres (100 yards), roughly the length of a football pitch.

It's not just texting or using apps that are the problem. Making or receiving a phone call is also seriously dangerous. Speaking on the phone amounts to a fourfold increase in a driver's likelihood of crashing, even if a hands-free device is used; it's not the physical holding of the phone that increases risk, it's the distraction of the conversation itself.[18] What we find especially worrying is that other studies have shown that talking on the phone while driving is comparable to driving with a blood-alcohol level over the legal limit.[19]

The "now generation"

Alongside changes in how we communicate, recent technological strides have also changed the expectations we place on each other. Once an instant message has been sent, we think it's safe to say that most of us would expect a reply within minutes; especially since many apps now show when our message has been read by the recipient.

We must accept that we're living in a world of instant gratification; we've become a "now generation" — we don't like having to wait for things. Drivers not only want to get from A to B as quickly as possible, but they also want to get as much done during the journey too. Hands-free and voice-activated technology allows drivers to stay on the right side of the law, but at what cost to the level of concentration needed for the driving task?

Delivery drivers are also risking their health and safety by meeting the tight delivery deadlines demanded by today's "now" consumer. The European Agency for Safety and Health at Work found that, "The time pressure resulting from competition is responsible for many of the hazards (accident risks) in the transport sector."[20]

Emotional state

Whether it's the sick feeling after a breakup, or tummy butterflies at the start of a relationship, extremes in emotion elicit significant changes in our physiology. These physiological changes can cause a major distraction from the driving task, resulting in drivers reacting differently to the events around them. A driver's emotional state is perhaps one of the biggest distractions with which they must contend.

Research has shown that driving under the influence of heightened negative or positive emotions can impair our ability to perceive hazards and the frequency and direction of our eye movements — critical capabilities needed when behind the wheel.[21] Also, a recent study found that driving while feeling sad is far more likely to result in a crash than driving while tired or when using a mobile phone.[22]

> I recall being about 21 years of age and having a huge row with my girlfriend at the time — long before I met Claire, I might add! Wanting to get as far away from her as I could, I grabbed the car keys, jumped into the car and screeched off in a rage. Before even reaching the road, I smashed my car door mirror on the gatepost. Fortunately, the clattering of the mirror against my window, followed by the crunch as the rear wheel of my car drove over it, was enough to make me stop driving and ask myself whether I was *really* in a fit state to be doing so.

As mood swings are more prevalent in adolescents than in adults, it's important that younger learner drivers are aware of how their emotions, or more accurately, how they unconsciously respond to them, can affect their behaviour on the road.

Root cause 3: Physiology

Young adults undergo significant biological changes between the ages of 17 and 24 that can affect behaviours and attitudes to risk-taking. Also, this period of socio-behavioural transition can also lead to an increased susceptibility to peer pressure, optimism bias, mood changes and attention-seeking behaviour.

Research has shown that a newly qualified 17-year-old driver is almost twice as likely to be involved in a crash as a newly qualified 60-year-old driver, proving that inexperience isn't the sole reason for young drivers being at risk.[23] Age is, of course, a major factor, but why?

> Think back to when you were 17 or 18 years old. Looking back, do you consider you were mature at that point in your life? Assuming you passed your driving test at that age, were you an impulsive driver who often took risks? I know I was. Out of my group of six or seven close friends, I was the only one not to crash within a year or two of passing my driving test. But, believe me, I came dangerously close quite a few times. Being completely honest, it horrifies me when I reflect on some of the things I did as a young driver.

Is this higher risk purely down to inexperience? Evidently not.

Recent advances in neuroscience have shown that the human brain matures at a much slower rate than previously thought. In infancy, the cerebellum — Latin for "little brain" — at the back of the brain forms first. It develops quickly and is most active in our infant years. The cerebellum is involved in cognition, hand-eye coordination and balance.

As we progress through adolescence, the middle part of the brain is highly active. This area of the brain is involved with things including bonding, friendships, wanting to "fit in" and self-esteem.

The last part of the brain to fully develop is the prefrontal cortex. This is a critical area, particularly when it comes to driving.[24] The executive function of the prefrontal cortex includes things such as:

- attention
- hazard perception
- risk assessment
- judgement
- impulse control
- abstract reasoning
- decision-making

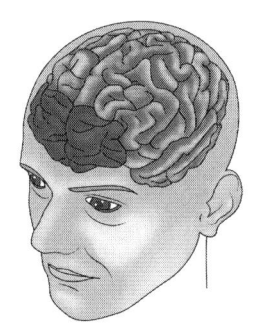

- empathy
- motivation
- working memory

Research has found that the prefrontal cortex isn't fully developed until the age of 25, which explains why people drive as they do in their late teens and early twenties. It also explains why there's a significant drop in the number of collisions involving those aged 25–29, compared to those aged 17–24.

The most natural reaction to hearing that brain development isn't complete until the age of 25 is to say, "Well, let's raise the driving age to 25 then." While that approach may offer a partial remedy, it's perhaps a little excessive to deny anyone under the age of 25 access to a car. It would severely affect our economy if young people were unable to travel more easily from home to work, for example, especially given the current state of our public transport system.

Tackling this cognitive disadvantage might almost seem impossible, as we obviously can't speed up the natural formation of the brain. But research, such as Isler and Starkey's 2008 study, found that training can help us to overcome some of the issues associated with the late development of the prefrontal cortex. They found that higher levels of skills training significantly improved visual search techniques in the study's participants. Such training also improved their attitude to speeding, overtaking and following too closely, and lowered their confidence levels in their driving skills.[25]

Fatigue

Research has found that almost a fifth of road traffic collisions on the main roads are sleep-related and more likely to result in a fatality or serious injury. Men under 30 have the highest risk of falling asleep at the wheel, meaning learner drivers, especially young male learner drivers, need to understand and minimise the risks of them dozing off while driving.[26]

> I have childhood memories of my dad driving us all to Spain for our annual family holiday. He used to drive all day from dawn until dusk, at which point we'd stop off at a campsite for the night. It took three and a half days to drive from our Cheshire home to our rental villa on the Costa Blanca — although as a child, that journey felt like more like three and a half weeks!
>
> I remember watching my dad slapping his face and neck every now and again to keep himself alert. As more time passed, he'd get a little bit more heavy-handed with his slaps, and then my mum would ask him to pull over for a break. At the time, I thought his actions were a bit strange, but now as an adult and a driver who has experienced fatigue first-hand, I can now understand how this tactic might have helped alleviate his tiredness for a few more minutes.

Our levels of sleepiness and alertness are essentially determined by two independent regulatory mechanisms.

The first mechanism is our circadian rhythm (sometimes referred to as our "body clock" or "sleep/wake cycle"). The circadian rhythm in sleepiness generally peaks in the early hours of the morning (between 2 a.m. and 6 a.m.) and mid-afternoon (between 2 p.m. and 4 p.m.). Our circadian rhythm changes as we age. Teenagers, for example, have a body clock which is "programmed" to sleep for longer, and also to go to bed and wake up later than adults.

The second mechanism which determines our sleepiness/alertness level is sleep pressure (or "sleep homeostasis"). It can be simply thought of as the brain's need for sleep, which is directly related to the amount of time that we have been awake. As waking duration increases, sleep pressure increases. This progressively increases our feelings of daytime sleepiness.[27a]

Seven to eight consecutive hours of sleep is generally recommended for adults, but many people simply aren't getting enough. Consistent research has shown that teenagers and young adults are getting insufficient sleep, making it hard for them to get up in the morning.[27b] School and college timetables don't typically allow for the circadian rhythm of this age group, leaving young adults with further sleep problems including daytime somnolence.

There's also evidence that suggests that the artificial light from smartphones, tablets, laptops and other electronic devices interferes with the brain cells that induce sleep, as well as stimulating the brain cells associated with alertness.[28]

Feeling groggy all day from sleep deprivation can result in grave consequences. Sleep deprivation limits our ability to concentrate and solve problems. It can also lead to aggressive behaviour, overeating, and as the body digests food, it can cause even more drowsiness or tiredness.[29]

Alcohol and drugs

The dangers of driving under the influence of alcohol and/or drugs are self-evident. Nevertheless, some young drivers are so susceptible to peer pressure and social conformity that they take the risk anyway, even though they're aware of the risks and potential consequences.

According to a survey of 1,000 drivers, one in three (32%) UK drivers admit to driving after drinking any amount of alcohol in the last year. Almost one in five (19%) admit to driving the morning after having a lot to drink when they're likely to still be over the limit.[30]

Although fewer people are taking the chance of drink-driving at night, others are risking driving in the morning, without realising that they may still be affected by the alcohol from the evening before. In general, our bodies can process only around one unit of alcohol per hour — one unit being equal to 10ml of pure alcohol. But this varies from person to person.

WHAT DOES 1 UNIT OF ALCOHOL LOOK LIKE?

STANDARD 4.5% CIDER	STANDARD 13% WINE	STANDARD 40% WHISKEY	STANDARD 4% BEER	STANDARD 4% ALCOPOP
218ml	76ml	25ml	250ml	250ml

To put this into context, here is what a young, female adult might typically consume on a big Saturday night out with friends:

- ½ a bottle of wine (before leaving the house) — five units
- Three cosmopolitan cocktails — six units
- Two shots of sambuca — two units
- Two bottles of cider/lager — five units

In total, this female will have consumed 18 units of alcohol, meaning it will take approximately 18 hours for her body to process the alcohol and clean it from her system. Assuming she finished drinking in the early hours of Sunday morning, she'll be impaired for the whole of Sunday and maybe even until the early hours of Monday morning.

It's not just those who go out drinking that are affected, either. More people are taking advantage of the low prices of alcohol at the supermarket and drinking at home. If someone finished drinking three pints of strong lager or a bottle of wine — both nine units — at midnight, they wouldn't be rid of the alcohol until at least 9 a.m.

Many people are ignorant of the effects of alcohol on their system. Do any of these justifications sound familiar?

- "I have a fast metabolism."
- "It's fine, I had a big meal."
- "It won't affect me."
- "I won't get caught." (the optimism bias)

- "I feel more confident driving with my mates when I've had a drink." (the pleasure principle)
- "I always have a couple of pints and it's never been a problem."
- "I'm fine after a night on the beers; I always sleep it off after a few hours." (the confidence feedback loop)

Dehydration

Recent research at Loughborough University has found that "drivers who are not properly hydrated make the same number of errors as people who are over the drink-drive limit."[31]

We all openly recognise the dangers of driving while under the influence of alcohol or drugs, but perhaps we should all take notice of our hydration levels, too; particularly on long journeys when people typically avoid drinking to minimise toilet stops. Dehydration affects our physiology and mental functions in many ways. Most notably, it leads to reduced alertness, fatigue, reduced concentration and changes in mood.

Root cause 4: Perceptual limits

As human beings, we have limits to what we can perceive at any one time. In our experience, driving instructors are good at developing a learner driver's anticipation and awareness skills. They ask things such as, "What can you see up ahead?" or "What's your next hazard?" and "How are you going to deal with it?" Questions such as these are great, but sometimes our learners appear to look directly at something, but still not see it. Why is this?

Well, there are two types of "blindness" which are innate characteristics of being human. Once you understand these properly and how they can be leading causes of crashes, it will enhance the way in which you develop your learners' anticipation skills even further.

Inattentional blindness

> *"Only those items which I notice shape my mind — without selective interest, experience is an utter chaos."*
> *— William James*[32]

"Inattentional blindness", a term coined by Arien Mack and Irvin Rock in 1992, describes a natural condition that we all have every minute of every waking day: the failure to see things that are beyond our focus.[33] It's one of the leading causes of road traffic collisions and driver error but is a normal, natural phenomenon.

All of us have something known as a reticular activating system (RAS), which lightens our mental burden by filtering irrelevant information from our conscious awareness. Without this filter, our brains would suffer from information overload — or, as psychologist William James puts it, "utter chaos". Our RAS lets through only the information which it decides is of value to us at any arbitrary point in time.

Several years ago, Daniel Simons and Christopher Chabris conducted a study of inattentional blindness. The video used in their research went viral, so there's a good chance you've seen it. In the video, two groups of people are passing basketballs between them. The subjects in the study had to watch the video and count the number of passes between the players wearing white.[34]

It's important that you have seen this video before reading any further, otherwise you'll spoil the whole point of the experiment. So, if you haven't seen it or would like a reminder, scan the QR code or watch the video at **http://gedclai.re/attention1** before turning to the next page.

Did you watch it? Okay, then read on!

In the middle of the video, a person wearing a gorilla suit walks unexpectedly into the midst of the scene, stops, thumps their chest, and then walks off screen. When asked if they noticed anything out of the ordinary in the video, only 50% of the subjects in the study reported seeing the gorilla, even though 90% of people are convinced they would notice it.[35]

Scan the QR code or visit **http://gedclai.re/attention2** to watch another interesting variant of the same experiment — see if you can spot the gorilla this time.

As weird and wonderful as our RAS is, it does create a serious problem for us as drivers. Because our RAS allows through only information which it feels is of value, we can easily miss important things. While looking left and right for a safe gap to emerge into traffic, for example, we can easily miss the pedestrian crossing the road. Driving on usual routes can lead to inattention blindness of roadside features and hazards.

Change blindness

Like inattention blindness, change blindness refers to another naturally occurring disruption in perception, but one which is caused by a brief disruption in visual continuity, such as a short change of scene or an eye movement.

We'll discuss eye movements — or saccades — as these can lead to lots of problems for drivers. An eye movement, when our eyes move from one fixation point to another, takes approximately 20-80 milliseconds. During this time, it would be logical to believe that we should perceive a blur of the scene in front of us, but we don't. Try it for yourself. Look around you now, do you see any blur? Better still, try this experiment:

1. Sit or stand in front of a mirror.
2. Look at your left eye, then at your right. Keep switching between them. Can you see your eyes moving?

Why Drivers Crash

3. Next, ask someone else to do the same, while you watch their eyes. Are their eyes moving as they alternate between looking at each eye? Can they see the movement of their eyes?

Of course, our eyes *do* move, but we don't see it happen. Neither do we see a blur as our eyes move, because during an eye movement, our brain blocks the image coming in from the eyes. This blocking is referred to as "saccadic masking". We're effectively blind during a saccade.

In addition, the amount of our visual field that's in focus at any one time is minuscule. To illustrate this, when you're next parked up in the car, look out of the window at a fixed object such as a vehicle registration plate or a sign. *Without moving your eyes,* try to read any other writing or number within your field of view, such as on a sign or billboard.

If you're sitting down at home reading this book, look around you. Look at a fixed point and notice just how little of your visual field is actually in sharp focus. When you extend your arm and look at your thumbnail, that's approximately the area that is focussed in your field of vision; to see something in focus our eyes need to look directly at it.

As impressive as these phenomena might sound, they can lead to disaster on the roads. While looking left and right for a safe gap to emerge at junctions, it's easy to miss things ahead of us, such as a car emerging from a road or driveway opposite, or a pedestrian stepping out into the road. That glance to the right, even when repeated for a second time before emerging, may not be enough for us to see a motorcyclist approaching. **Visual attention is needed to see change, and the smaller the object, the more likely we are to miss it.**

Change blindness and the limits of our visual focus pose such grave issues for the driver, so it's essential that we learn to scan efficiently.

Scan the QR code or visit **http://gedclai.re/fighterpilot** to read *A Fighter Pilot's Guide to Surviving on the Roads* — an excellent article by John Sullivan, an experienced

Royal Air Force pilot and crash investigator. He explains the issue of saccadic masking and gives some great tips on how to overcome the issues it can present to us as drivers.

Root cause 5: Inexperience

> *"The first few years of driving are crucial in determining the accident liability of new drivers — of all ages; accident liabilities fall by some 35-40 per cent due to experience alone in the first year of driving."*[36a]

It's a fact: the more driving experience a driver has, the lower their risk becomes. To get safe on the roads, a driver needs lots of experience driving under a variety of conditions, including:

- on different types of roads (rural, single track, urban, dual carriageways, motorways, etc.)
- in various situations (multi-storey car parks, drive-throughs, petrol station forecourts, etc.)
- at different times of the day (busy rush-hour traffic, as well as quieter times during the day or at weekends)
- during the daytime and at night in low-light conditions
- in adverse weather conditions (bright sun, wind, rain, fog, ice, snow, etc.)
- with distractions (radio, passengers, satnav, children, etc.)
- under varying emotional states

Although many instructors strive to give each learner as much experience in the above areas as possible, many others still focus too much on teaching to the requirements of the driving test. It's understandable, because learners (and their parents) often pile pressure on the instructor to get them through the driving test in the shortest possible time and at the lowest possible price. It's a shame when cost and time mean more to them than safety, but a shift in this mindset is unlikely unless more

Why Drivers Crash

emphasis is placed on the need for discussion on, and exposure to, the full range of conditions that drivers are likely to experience post-test.

Root cause 6: Absolving responsibility

A typical trait of many drivers is to instantly blame anything or anyone besides themselves for the negative things that happen to them. Conversely, they're quick to take responsibility when things go well.

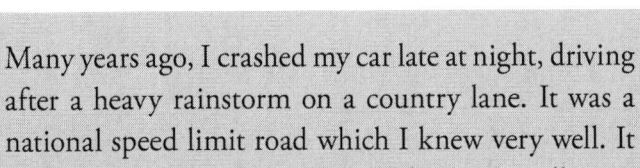

> Many years ago, I crashed my car late at night, driving after a heavy rainstorm on a country lane. It was a national speed limit road which I knew very well. It wasn't raining at the time of the crash, and I was travelling at just under 50mph. The left wheels of my car hit a deep patch of water gathered in a dip near the left-hand grass verge. I lost control and crashed. The vehicle was written off by the insurance company. For months — maybe even years — I blamed everything else but myself for the accident:
>
> - "The road was poorly lit."
> - "The drain on the side of the road was blocked, so it was flooded."
> - "I couldn't see the water because it was hidden from view in a dip."
> - "It could have happened to anyone."
> - "It wasn't my fault, it was just a freak accident."
>
> Looking back now, I know the crash was a result of my speed in the road conditions and my poor planning and anticipation skills. Those lies I told myself for years were not helpful to me. If I'd carried on thinking like that, my driving behaviour would never have improved because of the experience.

Awareness of the outside environment and ability to plan ahead are skills that driving instructors routinely develop with their learner drivers. What's less practised, however, is the skill of self-awareness — awareness of our internal state, knowledge, expertise and abilities — and the skill of self-evaluation, such as measuring our own performance.

Having self-awareness and the ability to self-evaluate are two critical components of a good, safe driver. Sadly, these components aren't adequately developed through traditional, instructor-centred methods.

Pre-driver-age education has failed us

It's been said that human beings start learning to drive from the age of two years old. From an extremely young age, we learn what's right and wrong, and how to behave behind the wheel from our parents (or other care-givers). Children are like sponges — they model everything a parent does and incorporate what they see into their own lives.

This informal education continues until the child reaches the legal driving age, at which point they come to us for driving lessons. We then try to undo all the bad habits, attitudes and behaviours they've learned from the School of Mum and Dad.

Sadly, there's no legal requirement to teach road safety in our schools at all; this must change. We believe that formal road safety education should start from as early an age as possible, and become a *mandatory* part of the school curriculum. Thankfully, local authorities have a duty to promote road safety and, as such, some may explicitly demand that schools in their area teach it. Other than road safety education in schools, what other opportunities do pre-driver-age people have?

Theory classes

Most of these courses seem to focus on technical elements of driving, such as signs, rules and regulations, rather than driver risk factors.

Under-17 driving opportunities

These mainly focus on vehicle control and manoeuvring skills rather than driver risk factors. Many pre-driver courses are advertised as a fun activity rather than an educational experience.

Peer-to-peer discussion groups

Typically coordinated by road safety societies, partnerships and charities such as the Royal Society for the Prevention of Accidents (RoSPA) and Brake, such discussion groups focus on specific topics which relate to current road safety issues. When run well, these groups can be very effective, but attendance is voluntary, and the numbers of young people reached through these groups is minimal.

Road safety campaigns & public information films

Road safety groups, charities, associations and local drama groups have created some excellent productions and interactive presentations which help to highlight safety issues. TV and radio campaigns also contribute by spreading road safety messages. The internet, and particularly the growth of viral video sharing on social media, also helps by spreading road safety messages from all over the world.

Passive watching of presentations and public information films is likely to have only a very short-term effect on the viewer. For the greatest effect, presentations and films must be engaging and, more importantly, they should have an interactive element. Presentations which form part of a workshop can be very influential in promoting safe driver attitudes, as delegates can explore the issues raised, consider how they could be directly affected by these matters and develop personal strategies to cope with them.

As good as some of these initiatives can be, in terms of the UK population, pre-driver-age people receive little to no education on the real risk factors that we have explored in this chapter. These are the factors that will, sadly, contribute to thousands of them being killed or sustaining life-changing injuries in the following years.

The National Driver Offender Retraining Scheme

Unique to the UK, the National Driver Offender Retraining Scheme (NDORS) is a programme which targets low level motoring offences, e.g. speeding a few miles per hour over the speed limit or using a mobile phone while driving. Visit **http://gedclai.re/NDORS** or scan the QR code to read more about this scheme.

Evidence shows that NDORS programmes are successful, in that those who attend such courses are less likely to reoffend.[36b] As such, it seems that post-test educational courses such as these are making a positive difference to road safety. However, we think it's important to educate drivers properly *before* they offend. This is where driving instructors fit in.

Adapting our current teaching methods

Ever since the introduction of the driving test in 1935, driver training and testing has focused on the knowledge of rules and regulations, how to control the car and how to interact with other road users. But now we have a deeper understanding of what causes crashes, we believe that the focus needs to change.

While there's no magic bullet, there are actions we can take to address these problems. We have a privileged position as educators in road safety — if we choose to use it. Driving instructors are in a perfect position to influence change and to help lead the future generation of drivers to reduce their road risk.

By developing your skills further and using the suggestions and scenarios in this book, you can not only increase your learners' engagement and understanding in their lessons, but also help make our roads safer.

Many of you reading this book recognise that only part of your role is to get people through their driving test. You aim to teach, "Safe driving for life", right? The question is, *how* do we help our learners to become safe drivers for life? We'll show you how to actively increase your learners' levels of knowledge, understanding, self-awareness and personal responsibility, in the hope that they won't be one of next year's road death statistics.

> I remember many a time sitting with learners and telling them the dangers of driving fast, not looking ahead, driving after they've been out drinking the night before, not wearing a seat belt, and so on. I told Carl — the learner driver I mentioned at the start of this book — repeatedly about the dangers of speeding, taking risks and his bad attitude. I remember lecturing him often about what could happen if he didn't listen to me. I think I even resorted to saying those immortal words, "You'll fail your test if you do that" to him on a few occasions. But he still knocked down that little girl.
>
> Thankfully, I've learned a lot since then. One of the main things I've learned through age, experience, parenting and marriage(!) is that people tend not to listen to you when you *tell* them what to do. It doesn't take a genius to work that out, I know, but at the time, it was the only way I knew.

We only need to look at the former ADI Part 3 test to see just how much things have changed over the years. Many ADIs today recognise that the instructor-led, negative, fault-based method of teaching just isn't a comfortable way of working, and instead seek to actively involve the learner in the learning process. Up until 2014, many DVSA examiners weren't sufficiently trained or able to acknowledge the use of coaching and client-centred techniques during a Check Test assessment.

Thankfully, the DVSA have now caught up, as the old style Check Test was replaced by the Standards Check in 2014. The Standards Check actively encourages the use of coaching and client-centred approaches and assesses an ADI's skills over a broader range of competencies. Also, the Part 3 test has been updated to mirror the Standards Check assessment. It's more important than ever for all PDIs and ADIs to understand coaching and client-centred learning fully, which is what we'll look at in the next few chapters.

Points for reflection

- Think back to a collision (or near collision) that you've experienced. Look back over the root causes of crashes that we've discussed in this chapter and consider which factors may have played a part in that situation.
- If you passed your driving test at the age of 17 or 18, think how you've changed over the years. How much of a risk-taker were you then? What about now? Have any changes in lifestyle affected the way you drive? How has your driving attitude changed?
- How many of the six root causes of crashes listed in this chapter do you successfully cover during a course of driving lessons? How do you address them with your learners? Consider those which you don't discuss – how could you introduce them into your lessons?
- If you've been qualified as a driving instructor for some time now, how has your instructional style evolved since you passed your Part 3 test?

CHAPTER 2

COACHING

"Coaching is unlocking a person's potential to maximize their own performance. It is helping them to learn rather than teaching them."[37]

Sir John Whitmore

> **Watch Video Message: Ged & Claire Introduce Chapter 2**
>
> http://gedclai.re/chapter2

What is coaching?

Coaching is one of the fastest-growing industries in the world. Today, people are receiving coaching across a range of sectors, from personal life and health coaching through to business and executive coaching. Coaching is also being adopted by educational establishments, from primary schools right through to universities. It was only a matter of time before it hit the driver training industry, too.

Some of the most significant developments in the education of new drivers stemmed from the work of many projects co-financed by the European Commission. CIECA, the International Commission for Driver Testing, either managed or participated in most of these studies. You can find links to their projects and research online at **www.cieca.eu**

HERMES

One of the most notable pieces of research was conducted via the HERMES project (**H**igh Impact Approach for **E**nhancing **R**oad Safety Through **M**ore **E**ffective Communications **S**kills). Of all the recent research projects that have been undertaken, this is the one we would most recommend that you read. As well as the final report and suggested training scenarios, the HERMES project produced an excellent video which explains in simple terms why and how we can improve our drivers using coaching. You can find all the HERMES resources by scanning this QR code or by visiting **http://gedclai.re/hermes**

Previous EU projects had discovered and outlined which methods are best to reduce road traffic collisions in new drivers. The aim of the

HERMES project, however, was to work out *how* to put these methods into practice — specifically, how driving instructors can deliver training to help reduce the number of people killed on our roads.

The outcome of the HERMES project was a highly practical training package containing suggested scenarios that new and experienced driving instructors could follow. The main recommendations were based on adopting coaching principles, rather than traditional teaching methods. Following the 2010 conclusion of the HERMES project, ADIs across Europe began to learn more about coaching.

Goals for Driver Education (GDE) Matrix

Many of the EU studies repeatedly refer to the skills gap left by current driver training and testing programmes throughout Europe, which have traditionally focused on teaching novice drivers to master the control of the vehicle and deal with various traffic situations (referred to as "lower level" competencies).

Research has found that there are more "higher level" competencies that need to be taken into account to be a safe driver. These involve taking into consideration:

- the context of the journey
- the vehicle's occupants
- route planning
- distractions
- physiological factors such as fatigue, alcohol, drink and drugs
- emotional factors
- personality characteristics and propensity to take risks
- personal goals, ambitions and habits
- other personal factors such as age, gender and lifestyle
- social factors such as position within group/work team
- self-awareness and self-evaluation skills

It's interesting to note how many of these considerations mirror the main crash factors in *Chapter 1: Why Drivers Crash*. The complete set of competencies were illustrated in the GDE Matrix. Our version of the matrix, in *Appendix B* of this book, is based on the four level framework first published by Hatakka et al. in 2002 and a proposed fifth level by Keskinen et al. in 2010.[38,39]

The GDE Matrix should ideally form an integral part of your training programme, but it often gets overlooked by PDIs, ADIs and trainers who are somewhat confused by its complexity. We've attempted to simplify it and make it a little more user-friendly in the hope that it makes more sense to you.

The remainder of this book is devoted to showing you how to cover all levels of the Matrix without needing to refer to it directly. We look at lots of self-evaluation strategies, as well as the content within levels three to five of the GDE Matrix, which aren't traditionally trained or tested in the UK. The HERMES project looked at how to cover the higher levels of the GDE Matrix; the resulting suggestions were that the optimal way to achieve this is through coaching.

Bringing coaching to the mainstream

We've delivered our own courses, workshops and conference presentations on the benefits of coaching in the driving instruction industry. We've spoken at many local driving school associations, with relatively mixed results. Most ADIs embraced the concept; some realised that they were already coaching to some degree and some rejected it as a fad. But our experience has shown us that those ADIs who were open-minded enough to look into coaching and use it in their work have reaped the benefits.

If you want your learners to become safer drivers, then we believe it's essential for you to become a good coach. That doesn't mean that traditional teaching methods can't make good drivers; it's just that our experience has shown us that coaching can help novice drivers to become even better.

The origins of coaching

Coaching isn't a new concept. Older and more experienced people have always shown youngsters what to do: how to find food, shelter and warmth; how to defend themselves against predators; how to protect themselves from the elements.

The word "coach" is derived from early forms of transportation, with "coaching" literally meaning to transport someone from one place to another. In its modern context, this literal meaning remains prevalent throughout all forms of coaching; the coach's role is to help you close the gap between where you are and where you want to be.

Driver coaching, a relatively new concept to many, also involves transporting someone from one place to another, not only in a moving car but also regarding their learning journey from a non-driver to a fully competent, safe and qualified driver.

One of the earliest known forms of coaching in the modern era was within the sporting industry. To improve their skill level and chances of winning, competitors would hire a coach to help them develop. Tennis coaches, golf coaches, snooker coaches, badminton coaches, football coaches: think of pretty much any sport, and there's a coach for it! However, these early forms of sports coaching were mostly direct instruction — "Do what I say and you'll get better."

The whole concept of coaching was transformed in 1974 when tennis coach Timothy Gallwey released his book, "The Inner Game of Tennis". Tim was frustrated by the limitations of conventional sports coaching methods and believed that *telling* players how to make improvements didn't bring about lasting change. According to Tim, "There is always an inner game being played in your mind no matter what outer game you are playing. How aware you are of this game can make the difference between success and failure."[40] In other words, the player's inner state and internal obstacles have more of a significant influence on achieving peak performance than focusing on technique alone.

Tim's work was the catalyst for a change in coaching, not just in the sports world, but also in the corporate world. People wanting to perform at the highest level hired executive coaches to help them overcome their inner obstacles and achieve peak performance.

Defining coaching

So, what exactly *is* coaching? Is it something radically new to ADIs, or is it just another label for what most of us are already doing?

Because coaching is used across many different sectors, including birth coaching, fitness coaching, life coaching, and executive coaching, defining what coaching is and isn't can be difficult. Some coaching interventions will take place in one-to-one situations, while others will be held in groups. Coaching has different degrees of formality and structure. Sometimes coaching will be on an informal, loosely structured basis; in other situations, it might be right to have a more formal, heavily structured approach.

There are various definitions of coaching in existence. Our personal favourite, used at the start of this chapter, is: "Coaching is unlocking a person's potential to maximize their own performance. It is helping them to learn rather than teaching them."[41] This definition of coaching makes a light distinction between teaching (or instructing), and coaching, which is a helpful place for us to start, given that most ADIs see the two as being different approaches.

The suggestion from this definition is that every learner has the potential within themselves and that the coach's role is to help the learner to maximise their performance. ADIs who coach support the learner's natural ability to learn.

The HERMES project defines coaching as, "a learner-centred method that engages body, mind and emotions to develop inner and outer awareness and responsibility with an equal relationship between the learner and coach."[42]

This great one-sentence definition encompasses five key components of coaching:

1. Coaching is **learner-centred**.
2. Coaching engages **body, mind** and **emotions**.
3. Coaching develops **inner** and **outer awareness**.
4. Coaching promotes **responsibility**.
5. Coaching is based on an **equal relationship** between learner and coach.

The coaching spectrum

In its broadest sense, coaching can include two different language styles: non-directive language and directive language. Traditional sports coaches, for example, will often use mostly directive language, where the professional teaches the novice what to do and how to do it. Life coaches, on the other hand, tend to use much more non-directive language, where the coach encourages the client to discover things for themselves.

Instruction
(Directive)
⟷
Coaching
(Non-Directive)

Understandably, the term coaching is therefore often confused with teaching or instruction. Some ADIs are of the view that coaching methods include directive methods such as instruction. However, most European research studies and definitions of coaching, within the context of driver training, see direct interventions such as teaching and instruction as being distinct from coaching. In fact, they'd consider teaching/instruction and coaching to be at opposite ends of the spectrum, as illustrated above. The DVSA also considers coaching and instruction to be different approaches.

In our experience as ADIs and ADI trainers, traditional driving instruction has been based on the driving instructor passing on their skills and knowledge to the learner driver in the form of instruction. The driving instructor is the one in control of most elements of the lesson, including the lesson plan, structure, route, teaching methods and feedback. They're also responsible for finding the learners' areas of weakness and for giving guidance on how to improve.

Coaching takes a different approach, one in which the learner driver takes more responsibility for the lesson plan, the learning process and their own development. The driving instructor is there to manage risk to the car, its occupants and other road users. The instructor acts as a *facilitator* of the learning, rather than a *director* of it.

Throughout this book, we'll consider instruction and coaching as fundamentally different styles.

Why coaching?

So how do people learn best? Is it better to teach or to coach? Why the recent shift towards coaching instead of the tried-and-tested direct approach? To answer those questions, let's first consider the famous phrase often attributed to Confucius (551 BC - 479 BC), China's most renowned teacher, philosopher and reformer:

> *"I hear and I forget.*
> *I see and I remember.*
> *I do and I understand."*
> — *Confucius*

Over the years, many theorists and researchers have tried to answer the question of how people best learn. Most appear to agree that learning through active involvement and experience works best, especially when learning a practical skill.[43]

Experiential learning theory

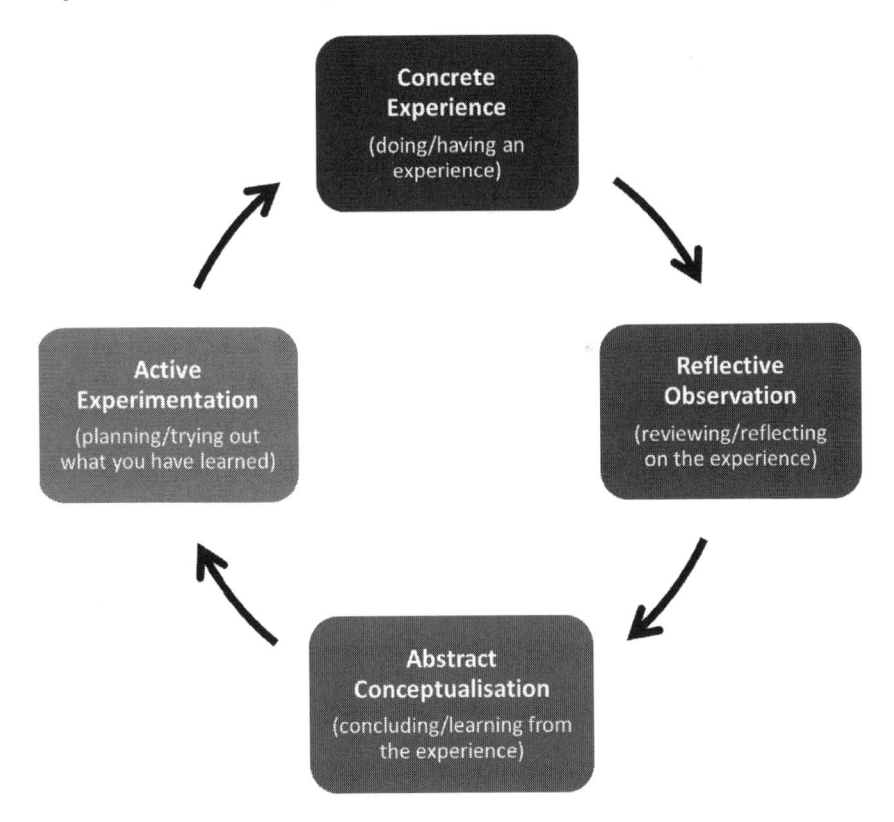

```
        Concrete
        Experience
        (doing/having an
         experience)

Active                      Reflective
Experimentation             Observation
(planning/trying out        (reviewing/reflecting
what you have learned)      on the experience)

        Abstract
        Conceptualisation
        (concluding/learning from
         the experience)
```

The idea that people learn best through active participation and experience was most notably expanded upon by David Kolb in the 1980s.[44] He built upon the earlier work of others, such as Carl Rogers,

Jean Piaget, Carl Jung and John Dewey, and developed a theory of experiential learning that provides a holistic model of the learning process. You can see Kolb's model illustrated above.

If we were to consider how we learn early life skills as a child, such as walking, or throwing and catching a ball, this theory fits nicely.

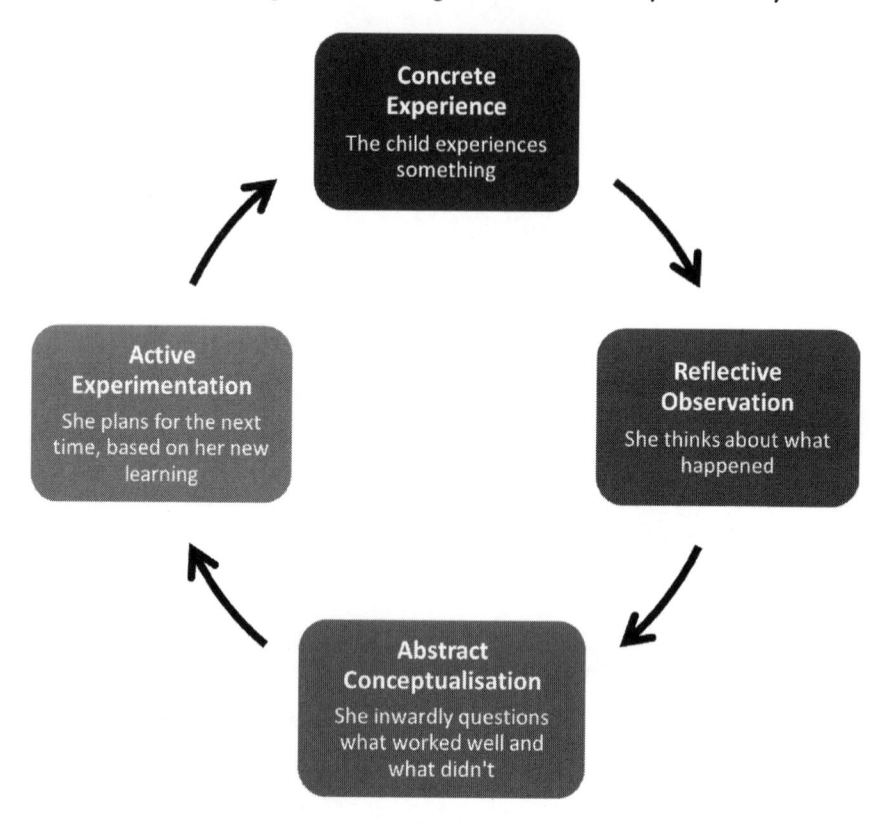

```
         Concrete
         Experience
    The child experiences
         something

Active                          Reflective
Experimentation                 Observation
She plans for the next          She thinks about what
time, based on her new          happened
learning

         Abstract
      Conceptualisation
    She inwardly questions
    what worked well and
         what didn't
```

Experience, **reflect**, **analyse** and **plan**. Through this process, a child will learn and develop naturally. After all, we weren't taught how to walk, throw or catch, were we? A parent or older sibling may have gently helped us along the way, and we may also have learned through imitation, but nobody placed one of our feet in front of the other.

Some have argued that Kolb's theory is far too simplistic and doesn't consider other ways in which we learn.[45] Furthermore, it doesn't account for *what* we're learning: are we learning behaviours or actions which are positive or negative? We only need to see how well a child can manipulate a parent into buying them sweets in a supermarket to see that this learning cycle can be used negatively, too!

Let's now consider Kolb's theory of experiential learning in the context of learning to drive a car. If you handed your car keys to a teenager who had never driven before, and then left them to figure out for themselves how to make it start, move and stop, they'd probably be able to do it. The main three problems with that approach, when compared with professional driving instruction, would be:

1. It would take a lot longer to figure out what to do.
2. The car is likely to get damaged.
3. It would be extremely dangerous!

Just because people *can* learn through experience doesn't mean that they'll learn to do the correct things in the safest ways.

Adverse driving behaviours, when left unchallenged or without consequence, are reinforced through this learning cycle (which is similar to the confidence feedback loop we discussed in *Chapter 1: Why Drivers Crash*). Consider texting while driving, speeding, tailgating and drink-driving. These are just a few examples of unsafe driving behaviours which are typically learned and reinforced through never experiencing an adverse outcome because of that behaviour.

Until those driving habits lead to a significant enough reason for the driver to stop doing them, such as receiving a hefty fine or points on their licence, crashing or even killing someone, those behaviours are likely to continue. Learning to eradicate unsafe driving behaviours through experiencing an adverse consequence isn't ideal.

- Does a driver need to wait until they kill someone through drink-driving before they consider making a change?
- Do drivers need to run over a child before they stop texting behind the wheel?

- Do drivers need to be involved in a serious collision on the motorway before they learn to increase the gap between them and the vehicle in front?

How coaching can help develop safer driving for life

A safe driver has a consistently high-level of awareness and excellent self-evaluation skills. They have pre-determined journey goals and can evaluate the risks such a trip may involve. These skills enable them to make the correct choices behind the wheel and take responsibility for the outcomes.

A driving instructor who's adequately able to develop these safe drivers needs to have several key coaching skills to help the learner driver achieve this aim. Their learner needs to be fully engaged in the learning process and feel comfortable enough to openly discuss their true thoughts and feelings.

A driving instructor who tells someone what to do, what to think and how to behave removes the need for their learner to be aware, to self-evaluate, to make correct choices and have responsibility for the outcomes of those decisions.

Ultimately, we don't want people to have to learn from crashes, injury and death. We don't want people to be in a prison cell or on their death bed before they realise the error of their ways. We want people to make responsible choices throughout their driving lives. We believe that coaching can help to achieve this outcome.

Nine fundamental principles of coaching

While performing a comprehensive analysis of traditional coaching models across a range of sectors, we collated what we believe to be the nine most important principles of coaching:

1. Establishing and maintaining rapport
2. Using a non-directive approach
3. Keeping to the client's agenda rather than the coach's agenda
4. Ensuring the coaching relationship is equal and that no hierarchy exists
5. Encouraging the client to set SMART or PRISM goals
6. Encouraging self-evaluation rather than giving feedback
7. Experiencing unconditional positive regard for the client
8. Believing that the client can succeed and that they have the resources to do so
9. Raising the client's levels of awareness and holding them responsible for the results they generate

Although we feel that all nine principles are vital to a successful coaching model, we firmly believe that "raising your client's levels of awareness and holding them responsible for the results they generate" should be at the heart of any driver coaching strategy. As such, a significant part of this chapter focuses on an in-depth look at this critical principle.

Let's now look at all these principles in the context of learning to drive.

1. Establishing and maintaining rapport

The level of rapport between the instructor and the learner refers to the warmth of their relationship and the extent of the connection between them. Learner drivers will be more enthusiastic and learn more effectively if they get along with their driving instructor. If you consider your favourite subjects from school or the ones you excelled in, it's very likely that the teacher connected well with you.

To achieve rapport with your learners, it can be a good idea to talk more about them than about you. Find out how *they* learn best, use *their* words and phrases, and learn about *their* interests. Have a sense of humour and make sure lessons are always fun and engaging. Another easy way to enhance rapport is to use your learner's name throughout the lesson, particularly when giving positive feedback or praise. We feel that rapport is so important that we've included it in *Chapter 4: The 5 Key Skills of a Client-Centred Instructor*.

2. Using a non-directive approach

A driving instructor striving to adopt a traditional coaching approach should hold back from giving direct instruction as much as possible. To be non-directive, you need to allow your learner to learn from experience where possible. Afterwards, you can ask questions and get them to reflect on their performance, encouraging them to come up with ways in which they could improve. Your goal is to hand responsibility for learning over to the learner driver.

3. Keeping to the client's agenda rather than the coach's agenda

There are two components to a driving lesson: the **content** and the **process**. When following a coaching approach, the learner would lead their learning — the content — not the instructor.

At the start of the driving lesson, the instructor should encourage the learner to describe what topics or skills they'd like to work on during that lesson. These skills are likely to be based on the goals set at the end of the last lesson (we discuss this further in *Chapter 5: What Does a Client-Centred Lesson Look Like?*).

Throughout the lesson, the instructor manages the process by checking on how well the learner thinks they're progressing, if the learner's still happy to continue with the topic or skill they're working on, or if they would like to develop in a different area. The instructor handles the lesson timekeeping and helps the learner maintain focus on achieving their short- and long-term goals.

4. Ensuring the coaching relationship is equal and that no hierarchy exists

Although they each have different roles, the relationship between instructor and learner is one of equal partnership and mutual respect. Both are co-active in the relationship; the instructor isn't the one in a position of power.

Kimsey-House et al. remarked that "The power … comes from the relationship — from the synergy of the energy clients bring in the form of desire and motivation and the energy coaches bring in the shape of their commitment, skills, and understanding of human change."[46] By adopting a superior position in a coaching relationship, the instructor can alienate the learner. In turn, the learner can lose confidence in the instructor and even begin to resent them.

Driving instructors often find this quite challenging. After all, they're "the driving expert", aren't they? Firstly, it's important to recognise that there's a difference between giving information, for example, information on what the clutch pedal is and how it works, and coaching. It can be helpful for an instructor to provide information, of course, but coaching can be a more effective method when exploring goals, progress, mistakes, attitudes, beliefs and next steps.

Taking an equal position in the relationship allows the learner to:

- feel comfortable in making mistakes without fear of being "told off"
- share their thoughts, concerns and questions without fear of being judged
- freely express their feelings and emotions

- take a more active role in the learning process
- self-evaluate and look for ways to improve further
- accept responsibility for the results of their actions

5. Encouraging the client to set SMART or PRISM goals

Earl Nightingale famously said that "People with goals succeed because they know where they're going."[47] Traditional goal setting within coaching is often based around the SMART or PRISM acronyms. There are different variations to each of these acronyms, but the ones we prefer to use are:

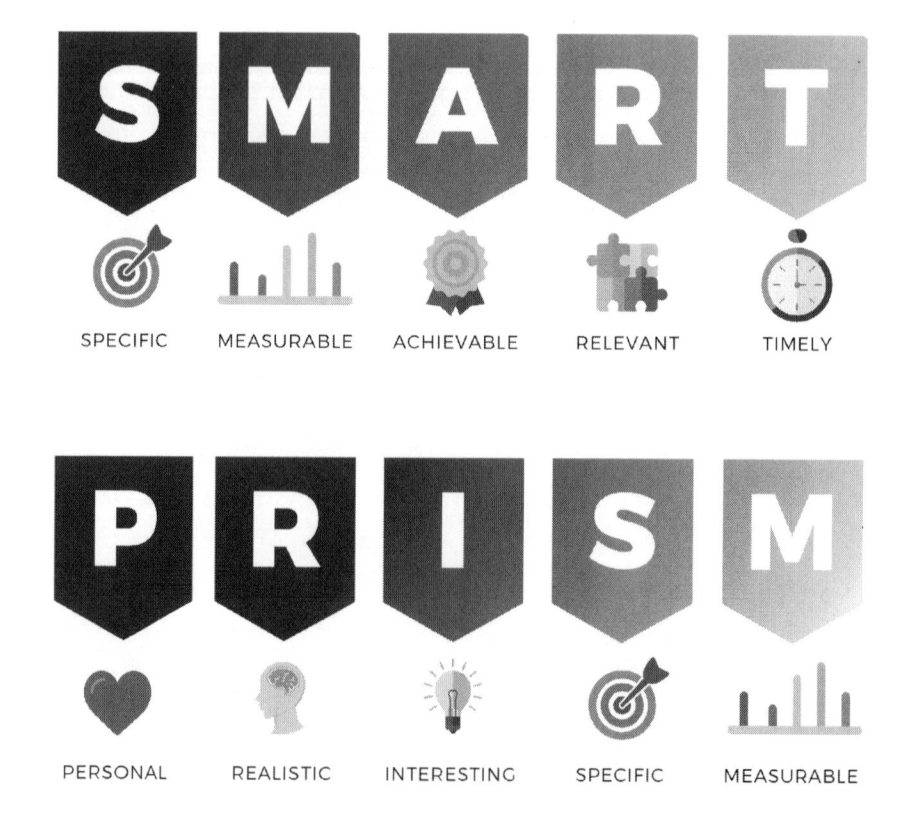

SMART
- SPECIFIC
- MEASURABLE
- ACHIEVABLE
- RELEVANT
- TIMELY

PRISM
- PERSONAL
- REALISTIC
- INTERESTING
- SPECIFIC
- MEASURABLE

In either case, the goal-setting approach is broadly designed to focus the learner's mind on what specific outcomes they'd like to achieve. The learner sets the goals, not the instructor, although the instructor is there to help ensure the goal setting is completed thoroughly.

For example, a learner's SMART or PRISM goals for a lesson might be:

- to be able to make efficient use of the mirrors before signalling — without needing any help from the instructor
- to learn, in theory, how to approach roundabouts safely using the MSPSL routine
- to have approached and taken the first exit at two roundabouts — with help from the instructor
- to stall the car no more than once
- to have achieved all the above by the end of the day's driving lesson

Goal setting is explored further in *Chapter 5: What Does a Client-Centred Lesson Look Like?*

6. Encouraging self-evaluation rather than giving feedback

Feedback is information that the learner driver receives about their performance. There are two forms of feedback they can receive: intrinsic feedback and extrinsic feedback.

Intrinsic feedback is the information that the learner driver receives from his or her own experiences (thoughts, feelings and emotions) and senses. For example, consider the visual cues, sound and feel of the biting point. Driving instructors are also often familiar with the *smell* of a high biting point, or one that is held for too long!

Extrinsic feedback can come in many forms and from various sources:

- the driving instructor
- other drivers/passing pedestrians
- friends and family during private practice

- observations from a person in the back of the car during a driving lesson
- video-recorded lessons
- self-reflection and self-evaluation

It's important that the driving instructor isn't always the one giving feedback on what's going well and what needs further improvement. Instead, the instructor should be encouraging the learner to spend more time paying attention to their intrinsic feedback and reflecting, evaluating and planning a way forward for themselves. Ultimately, this will help them to become a more capable and responsible driver.

When the instructor offers feedback, it should be presented positively, at least in the early stages of the relationship. In "Coaching for Performance", John Whitmore states that "Generating high-quality, relevant feedback, as far as possible from within rather than from experts, is essential for continuous improvement."[48]

We elaborate on the importance of feedback in *Chapter 4: The 5 Key Skills of a Client-Centred Instructor.*

7. Experiencing unconditional positive regard for the client

The term "unconditional positive regard" was used by Carl Rogers, the humanistic psychologist who developed the concept of person-centred therapy, an approach which many would agree influenced today's coaching models.[49] Unconditional positive regard involves the complete acceptance of and support for the other person, regardless of what they think, say or do.

The instructor should never judge or criticise the learner, regardless of their thoughts, opinions or beliefs. Instead, they should always strive to support them in their learning, to be compassionate and to understand their perspectives, struggles and issues.

Throughout their training with us, we encourage PDIs and ADIs to remember that generally speaking, learners don't do things wrong on purpose. Physical mistakes, poor attitudes or verbal outbursts are things we should seek to *understand* rather than criticise. Once we figure out what's behind the action, attitude or behaviour, we can then coach our learners to help them find better or safer ways of thinking or behaving. This approach might not always work, of course, but it's certainly more effective than just telling someone that they're wrong. We take a look at offering extra support for your learners in *Chapter 7: Addressing Limiting Beliefs* and *Chapter 8: Dealing with Negative Attitudes.*

8. Believing that the client can succeed and that they have the resources to do so

Central to any coaching relationship is the coach's belief in the client's ability to be successful. When interviewed by Forbes.com, Anisa Kamadoli Costa said that "If you believe passionately in what you are doing and whom you are doing it with, success is bound to follow." [50] Holding high expectations of your learner drivers can lead to enhanced performance, while low expectations may result in weak performance. The driving instructor's role is to help the learner to develop and grow; therefore, the instructor needs to see potential where nobody else can. It's essential that the instructor is genuine in their belief. If they say one thing but think another, this will be communicated non-verbally and unconsciously picked up by the learner.

We appreciate that some ADIs might find this a challenge at times; some learners appear to have a natural driving ability, while others seem to find learning to drive tough. We believe that there are very few people in this world who are incapable of ultimately passing their driving test. Chances are you might have met someone you thought would never make it. The problem is, this can become a self-fulfilling prophecy. Change your attitude towards that individual: don't just change your *thoughts* about that person — you need to change your *beliefs* about them and their ability to succeed.

If all else fails, and you still can't help the learner become successful, try to recognise that it might not be them that's the issue. It's not personal; it's just a fact that not all learners and their instructors are a perfect fit for each other. A different instructor with a different style or approach might be able to help them where you couldn't.

The driving instructor should also genuinely believe that the learner driver has all the resources they need to achieve their goals and can come up with solutions for themselves. The instructor is there to help the learner find those keys to success.

As well as believing in your learner's ultimate success, trust in their ability to analyse their own performance and to know how to improve on it. While it's true that some won't be open to you using a coaching approach, those that *are* open to it will thrive if you ask the right questions to help them self-evaluate and develop strategies for coping with situations better next time.

9. Raising the client's levels of awareness and holding them responsible for the results they generate

Coaching in its truest sense can help a driver become better and safer with a high level of internal and external awareness. A driver with a high level of awareness takes responsibility for the choices they make and accepts responsibility for the outcome of those choices.

To develop good, safe drivers, it's important that we strive to increase awareness and responsibility in all our learners at the earliest possible stage. As ADIs, we need to recognise the influences that a learner's internal thoughts, feelings and emotions will have on their behaviour. By helping our learners become more aware of these influences, we can encourage them to recognise how and why their behaviour is affected, intentionally or otherwise. Developing their ability to reflect and learn from experiences will help our learners become better equipped to make safe decisions throughout their driving life.

Let's now take an in-depth look at practical ways in which you can increase your learners' levels of awareness and encourage them to develop a greater level of responsibility for their choices, and therefore, their learning.

Raising awareness

> *"The first key element of coaching is awareness, which is the product of focused attention, concentration, and clarity."*
> — *Sir John Whitmore*[51]

Although we're taking in information about our surroundings all the time, our brain filters out a significant proportion of our internal and external environment. This means that we're only consciously aware of a small fraction of this information.

Many factors drive behaviour. If we want our learners to demonstrate positive driver behaviour which lasts well beyond passing the driving test, we really should be helping them to recognise how these factors influence and ultimately determine their choices and actions. To achieve this goal, knowing the rules and understanding the potential consequences of not following those rules isn't enough. Telling someone *what* to think and *how* to behave might be sufficient to get them through a driving test, but we don't believe this approach promotes change for the long term. To have the best chance of achieving long-term safe driving attitudes and behaviours, we need to raise our learners' awareness of these behaviour-driving factors and, where appropriate, challenge them to invoke positive change.

Awareness of external environment

We spend a significant proportion of our time developing a learner's awareness of their external environment — the planning and anticipation of situations that could develop ahead. We ask questions such as:

- "What's our next major hazard?"
- "What could be around this corner?"
- "What hazards could we expect along here?"
- "How are you going to deal with this?"
- "Who has priority here?"

By using these questions, the learner is encouraged to develop a strategy for tackling that situation, which may involve checking the mirrors and changing speed and/or direction. It's also important that we check our learners' levels of awareness *after* an incident or situation, particularly one in which the learner made an error. Here are some examples of useful questions which can enhance your learner's awareness of their external environment:

- "What did you notice about…?"
- "What did you see/hear/feel…?"
- "Where was the car…?"
- "How did you know when…?"
- "Where were you looking while…?"

In many of the cases above, you might well know the answer because you probably saw/heard/felt the same things. It's important to check, however, that the learner was aware as well.

We need to instil in our learners the ability to reflect on a situation, learn from it and then decide how better to deal with that situation in the future; this is true self-directed learning, which is much more effective than simply being told what to do. Remember Kolb's experiential learning cycle? Well, this is experiential learning in action, but the coach streamlines the learning process and directs the learning according to best, safe practice.

Awareness of internal environment

A learner's internal environment relates to their internal state. Although the learner's body language and behaviour can sometimes give us a clue as to what's happening inside, we can't know for sure unless we ask. To be truly self-aware, a driver needs to become skilled in the art of observing and monitoring their own internal state.

Enhancing a learner driver's awareness of their internal state is much more than just asking them what they can see, hear and feel. We can encourage our learners to become more aware of their:

- thoughts and feelings
- emotional and physical condition
- needs and desires
- values and beliefs (and from where/whom they came from)
- strengths and weaknesses
- frustrations, concerns and anxieties
- prejudices

Encouraging self-awareness helps the learner to identify the "gap" — not gaps in their knowledge and skills — the gap between where they are and where they want (or need) to be. Here are some questions you can use to learn more about your learners' internal states:

- "How did you feel about…?"
- "Where was your focus of attention when…?"
- "What was going through your mind when…?"
- "What were you saying to yourself…?"
- "What would you like to…?"
- "What are your thoughts on…?"
- "I notice you seem to be a little upset/frustrated/angry/irritated/confused. Tell me more about that."
- "What's going on for you right now?"
- "How did that make you feel?"
- "What do you feel you would benefit from working on next?"

By asking questions like these, we bring unconscious thoughts, feelings, emotions, beliefs and values to the surface, and into our learner's conscious awareness. We help our learners to become critical thinkers, in that they can look inwards for the answers rather than relying on you to provide guidance or feedback. It's fine receiving guidance and feedback while learning to drive, but after the learner passes their driving test, you won't be there — who's responsible for feedback then?

So why don't we spend more time asking questions that help our learners to become more aware of their internal state? We think the answer, often, is fear. Fear that we won't know how to deal with the response we get.

ADI: "Where was your focus of attention just before we stalled at the traffic lights, Mary?"
Mary: "I was thinking about the guy in the car behind and how close he was."
ADI: "Ah, don't worry about other people — he probably just doesn't know how much distance to keep in front of him."
Mary: "Yeah, I guess."

Did the instructor's feedback help? Maybe. Is it likely to stop Mary worrying in the future and stalling again? I doubt it.

We're not traditionally trained in how to handle this stuff, are we?

If you've been qualified as a driving instructor for a while now, think back to the old ADI Part 3 test, where the "learner" (role played by the examiner) made faults which were caused by a lack of knowledge or understanding or difficulty in judgement. These errors were relatively easy for the PDI to fix if they had been trained in how to address them properly. The "learner" rarely made mistakes based on internal dialogue, anxieties about other road users or limiting beliefs, but real learners do!

The "Learning Ladder"

Because each stage of learning brings with it different physical and emotional challenges for both the learner and the instructor, ADIs, and indeed learners themselves, will find it helpful to fully understand the different stages of learning we go through when we're learning something new.

When learning any new skill, a learner's emotions change throughout the process. At times, it feels like they're riding an emotional rollercoaster: one minute they're feeling ecstatic at having mastered a new skill, and the next minute they feel down because they've made a mistake or are finding something challenging. I'm sure you can think of a few learners who've openly expressed their frustration at not being able to master something as quickly as they'd hoped.

Noel Burch, an employee of Gordon Training International in the 1970s, outlined the four stages of learning.[52] The "Learning Ladder", illustrated on the next page, highlights the four stages of learning a new skill and the two factors (**awareness** and **competence**) that affect our thinking as we learn that new skill.

The Learning Ladder is helpful to both the learner and the instructor.

For the learner, it can help them to understand the reasons behind their emotions. Knowing how far up the ladder they are can help motivate them when they're feeling frustrated or down. It can also help them manage their expectations, especially if they're perfectionists who try to achieve too much too soon. Recognising how much they have achieved so far can help reassure them that they'll soon reach the level they desire.

For the instructor, the Learning Ladder is useful in helping to recognise how your learners may be feeling at that point in their learning. It assists with your patience, too — some people will take longer to ascend the ladder than others, and that's okay! Being aware of this framework can enable you to encourage your learners along their learning path.

```
         Level 4:
   Unconsciously Skilled


         Level 3:
    Consciously Skilled


         Level 2:
   Consciously Unskilled


         Level 1:
  Unconsciously Unskilled
```

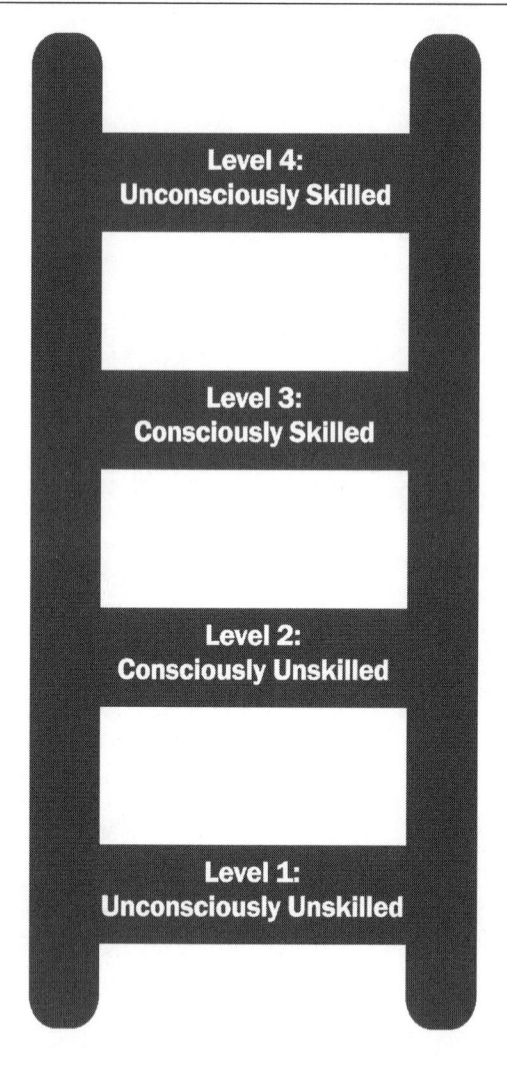

(Reproduced with permission from Gordon Training International)

Level 1: Unconsciously unskilled

The unconsciously unskilled — or unconsciously incompetent — person is blissfully unaware that they can't drive. They lack the knowledge and skills to do so but they're not even aware of it. Their confidence far exceeds their ability.

> When I was fifteen, my dad decided to give me some driving experience in an empty private car park. I insisted that I didn't need any help — after all, "If you and Mum can do it, it must be easy!" Within seconds of starting the engine, I swiftly moved to level 2 of the Learning Ladder — "Oh... Wait, this is *much* harder than I thought!"

Level 1 doesn't just apply to those who can't yet drive; sometimes your current learners will be at level 1 for a skill they haven't yet learned. For example, take the absolute beginner who, at the end of their first lesson, tells you that they've booked their driving test for three weeks' time. Or the learner who seems to know it all — they think they're fantastic at planning and have a great sense of all-round awareness when it's plain for you to see that they haven't. As the ADI, you need to deal with these situations tactfully to have the biggest impact. The trick is to help your learner drivers become more self-aware of their current level of skill at this stage, rather than telling them that they're deluded. This is where coaching fits in.

When it comes to absolute beginners, you can guide them to better self-awareness by perhaps showing them your whole syllabus (or all the topics and skills you intend to cover) and asking them what knowledge or skills they feel they already have, and how much more they need to learn before taking their test. For learners who suffer from an abundance of confidence in their planning skills, you could try giving them a top-level commentary drive for 5-10 minutes. After pulling up, you could ask them for feedback; what did they notice and what did they learn? Then ask them to have a go at giving a commentary of their own and to self-evaluate their performance at the end of the exercise. Discuss what went well and what could be improved upon to help with their planning and awareness on the road.

Level 2: Consciously unskilled

The consciously unskilled — or consciously incompetent — learner recognises the need to learn new skills to become a "proper" driver and reach the standard to pass a driving test. They see that others are much more competent at driving than they are.

This level can be quite tough for most learner drivers as they're at risk of losing confidence or even giving up altogether. The goal of being able to drive well and pass the driving test might seem impossible, or too much like hard work. For this reason, it's essential for you to encourage them and help them stay positive, highlighting each small step towards success. You must also help your learner to remain self-aware and to notice their own small steps towards success.

Level 2 is an ideal stage at which to explain the idea of the Learning Ladder to your learner drivers. We always show this to our PDIs so that they don't become disheartened during the challenging Part 3 training element of the course. It helps them to understand any feelings of discouragement that they might be experiencing.

Some learners will naturally see this level as a positive challenge for them; "I can't do it yet, but if I practise enough, I *will* master it!"; this is how we want all our learners to think, but it doesn't come naturally to the majority.

Level 3: Consciously skilled

At the consciously skilled — or consciously competent — stage, driving is still very much a conscious activity. The learner can drive well, but only while fully concentrating and giving the task 100% focus. Their confidence grows through practice and skills start to become increasingly automatic. This stage can last for quite a long time as there are so many skills to master. Some drivers find that challenging skills, such as a reverse manoeuvre, might remain a conscious activity for years.

Coaching fits in well at level 3, although the lesson goals need to be balanced between what the learner *wants* to do with what they *need* to do. Again, your aim here is to coach them around to the best option. You can gain their agreement by increasing their level of self-awareness on which skills or topics still require a lot of conscious effort.

Regular self-evaluation is important at this level as learner drivers need to recognise for themselves where they're doing well and where improvements could be made. Giving them choices about what to work on next, the lesson route and so on will increase their overall sense of responsibility.

Level 4: Unconsciously skilled

At the unconsciously skilled — or unconsciously competent — stage, driving becomes an effortless, subconscious activity. Simple skills, such as operating the pedals and hand controls, rarely need any conscious thought after having passed the driving test. They almost become an integral part of the driver, in the same way that blinking or breathing doesn't require conscious thought.

Our brains have evolved to help us out; once basic vehicle control skills have become automated, we can focus more on other complex tasks such as handling other road users and approaching unusual traffic situations. This automation is where "muscle memory" fits into learning to drive a car because repeated practice allows the brain and body to automate the skills required. Imagine having to think about every physical action as you do it; the placement of your foot on the pedals, the pressure you apply and the timing of when you press each one down or bring one up. At the same time, you must focus on the movement of your hand to the gear stick, the pressure you apply and the direction in which you move it. Imagine having to consciously focus on all that for the rest of your driving life? How hard would that be?!

As an experienced driver, it's likely that most aspects of driving have become automated. For example, think of a recent journey you made, particularly one involving a long drive on a motorway. It's unlikely that you can recall the whole trip. Frequently, it almost seems like we drive on autopilot, and suddenly realise that we need to be taking the next exit off the motorway. Sound familiar? This autopilot feeling happens because, for you, motorway driving has become an unconsciously skilled activity.

While automation is fantastic for letting us focus on other tasks, it only works if the skills in question are used regularly. The Learning Ladder doesn't move in only one direction; it's possible to slip down if vital skills aren't practised. And while automation might seem like the perfect end goal to aim for, it has a severe dark side: the risk of complacency.

Defined by the Oxford English Dictionary as, "A feeling of smug or uncritical satisfaction with oneself or one's achievements", complacency accounts for the fact that drivers are far more likely to have a crash within a few miles of their home than they are when driving on more unfamiliar roads.[53] A study carried out by elephant.co.uk found that two-thirds of road traffic collisions occur within 5 miles of a driver's home. The study also showed that nearly a third of crashes happen less than a mile from home.[54]

> About 100 metres from our house is a T-junction at which I always turn left. Nobody ever comes from the right. At least, that was my belief, having emerged from that same junction thousands of times and never encountered any vehicles coming from the right. This belief inevitably led to complacency, so much so that my observation to the right became little more than a cursory glance, and I unconsciously approached the junction a bit too quickly. Well, one morning on my way to work recently, a car *was* coming from the right.

> By the time my conscious brain had kicked in and told my right foot to get off the accelerator pedal, I was stopping in a fashion akin to the emergency stop and ended up over the give way line. I sheepishly waved an apology to the other driver.
>
> A few seconds after the incident, I reflected on why this situation had happened and immediately recognised that my behaviour and my complacency had been directly driven by my belief that "Nobody ever comes from the right at this junction." Now that I'm aware of this belief, I've chosen to change it to "Vehicles *could* come from the right at this junction." This has meant that I now approach it at a much slower speed so I have time to look properly, and I am always prepared to give way.

Self-reflection

We can all be guilty of complacency from time to time, but it's recognising and reflecting on those times of complacency that holds the key to becoming a better driver. Driver complacency can be driven by confidence in our skills, but also by the personality factors we discussed in *Chapter 1: Why Drivers Crash*, such as optimism bias and the confidence feedback loop.

Also, a driver's internal and external environment can quickly bring a skill that they were unconsciously or consciously skilled at right down to the consciously unskilled level. As we also discussed in *Chapter 1: Why Drivers Crash*, we can easily be overwhelmed by our internal and external environment, rendering us almost unable to perform a task which we could usually carry out with ease. Consider how your driving is affected when you're driving in an unfamiliar town and are looking for a destination, while the radio is on. Chances are, you have developed a strategy to deal with it, such as turning the volume down or switching the radio off.

Self-reflection is the ability to look back and analyse our experiences and realise what lessons can be learned for the future. For many drivers, however, this doesn't come naturally. When something goes wrong, they immediately look to place blame on something or someone else, rather than thinking about how they could have thought or behaved differently. Even when a collision is the fault of another road user, a good driver will always look within and ask themselves if they could have done anything differently to have prevented the crash.

As a driving instructor, you need to help your learner drivers to develop the critical skill of self-reflection. As well as reflecting on their driving skills and abilities, learners need to be able to identify how internal and external factors influence their driving performance. Once they've recognised these factors, they can, where necessary, develop coping strategies for them. Self-reflection ultimately gives learners more personal choice and control over their future thoughts and actions.

If the driving instructor makes all the decisions throughout a learner's course of lessons and takes responsibility for giving feedback to the learner, it's inevitable that the learner will blame the instructor when things go wrong. Should the learner fail their driving test, they'll often look to blame the examiner, the weather, the car, another road user or some other external factor. Assuming the learner passes their driving test, they're likely to continue blaming other people or external factors when things go wrong, therefore shirking responsibility for their actions.

Self-reflection isn't only useful for when things go wrong; it's just as important for your learners to reflect on their successes. Recognising when a positive attitude, belief or action resulted in a positive outcome is important, as doing so helps to reinforce that opinion, belief or action.

- "What did I do?"
- "Which parts went well?"
- "Which elements did I enjoy?"
- "How could it be better?"

- "Who was affected?"
- "Who else *could* have been affected?"
- "What was I thinking or feeling just before it happened?"
- "Where did that thought (or belief) come from?"
- "How could I have handled it differently?"
- "What, if anything, will I do differently next time?"

You can assist your learners with self-reflection by posing the above questions to them, swapping the word "I" for "you".

Self-reflection is also an instrumental technique for developing awareness of our depth of knowledge and understanding. Once we know where our "blind spots" are, we can seek the necessary resources to learn more.

- "What do I already know about…?"
- "What do I need to know about…?"
- "Do I know enough, or do I need to learn more?"
- "Why might I need to know more about…?"
- "How could it benefit me?"
- "Where could I find the information?"
- "What external help do I need, if any?"
- "Who could I ask for help?"

Encourage your learners to become self-aware and to reflect on their performance even from the very first lesson. These invaluable skills should last well beyond driving test day and help your learners to become safer and more responsible drivers for life.

Developing responsibility

> *"When we truly accept, choose, or take responsibility for our thoughts and our actions, our commitment to them rises and so does our performance."*
> *— Sir John Whitmore*[55]

Developing responsibility is another crucial element of coaching. Responsibility is empowering as it allows a learner to take ownership of their learning process and the outcomes that follow. Increased responsibility builds confidence and self-esteem, and ultimately your learner's performance improves.

Giving your learner driver this type of responsibility from the outset will develop their critical thinking and self-evaluation skills. They'll begin to recognise the extent of their capabilities and the limit of their current skill level. Giving your learners more responsibility will help build the self-confidence in your nervous, uncertain learners and reduce the likelihood of over-confidence in your self-assured, thrill-seeking ones.

Of course, this doesn't mean that you should just allow your learner drivers to drive the car unsafely, make dangerous mistakes, or to break the law. But there are some things you could perhaps let them have control over as long as it doesn't compromise safety or laws.

Traditionally speaking, the very first driving lesson starts with the instructor telling the learner how to carry out the cockpit drill, explaining all the main car controls and giving detailed guidance on how to get the car to move off and stop safely. It's very much an "instructor-led" experience, but it needn't be. You can begin to develop your learner's responsibility by first finding out what they already know about the various seating adjustments, the car controls or how to move off and stop. You can then, where appropriate, give them further technical information to fill in the gaps in their knowledge. This additional information could include airbag placement and consequently the optimal seating distance from the steering wheel, or the technical aspects of the foot pedals, for example.

Another interactive way of discussing the car controls with your learner is to say something like, "Point at something which *isn't* familiar to you and we'll discuss it". This invites the learner to share the responsibility for their learning and the direction of the driving lesson.

When it comes to adjusting the seat for optimum driving position, or getting the car moving, you might start by explaining the important safety principles. But then allow the learner to try these things for themselves without intervening too much. After all, only *they* know what feels comfortable to them when adjusting the seat. By letting your learner experiment in moving off from the roadside without too much input from you, you empower them and give them responsibility for the results. If they stall the car, hold back from immediately telling them what went wrong, why it happened and what to do next time. Instead, give *them* the responsibility to try analysing and correcting the problem first, as this will greatly enhance their learning and understanding. Encourage them to figure out what might have caused it (raising awareness) and ask them what they could try differently next time (developing responsibility). Then, try moving off and stopping again.

In later lessons, instead of giving a detailed briefing before your learner carries out a manoeuvre, you could allow your learner to hold the visual aid for themselves and explain to you how they intend to go about it. Allow them more opportunities to learn experientially. By letting a more experienced learner attempt a manoeuvre unaided, you give them responsibility for the outcome. For example, if a learner ends up positioned wide from the kerb after a parallel park, hold back from explaining where they went wrong. Instead, ask the learner what they could try doing differently on the next attempt to get closer to the kerb.

> Amy came to me for driving lessons with her practical test already booked. After the usual preliminaries, she drove away from her house, and I asked her to turn right out of her road onto a faster main road. Amy stopped at the give way line and just looked forward. Surprised by her lack of observation to the left and right, I asked "Amy, are you going to look for a gap to get out in?" She replied, in a matter-of-fact tone, "Oh, my instructor normally does that for me."

I very much doubt that Amy's previous instructor told her not to look because he would check for her. What's more likely is that he was looking for a gap in the traffic and saying things like, "Okay Amy, we've got a gap after this red car… Get prepared… Okay let's go!" or "Okay, it's clear, let's go now."

If this was the case, he was inadvertently taking responsibility for observing and judging a safe gap for Amy, and two things were probably happening:

1. He was taking responsibility away from Amy; he was so busy looking left and right himself that he didn't notice that Amy wasn't looking effectively (or at all).

2. Amy was becoming less aware; she could see that her instructor was looking for a safe gap and wouldn't let her emerge if it wasn't safe. She, therefore, became reliant on him looking and telling her when it was safe to go.

The more the instructor took responsibility, the less aware Amy became. By encouraging Amy to understand the need for her to make the choices for herself, she agreed that she needed to go when she felt it was safe. We discussed how, as a pedestrian, Amy had crossed the road several thousand times in her life and not been knocked over up to this point. She agreed that it might be helpful to use a similar method of judgement to help her find a safe gap to emerge from a junction.

At the next junction, I just watched Amy's observations. I didn't look at the road, just her observations. She was slightly uncomfortable with me not looking for her and was in disbelief that I wouldn't check for her at all. As soon as she realised that it was her responsibility to look and to decide on a safe gap, she took that responsibility and became instantly more aware.

> She took that first junction with full responsibility. Without Amy noticing, I naturally checked for myself that she had a safe gap just before she pulled out, but the ultimate decision was hers. It took her a while to choose the safe gap but the next emerge was better and the one after that even better again. Her responsibility was increasing with each emerge, and as a result, she was far more aware of what was around her, not just when emerging from junctions, but throughout all her driving.

Put your learner in the driving seat

Amy's story is just one example to illustrate the relationship between awareness and responsibility when working on a practical skill. There are many other elements of the driving lesson in which your learner can take a more active role. Here are just a few examples of things we can give our learners responsibility (or at least, *more* responsibility) for:

- Being aware of their mental and physical state and how that might affect their driving
- Asking the driving instructor (and any other passengers) to put their seat belts on
- Recognising their current strengths and weaknesses
- The training areas and lesson routes
- How much help (input) the instructor should provide
- Evaluating performance
- Working out where and how to improve
- Identifying concerns, anxieties or frustrations
- Coming up with alternative options for thinking or behaving
- Planning the goals for next lesson

If you're thinking, "Wait a minute, are you really saying that my learner should take responsibility for all those things?", "Where do I fit in?" or "The learner is paying for me to teach them — aren't those things *my* job?", then you're not alone; many driving instructors have those reservations. If you are to provide lessons using a traditional coaching approach, then yes, the balance of responsibility for the content should shift to the learner as you're there to manage the process. However, there are some situations where coaching isn't always the best approach.

Is coaching always the answer?

Are you all geared up to go out and coach? It sounds great, right? Unfortunately, coaching isn't a cure-all for all the challenges ADIs face when it comes to engaging their learner drivers. Earlier, we outlined how instruction and coaching would be considered entirely different approaches. A purely instructional approach uses directive language, and an exclusively coaching approach uses non-directive language.

Instruction (Directive) ⟷ Coaching (Non-Directive)

Instruction: Instructor-led

Traditionally speaking, the driving instructor is the one in control, choosing what to do, when to do it, where to do it and how the lesson should be conducted. From leading the discussion on the lesson topic and choosing the location for a reverse manoeuvre, to deciding how much time should be spent working on a particular skill to providing ongoing feedback on performance.

A driving instructor with a purely directive style assumes a position of authority in the relationship as the one with superior knowledge. They'll be the one to set the goals for the driving lesson and the one responsible for changing those goals if they consider it necessary. They'll give specific instructions, which the learner is expected to follow. They always bear the responsibility of all risks, finding and analysing weaknesses in the learner's driving, then providing solutions to resolve those shortcomings.

The instructor will be doing most of the talking during the driving lesson. They'll give feedback to the learner, both throughout the lesson and at the end. Specific goals for the next lesson will be set by the instructor, who will also tell the learner what to read, learn or practice before the next lesson. New skills are taught, and the learner repeatedly practises with decreasing help from the instructor until they eventually get it right by themselves.

This procedure is referred to as an instructor-led approach. Such an approach reduces the learner's need to be self-aware since all they need to do is watch, listen and learn. The learner is viewed as an empty vessel, a receptor for information and knowledge. In effect, they're passive in the learning process.

The instructor-led approach creates a "remembering driver", the type of driver that, when faced with a situation on the road, reverts to memory for guidance. Learning this way, almost by rote, means that when a driver faces a new situation for the first time, they don't know what to do.

- "What did my instructor say I needed to do here?"
- "What am I supposed to do here?"
- "I've never done anything like this in my lessons; what should I do?"

A new driver will encounter many new situations after passing their driving test, and if they haven't been told how to deal with a situation, or have no memory of what to do, then their decisions can end disastrously.

Coaching: Learner-led

Learner-led learning is exactly the opposite of instructor-led learning. In other words, the learner is the one who leads the core elements of the driving lesson. The learner handles choosing the lesson goals, plan, route, practice and feedback. The learner is active in the learning process.

A driving instructor with a purely non-directive style — an instructor who coaches — assumes an equal position in the relationship. They keep the belief that the learner has all the answers within themselves, their own position being one of "teasing" those answers out of the learner. A non-directive instructor will encourage their learner to set their own goals for the lesson and to handle changing those goals when necessary. They'll help the learner to plan their own lesson routes and drive to areas they feel are best suited to their learning goals. The driving instructor acts as a facilitator and a guide instead of the expert and the primary source of knowledge.

Responsibility for risk remains in the hands of the learner. The learner deals with situations themselves and then evaluates their own performance. They then come up with their own solutions to resolve those weaknesses. The learner will be doing most of the talking during the driving lesson, but they're also encouraged to be inquisitive and to ask questions. The instructor elicits feedback from the learner, both throughout the lesson and at the end. Specific goals for the next lesson will be set by the learner, who will also decide on what to read, learn or practice before the next driving lesson.

Such an approach enhances the learner's levels of awareness and responsibility. Learner-led approaches are believed to enhance learning much more than an instructor-led approach, as the learner takes ownership of their learning.[56] This approach helps to develop a "thinking driver." When this type of driver faces a new situation, they can analyse and calmly make a responsible decision based on all the information available to them at the time. The outcome of that decision, therefore, is more likely to end favourably.

- "What options do I have for handling this situation?"
- "What would be my best course of action here?"
- "How can I solve this problem?"

When coaching doesn't work

Having read the above two styles of instruction, which one do you prefer? Chances are it's a mixture of the two, but one may seem closer to your style than the other. The instructor-led approach will almost certainly seem familiar to many experienced ADIs, as this is generally how the old-style ADI Part 3 test was presented, at least during the first half of the examination ('Phase 1').

The former Part 3 test was first introduced in 1985. Due to the nature of that assessment and the style of teaching which was the norm at that time, instruction at Phase 1, where the learner being portrayed was in the early stages of learning, was expected to be "traditional" — that is, instructor-led. The instructor was expected to maintain tight control of the lesson along with identifying, analysing and correcting "faults". The lesson plan was fixed and didn't change as the "learner" only showed weaknesses related to the specific lesson topic being tested. It's hardly surprising, therefore, that many ADIs continue to work in a very much instructor-led way, even though they might not be aware of it.

Remaining non-directive is unrealistic

How did you feel about our earlier description of an exclusively learner-led lesson? Uncomfortable? Let's face it, as driving instructors we're in a time- and a safety-critical environment. Giving full responsibility for your £10,000+ car to someone without the skills to control it would be insane!

Even life coaches and business coaches don't always stick to using a non-directive approach — the three life and business coaches we work with direct the coaching sessions from time to time and suggest areas where we need the most focus. They're the coaching experts, and they need to steer the coaching session in the correct direction to achieve our desired outcomes. Our business coach, for example, has expert knowledge of what works in business, so we want him to share his expertise and advice with us. He is able to uncover our business blind spots — things we wouldn't otherwise notice without him pointing them out.

In the same way, when a learner driver reaches a learning plateau or struggles with a topic or skill, you remaining non-directive can lead to them becoming even more frustrated and being "stuck" for much longer than necessary. In such situations, you shouldn't be afraid to use your expertise to make suggestions or guide them towards success.

It's about using the most suitable approach at the most appropriate time. Neither language style or approach is ultimately correct — each has its place — so try to adopt a flexible approach and use whatever method you feel is best for the situation.

Sticking to the learner's agenda isn't always the best strategy

The essence of traditional coaching is that the session should centre around the client's plan; the client handles the content, and the coach controls the process. In the context of learning to drive, however, what the learner driver *wants* to cover might not align with what they *need* to cover.

Some learner drivers will want to move on too quickly, beyond the boundaries of their current ability. Consider the learner who tells you at the start of their second-ever driving lesson that they want to drive on the national speed limit dual carriageway in that lesson, even though they've only ever driven on a quiet side road up to 15mph in second gear.

Some learner drivers will want to play it safe, repeating the same lesson topics repeatedly until they're perfect. For example, the learner who wants to continually practise left turns, even though you know they'll improve over time on those and would benefit from moving on to right turns. Others will avoid certain topics or manoeuvres because they find them boring or too challenging. For example, the learner who's one lesson away from their driving test expresses a desire to "chill out" on this lesson and drive on some open country roads — when you know they really need to develop their skills at handling meeting situations and emerging onto busy roundabouts.

An instructor skilled in asking open questions will sometimes manage to gently coach the learner around to a more productive lesson agenda. Although this is a good way to help your learner to recognise where they are and where they need to be, a directive approach can sometimes be a lot quicker, especially if the learner is adamant about their plan.

Don't be afraid to break out of the comfort zone

"A comfort zone is a beautiful place,
but nothing ever grows there."
— Unknown

It can be difficult to work with a learner driver who isn't keen to move on to a new topic, even though you might consider them ready to do so. Traditional coaching models place a lot of emphasis on allowing the client to set goals and lead the agenda, and on the coach supporting the client in achieving those goals. By helping our learner drivers with their desires to stay working on one topic or issue, we could also be doing them a disservice by not pushing them towards their end goal. When it comes to learning, the challenge is just as important as the support.

In their excellent book, "Challenging Coaching", John Blakey and Ian Day describe how both support and challenge can be used together.[57] Their concept is illustrated in the "support/challenge matrix" below. It was based on the original work of Nevitt Sanford and later developed by Laurent Daloz.

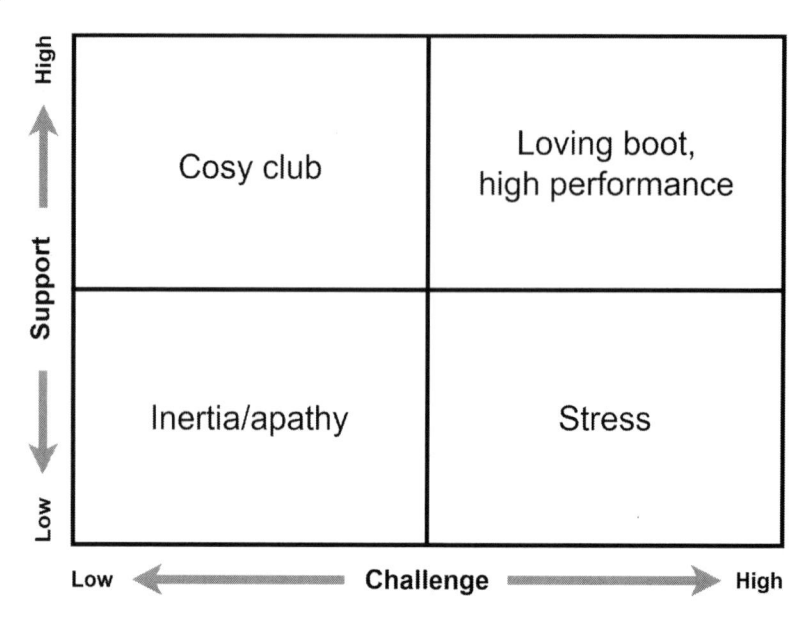

	Low Challenge	High Challenge
High Support	Cosy club	Loving boot, high performance
Low Support	Inertia/apathy	Stress

Low-challenge/low-support quadrant

The learner driver experiences inertia and apathy; this is the place of boredom, where the learner driver becomes disinterested in the learning process. They don't seem to be getting very far or progressing at the rate they'd hoped. The learner loses their motivation for learning, and they begin to question whether they can be bothered learning to drive after all. Alternatively, they might decide to look for a different instructor.

Low-challenge/high-support quadrant

This section is the "cosy club", a comfortable place for the learner driver to be. Their instructor has high empathy, and great listening and questioning skills, but the learner doesn't feel they're learning or progressing as quickly as perhaps they should.

High-challenge/low-support quadrant

The learner feels stressed, perhaps even scared at times. They're being pushed beyond the boundaries of where they feel comfortable and are making lots of mistakes because their instructor isn't providing them with much support.

High-challenge/high-support quadrant

This section is where the magic happens! The perfect balance of challenge and support allows the learner to grow and develop at their best rate. Blakey and Day describe this area as "The 'loving boot' that can stimulate and 'kick' a person to pursue a new direction or goal and achieve high performance."[58]

We think the support/challenge balance is of significant relevance to our industry. Take some time to consider which quadrant you tend to work within and how you could work towards positioning your lessons within the top-right quadrant. It's entirely possible to be both challenging and supportive whilst coaching. However, many learner drivers need that "loving boot" occasionally, so you'll need to be directive at times, too.

As a learner's level of competence increases with each new challenge, you'll find your level of support for that particular challenge will naturally reduce as the learner begins to take more responsibility.

Beware of the fun factor

I'm sure most ADIs would agree that learners like their lessons to be enjoyable. After all, we learn best when we're enjoying the process, don't we? To that question, we would answer, "Yes, *if* the balance is right."

We've observed ADIs on hundreds of driving lessons, many of which involved lots of laughter and fun. It's great to watch the connection between instructor and learner, some of whom have formed a friendship.

Lessons full of laughter and joy might be entertaining for the learner and make our working days enjoyable, but in doing so are we still effectively and efficiently helping our learner achieve their end goal? If so, then great. If not, it might be better for us to focus more on challenging our learners and tackling their weaknesses rather than on keeping them entertained. Rapport is a fundamental element in creating and supporting a positive coaching relationship but, like support, we should remember that a good relationship must be balanced with the right amount of challenge.

Your feedback is vital

An all-too-common issue with traditional coaching approaches is that the coach holds off from giving feedback; this is something we've seen first-hand while observing driving lessons. Many ADIs who have attended a coaching course seem to believe that they shouldn't be giving any feedback, so instead, they mimic the behaviour of politicians, who avoid answering questions.

Example: Alex has just completed a manoeuvre. She has pulled up on the left and turned to look at her instructor for some feedback.

Alex:	"So how was that? Any better?"
ADI:	"What do you think?"
Alex:	"Well, I think it was, but you're the expert!"
ADI:	"I appreciate that, I'm just wondering how you felt about it?"
Alex:	"Oh. Well, would I have got any faults if that was on my driving test?"
ADI:	"Do you think you would have got any faults?"
Alex:	"Hmm, I don't know. That's what I'm asking!"
ADI:	"Well, if you were an examiner and you'd been assessing yourself, what faults would you have picked up on?"
Alex:	"You're really beginning to annoy me now!"

Another approach ADIs use is the scaling technique, a popular and extremely beneficial self-evaluation tool, which we cover in more detail in *Chapter 6: Learning Styles*.

ADI: "Okay, Alex, so that's the end of the lesson. How do you think you got on today?"
Alex: "Okay, I think."
ADI: "So on a scale of 1 to 10, where 1 is the worst performance ever, and 10 is the best, what number would you give that lesson?"
Alex: "Not sure. You're the instructor — what do you think?"
ADI: "What I think isn't important, though. I'm asking you."
Alex: "What? I thought I was paying you to teach me to drive and tell me where I'm going wrong. What the heck are you asking me for?"

Admittedly, part of the issue in the above examples might be that the learner hasn't understood the benefits of self-evaluation, and the reasons why their ADI is trying to raise their levels of awareness and responsibility. But put yourself in the learner's situation for a moment: how massively irritated would you feel in each of the above examples?

If a learner directly asks you for your feedback or an opinion on something, don't be afraid to give it. Coaching is a voluntary process; you can't force reflection and self-evaluation on someone who only wants your feedback. Your feedback is essential in optimising the learner's progress. Your comments could help uncover problems, mistakes or issues of which the learner is unaware.

Feedback from you is often the fastest way of bringing an issue to light. If your learner has made a mistake which will, or could, potentially result in something more serious happening, it's important that you step in to give some feedback. For example, you might have noticed your learner has mistakenly selected third gear instead of first when they're just about to move away at a set of traffic lights. Asking your learner to give feedback on their gear choice at this point would be inappropriate.

Instead, you might say, "Just check we're in the correct gear there, John" or "We're in third gear, John. Try selecting first again."

Feedback is also an excellent way to reinforce positive actions. If a learner does something well, it can be tremendously rewarding for them to hear positive words of encouragement from you.

We discuss the use of feedback in much more detail in *Chapter 4: The 5 Key Skills of a Client-Centred Instructor*.

Points for reflection

- Which of the nine key principles of coaching resonate with you most? Which of them do you already follow in your driving lessons? Do you disagree with any of the nine principles? Which of them are absent from your driving lessons?
- If you don't already incorporate coaching into your lessons, what are your objections to trying it? If you've used coaching methods with your learner drivers, what objections have you had from them? Have you managed to overcome these objections? If so, how? Are there any other situations where you feel a more direct instructional approach would be more suited?
- How often do you help your learner drivers become aware of their internal environment?
- If your learner is struggling to master a topic or skill, are you more likely to place the blame on your learner, or self-reflect and see what you could do differently?
- How much responsibility do you give your learners? How could you pass on more responsibility?

CHAPTER 3

AN INTRODUCTION TO CLIENT-CENTRED LEARNING

Client-centred learning is based on the needs, abilities and learning style of the learner. The driving instructor is a facilitator in the learning environment. The learner driver is encouraged to be an active, responsible participant in their learning.

| Watch Video Message: Ged & Claire Introduce Chapter 3 |
| http://gedclai.re/chapter3 |

The origins of client-centred learning

Student-centred philosophies are nothing new; in fact, they've been around for well over a hundred years. Frank Herbert Hayward has been credited with coining the student-centred concept back in 1905.[59] Later in the twentieth century, esteemed psychologists Jean Piaget and John Dewey advocated for student-centred learning.[60,61] American Psychologist Carl Rogers developed the theory of person-centred therapy. The term client-centred was also used by Rogers, although he used this for where commerce was involved.

Through his work on personality theory, Rogers believed that a person exists in a continually changing world of experience, at which he — or she — is the centre. The way the person reacts and responds to situations is based on their perception and experience. Regarding teaching, Rogers believed that the student is at the centre of any learning experience and that what the student does is more important than what the teacher does: "We cannot teach another person directly; we can only facilitate his learning."[62]

Is client-centred learning the same as coaching?

For most driving instructors, coaching was a concept which was introduced well before client-centred learning was ever on our radar. Coaching seemed to divide the industry, which was a shame, as it does have a lot to offer. At one end of the scale, we have instructors who have rejected coaching as nothing more than a fad. Some of these ADIs have been instructing for many years and don't feel inclined to change their teaching style or even learn about alternatives. Their way has always worked and has previously been confirmed by the DVSA as satisfactory.

An Introduction To Client-Centred Learning

Some instructors have heard rumours about what coaching is, or have a vague gist of the concept, rejecting it before learning more because they don't feel it could work in the in-car environment.

At the other end of the scale, we have curious ADIs who have learned more about coaching and what it can offer. From going on courses to reading books, they've embraced the coaching approach in its entirety, becoming huge advocates and insisting that coaching is the best approach. In more recent years, the DVSA have introduced a relatively new concept to the driver training industry, that of client-centred learning. So how does coaching compare to client-centred learning? Are they different, or are they the same? We believe that coaching methods can be viewed as a subset of a client-centred approach, so they are not the same, and as such, the two terms shouldn't be used interchangeably.

The DVSA also make the distinction between instruction, coaching and client-centred learning in the following section of the DVSA's guidance for driving examiners carrying out instructor tests (ADI1):

4.44 Teaching and learning strategies

The important thing to remember when considering teaching and learning styles is that it is not just about coaching. It is about client-centred learning. Our judgement should be about whether the ADI can help the pupil to learn in an active way ...

... There will be many times when it is useful to use a coaching technique. The principle that underpins coaching is that an engaged pupil is likely to achieve a higher level of understanding and that self-directed solutions will seem far more relevant. This applies in every situation, including instruction. Direct instruction is useful in helping a pupil in the early stages cope with new situations or supporting a pupil who is clearly struggling in a certain situation. Good coaching will use the correct technique at the correct time, matching the pupil's needs. In some cases, the ADI may need to give direct instruction through a particularly difficult situation.

That instruction forms part of a coaching process if the ADI then encourages the pupil to analyse the problem and take responsibility for learning from it.[63]

By their very nature, coaching methods are wholly client-centred. We believe that if an ADI is to be truly client-centred, a good understanding of coaching is essential. However, to be client-centred doesn't necessarily mean that you must always use a coaching approach. A good ADI has a range of methods at their disposal. Being client-centred may, at times, require that the instructor takes the lead and instruct rather than coach with questions. When a learner is approaching a particularly challenging situation, direct instruction might be necessary; some learners may welcome a coaching approach but might prefer you to take the lead at times, to teach them and to provide them with feedback.

> A few years ago, I took some advanced driver training with a specialist advanced driving instructor who had a background in police driver training. We had only limited training time together, so I wanted to get the most from the day. The day started with the trainer discussing my goals for the day. I told him that although I'd passed many advanced driving tests in the past, I was keen to learn more about applying the Roadcraft system of car control.*
>
> The trainer observed my driving for a short period. He then provided me with feedback on my performance and spent the rest of the day instructing me on how to perform better. He showed me how to achieve peak driving performance, using trainer-led (or "instructor-led") methods; which was the exact outcome I wanted.

---

* Coyne, P., Mares, P. and MacDonald, B. (2013). *Roadcraft*. New edition 2013, London: Stationery Office [for] the Police Foundation.

An Introduction To Client-Centred Learning

> Had the trainer coached me and encouraged me to self-reflect when I had hardly any concept of what I was aiming to achieve, I would have finished the day frustrated and annoyed that I didn't take away what I wanted from our time together. In this situation, by being instructor-led, he was being client-centred.

The DVSA's definition of client-centred learning

Carl Rogers offered no specific definition for the term "client-centred learning", but the DVSA give their view on its meaning in the National Standard for Driver and Rider Training (Role 6 Unit 3):

Client-centred learning is not about the learner taking charge of the learning process and deciding what is going to happen. Instead it is about creating a conversation between the learner and the instructor that is based on mutual respect. This approach is based on the idea that people resist taking on new understandings and resist modifying their behaviour if:

- *the person who is trying to teach them fails to respect and value their idea of who they are*
- *the person delivering the learning is not seen as "genuine"*
- *the person delivering the learning is not seen as having legitimate authority*

In the context of learning to drive or ride, the instructor brings to the learning process their hard-earned knowledge, understanding and experience. If they rely simply on telling the learner what they should do, they will probably be able to teach them enough to pass their test. However, all the evidence suggests that learners in this sort of relationship do not really change the way they think and quickly forget what they have been taught. There is a better chance of a long-lasting change in understanding and behaviour if the instructor:

- *presents their knowledge, understanding and experience clearly and effectively*
- *listens to the learner's reactions to that input*
- *helps the learner to identify any obstacles to understanding and change*
- *supports the learner to identify strategies for overcoming those obstacles for themselves.*[64]

Instructor-centred teaching vs client-centred learning

The following table illustrates the main differences between instructor-centred teaching and client-centred learning:

Instructor-centred teaching	Client-centred learning
The instructor's role is that of primary information giver and evaluator.	The instructor's role is to facilitate learning and for the instructor and learner to learn together.
The instructor is the authority figure. The learner is subordinate in the relationship and regarded as an empty vessel. The instructor is the expert and the one in power, who passes on knowledge and information to the learner.	Although the nature of driving lessons means the driving instructor is inevitably still viewed as the authority figure, there's an equally active role in the learning process. The instructor coaches and facilitates the learner's learning and understanding.

An Introduction To Client-Centred Learning

The focus is on what the instructor wants and/or needs to cover.	The focus is on what the learner wants and/or needs to cover.
The instructor chooses the topic and decides on the lesson goals without the learner's input.	The learner is encouraged to share their input when deciding on the lesson goals with the instructor.
The instructor talks and the learner listens.	The learner is encouraged to interact in a two-way discussion.
The focus is on giving directive instruction. Those learners who can learn will learn.	The instructor engages the learner and uses a range of directive and/or non-directive methods and techniques to suit the learner's preferred methods of learning.
The instructor monitors, identifies, analyses and corrects every mistake the learner makes. They tell the learner where they went wrong and why, and how to correct it.	The learner monitors their performance, and the instructor encourages the learner to identify and analyse any areas for improvement and to develop a strategy to solve the problem.
Emphasis is on giving the learner the right answers.	Emphasis is on generating self-awareness and responsibility and helping the learner choose the most appropriate action from a range of possible options. Learning is achieved with the help of reflection and self-evaluation.
The learning environment is one-sided and contradictory.	The learning environment is supportive, cooperative and collaborative.

Emphasis is on the instructor's syllabus and the requirements of the driving test.	Emphasis is on discussing situations, issues and problems in real-life contexts relating to an individual learner. The learner is aware of the syllabus and driving test requirements and is encouraged by the instructor to ensure they feel comfortable in all those areas.
The instructor evaluates the learner's performance and gives feedback to the learner.	The learner is encouraged to reflect on their own performance, with added feedback from the instructor.

The term "instructor-centred" could be considered synonymous with "instructor-led". An instructor-centred approach means that the lesson revolves around the needs and desires of the driving instructor, which are often based on the DVSA's driving syllabus or standards, the requirements of the practical driving test and anything else the instructor wishes to cover. Instructor-centred teaching, therefore, uses an instructor-led approach.

The focus of client-centred learning is on placing the learner at the centre of the process, encouraging them to shape their learning paths and actively take part in the educational process. The learner will be made aware of the contents of the driving syllabus and the requirements of the driving test by their instructor. The instructor encourages their learner to take joint responsibility for ensuring that all the elements are covered thoroughly, to a standard with which both the learner and the instructor are happy. The emphasis is on learning rather than teaching. Client-centred methods may include both client-led and instructor-led approaches, depending on whichever approach is most beneficial for the learner at any given moment.

An Introduction To Client-Centred Learning

Instructor-centred approaches focus on teaching the learner *what* to think.

Client-centred approaches help the learner to understand *how* to think.

Knowing what to do is fine in the short term; in the case of driving lessons, knowing what to think will often be enough to pass a driving test. Knowing how to think, on the other hand, is a skill that lasts for life.

> *"Give a man a fish, and you feed him for a day; teach a man to fish, and you feed him for a lifetime."*
> — Proverb

A blended approach

In our opinion, we shouldn't be looking for an either/or approach when it comes to coaching or instructing. As we outlined towards the end of *Chapter 2: Coaching,* some learners and some situations will benefit from a blended approach, where the instructor uses a mixture of directive instruction and non-directive coaching methods. For example, when the car is in motion, and the person behind the wheel is inexperienced and therefore giving the driving task their full attention, an exclusive coaching approach would be tough and, at times, unsafe.

Being client-centred requires us to accommodate the learner and their learning preferences, but we also need to adapt and use whatever teaching/learning methods we feel are appropriate to get the best outcome at that moment in time. In addition to the learner's wants, we're there to support their needs and to provide some form of structure to the learning process. In some time-critical situations, like the meeting situation with the lorry, they require more help and instruction so that they don't crash. Once through the situation, the instructor can then use a coaching approach to encourage the learner to reflect on the situation and develop a strategy for when they encounter a similar situation in the future.

How to decide which approach to use

Which approach a driving instructor should use at any given moment will depend upon a range of factors. These include the learner's willingness to communicate, the approach the learner prefers you to take, the learner's expectations, the external environment, the internal environment, time, knowledge gaps or basic skills transfer and motivation levels.

Let's now take a look at each of these factors in more detail.

The learner's willingness to communicate

While many learner drivers ask lots of questions and enjoy interacting with their driving instructor, we're sure you've come across some learners who are completely the opposite. Some learner drivers are very introverted, never instigate a conversation or ask questions and rarely give you more than one-word answers to your questions. They may even blush and avoid making eye contact when they speak or show signs of extreme discomfort when you ask them questions.

For coaching to be effective, the learner must want to be coached. Sure, some introverted learners may begin to open up after a few lessons, in which case coaching approaches might start to work well, but others will remain pretty much silent for the duration of the driving course. You need to decide which method would work best for that individual.

The approach the learner prefers you to take

Like the first point, some learners may openly enjoy assuming responsibility for the learning process; others would rather you took control. It would

An Introduction To Client-Centred Learning

be helpful from the outset of a course of driving lessons to find out which approach they'd prefer. Throughout their lessons, pay attention to their response to your approach. If you're using more instruction than coaching and you notice that they're struggling to get a word in edgeways, perhaps you need to take a step back and move to more of a coaching approach.

On the other hand, if your coaching approach is being met with sighs, shrugged shoulders, repeated "I don't know" replies and statements such as, "You're the instructor — you tell me!" then perhaps your learner would prefer you to take a more directive, instructional approach.

The learner's expectations

Many learner drivers will have preconceived ideas about the way driving instructors "usually" teach. These may be based on any former instructor's teaching methods, the way they've been taught in school, music lessons or sports, what their parents/family/friends have told them, and what they may have seen on TV or online.

A conversation at the start of the learning process will help you discover your learner's expectations. What preconceptions do they have from the outset? Perhaps their parents passed in less than seven lessons and they think that's a suitable time frame for them. Maybe their friend has told them that their instructor shouts a lot, so they're feeling apprehensive. This conversation can be very enlightening. It will help you understand your learner and to decide on the best approach for them. Now would also be a good time to introduce your learner to coaching, helping them understand the benefits of active learning on or before the first lesson. That way, they're more likely to buy-in to the process and not question it further down the line. We explain the active learning agreement in detail in *Chapter 5: What Does a Client-Centred Lesson Look Like?*

The external environment

Using coaching approaches while the car is in motion can be challenging. By their very nature, non-directive questions require thought and consideration from the learner. Sometimes the external environment isn't conducive to this — busy traffic, challenging junctions/traffic situations, or a potential safety-critical situation. In these cases, a more directive approach would be appropriate — verbal guidance from the driving instructor. A more coaching-style discussion could ensue once parked in a safe position at the roadside.

To illustrate this point, imagine this situation: your learner is driving along the road at 28mph towards a meeting situation, there are parked vehicles up ahead on both sides of the road, and in the distance, you see a large heavy goods vehicle approaching from the opposite direction. The lorry is moving out to take priority in the situation, but your learner is showing no signs of having recognised this; their speed isn't dropping, and they're using their mirrors in preparation to move out to proceed. You're only a few seconds away from having a head-on collision with the heavy goods vehicle. In this example, the external environment dictates that you should tell your learner to brake to a stop and hold back (directive), rather than ask them how they feel about the meeting situation ahead (non-directive).

The internal environment

The learner's internal environment may direct the driving instructor's style of language at any given moment. For example, if the instructor senses that the learner is anxious, embarrassed, scared, frustrated or emotional, or indeed if the learner expresses that they are, this will affect the instructor's chosen style. Using a non-directive coaching approach in this situation is more helpful, as it will uncover more about the issue so that the instructor can look to help the learner resolve it.

But we need to be careful in these kinds of situations — sometimes we can risk opening a can of worms which might take us out of our depth. If a learner's conversation starts to go off on a tangent, one which isn't conducive to achieving their short- or long-term learning goals, then a directive approach might be more appropriate to get them back on track.

Time

In therapeutic coaching situations, time isn't usually of primary concern. In driver training, however, time can often be a significant barrier to success with coaching. In the short-term, coaching can take longer than traditional teaching, since the driving instructor will often be exploring the thoughts, feelings and experiences of the learner using open questions. This difference means that exploratory chats at the start of the lesson and throughout can take a little longer when compared to a situation where the ADI controls and directs the conversation.

It's important to strike a balance between theory and practice in order to maximise learning. Some situations will require more time at the roadside than others. Give your learner sufficient time to explore, reflect, self-evaluate and come up with solutions, but ensure you allow sufficient on-road time to put that learning into practice.

Although coaching is tremendously useful in dealing with issues thoroughly and efficiently, the problem is that most of the lesson is spent in a moving vehicle. In a safety-critical situation, it might not be an excellent time to start asking questions. If time is of the essence, it can be better to take a directive approach. Coaching can then be used at the roadside to explore situations further.

You may also need to consider the duration of the learner's driving course. In some exceptional circumstances, where you might be limited to getting a learner to test standard within a very specific time frame, you may need to adapt your approach. This constraint is certainly not ideal, but you need to approach each situation with a flexible mindset.

Knowledge gaps or basic skills transfer

When a learner driver gets into the driving seat for the first time, the driving instructor needs to assess the learner's current level of knowledge and understanding about the main car controls. If it's clear that the learner has no idea whatsoever about the clutch pedal, non-directive approaches probably won't work.

ADI: "Any idea what the pedal on the left is called?"
Joe: "Err, no."
ADI: "And if you did know?"
Joe: "What? I don't know, though."
ADI: "Take a guess."
Joe: "Look, I already told you, I've no idea. Can you take me home now?"

Instead, a more directive approach might be more useful.

ADI: "Any idea what the pedal on the left is called?"
Joe: "Err, no."
ADI: "Okay, well that pedal is called the clutch. Have you any idea what that might be used for?"
Joe: "I'm not sure. Is it something to do with the gears?"
ADI: "Yes, that's right. Well basically, the clutch pedal is used to connect and disconnect the engine from the drive wheels on the car. The way it works is …"

Trying to encourage a learner driver to explain how something works, when they have no idea, is futile — not to mention tremendously frustrating for them.

Since skills transfer is such a significant part of a driving instructor's role, directive instruction will be necessary at times, especially with a learner in the early stages of learning to drive.

Motivation levels

As ADIs, we come across all sorts of learners with varying degrees of motivation. Some seem keen to learn and develop; others seem less interested in the learning process and more in the outcome — getting their driving licence. On our blog at **gedandclaire.com**, we've written an article entitled, *Motivating the Unmotivated* that you might find helpful.[65] In it, we explore some techniques to help those with low motivation levels to find their "spark" and desire for learning. Scan the QR code or visit **http://gedclai.re/motivating** to read the article in full.

Learners will perform better when they're motivated to learn. If you're struggling to help a learner find their motivation, you might be wondering whether to use directive or non-directive methods — is it better to instruct or coach? In "Coaching for Performance", John Whitmore states that, "When I want to, I perform better than when I have to. I want to for me, I have to for you. Self-motivation is a matter of choice."[66]

As a general guideline, if you're working with someone with low motivation in the early stages of learning to drive, directive approaches will probably work best in helping them to achieve more, and thus feel inspired by their progress to continue to improve. As they develop, they may benefit from using more of a blended approach. Someone in the early stages of learning to drive who's highly motivated to learn will benefit from more of a blended approach too. A blended approach can accelerate the learning process for the learner, but at the same time, leave them in control of their learning. As they develop, a highly-motivated learner will thrive when the instructor uses more non-directive approaches, as they'll enjoy working things out for themselves, reflecting on their performance and planning a way forward.

The client-centred ADI

Take a few moments to think about an adult who you knew personally from your childhood, someone whom you remember with affection. This person should preferably not be a parent, but instead someone else with whom you had a fond connection. It might be a grandparent, teacher or family friend. If you struggle to think of someone from your childhood, then think of someone from your young adult years — a colleague, boss, trainer or mentor, perhaps. Once you have a clear picture of this person in your mind, consider what personality traits or characteristics that person had which made them more memorable than all the other people in your life at that time. What made them stand out?

We learned this exercise on a course with Sir John Whitmore, author of "Coaching for Performance". As we found it so compelling, we also used the exercise on our coaching courses for ADIs. We consistently heard the same characteristics mentioned, such as:

- "They **listened** to me."
- "They were **interested** in my thoughts and opinions."
- "They **respected** me."
- "They treated me as an **equal**."
- "They made me feel **special**."
- "They **inspired** me."
- "They **believed** in me."
- "They **challenged** me."
- "They **built my self-confidence**."
- "They were **fun**."

Chances are the person you're thinking about has many of those characteristics listed above, too. Aren't these traits something that we should all strive towards? What can we do to become that person? For a start, we can pay attention to the way we interact with our learners and ask ourselves these questions:

An Introduction To Client-Centred Learning

- "Am I listening as well as I could be? How could I listen better?"
- "Am I paying attention or is my mind on other things?"
- "Am I genuinely interested in what my learners are thinking and feeling?"
- "Am I aware of my learners' emotional states? How might they be feeling?"
- "Do I always speak to my learners in a respectful way?"
- "Do I turn up on time for my learners' driving lessons?"
- "Do I treat my learners as my equal, or do I view myself as being superior in some way?"
- "Do I make my learners feel special?"
- "How could I inspire my learners to perform at their best?"
- "How could I help them become more motivated to practice and succeed?"
- "Do I honestly believe that all my learners can achieve success?"
- "How could I change my attitudes towards the learners I doubt?"
- "Am I supportive to all my learners? How could I be more supportive?"
- "Do I provide enough of a challenge? Do I expect too much of them?"
- "Are my learners self-confident? How could I build on their confidence, if they need it?"
- "Are my lessons fun and engaging? Do my learners look forward to their lessons?"

Asking ourselves these questions will help us recognise areas that we can improve on, and uncover our coaching blind spots. When we know what our weaknesses are, we can then consciously work on them until we become better. Reflection and self-evaluation are the keys to growth and development.

Points for reflection

- Consider the overall balance of control within your driving lessons. Are your lessons more instructor-led or client-led?
- How could you make your lessons more client-centred? In what parts of your lesson could your learners have more control?
- Look back over the list of role model characteristics. Which characteristics would your learners attribute to you? Which characteristics would they say you don't possess?
- How could you improve or develop these characteristics to become more of a role model to others in your life, not just your learners?

CHAPTER 4

THE 5 KEY SKILLS OF A CLIENT-CENTRED INSTRUCTOR

"People are just as wonderful as sunsets if you let them be. When I look at a sunset, I don't find myself saying, 'Soften the orange a bit on the right-hand corner.' I don't try to control a sunset. I watch with awe as it unfolds."[67]

Carl R. Rogers

Watch Video Message: Ged & Claire Introduce Chapter 4

http://gedclai.re/chapter4

How we communicate

Communication can be broken down into three elements:

1. **Words** — what is said
2. **Tone of voice** — how it's said
3. **Body language** — conscious and unconscious movements, gestures, posture, facial expressions, etc.

To understand the full and genuine meaning of a message, we ideally need all three of these elements.

The most challenging form of communication to interpret correctly and accurately comes in written format, as we only have access to one of the above elements: the words. Those who frequent online forums and Facebook groups will notice just how quickly forum posts and social media discussions can turn nasty, as people misunderstand or misconstrue the meaning of someone's words.

These misunderstandings occur when non-verbal communication, a person's tone of voice and body language, is completely absent. It's for this reason that we recommend refraining from texting, messaging or emailing learners when needing to communicate more sensitive issues, such as the need to cancel a driving lesson or reschedule a driving test. Using emoticons and emojis to try and help to convey the emotional tone of what we're saying can be useful, but speaking over the phone is usually a better choice.

During a phone conversation, we can communicate using two out of the three communication elements: words and tone of voice. These two forms of communication enable us to express emotion and meaning much more efficiently than using words alone.

Communicating face-to-face is the best form of communication, as we can use words, tonality and body language — gestures, facial expressions and body posture — to convey messages; this means it's less likely that we'll be misunderstood or that we'll misunderstand others. Communicating face-to-face does have a downside, however, and that's that our body language "leaks" the truth — if what we say isn't congruent with what we're thinking, our non-verbal communication will give the game away.

It's impossible not to communicate; even when you're avoiding communication, such as no eye contact or sitting in silence, you're still communicating something. This communication avoidance could be interpreted in the listener's mind as, "This person is avoiding eye contact, so this means that they are hiding something/are lying/are shy/don't like me." Or it could be interpreted as "This person isn't saying anything, so this means that they're ignorant/introverted/not listening."

It's important to remember that communication goes two ways — it doesn't just involve speaking, but also listening. When it comes to successful communication, there are five key skills which a good coach will have, use and seek to develop:

1. Rapport
2. Active listening
3. Asking questions
4. Feedback
5. Intuition

Key skill 1: Rapport

Have you ever met someone for the first time and within a few minutes of chatting felt like you've known the person for years? You might have even noticed that you've unconsciously adopted the same posture. We call this being 'in rapport' with someone. The Oxford English Dictionary defines rapport as, "A close and harmonious relationship in which the people or groups concerned understand each other's feelings or ideas and communicate well."[68]

Rapport is an essential foundation for effective coaching. But don't worry, this isn't some new technique you need to learn, rapport is a very natural and unconscious part of communication. However, there are ways in which you can accelerate and enhance levels of rapport with anyone.

In the context of driver training, rapport creates a sense of warmth, comfort, trust and connection between instructor and learner. From a coaching perspective, building rapport with your learners encourages them to communicate more openly and honestly with you. High levels of rapport and a relaxed connection with your learner will enable you to discuss more severe or sensitive issues more easily than without it. Learners are more likely to discuss their inner thoughts, feelings, values and beliefs with someone they connect with than someone they don't. Furthermore, your learners will be more apt to enjoy taking an active role in the learning to drive experience.

Mirroring and matching

NLP trainers Joseph O'Connor and John Seymour remarked that "When people are like each other, they like each other."[69] In other words, the more similar you are to another person, the more you like them. A good way of establishing rapport is to mirror or match the other person. Often used interchangeably, the terms 'mirroring' and 'matching' refer to the subtle and respectful copying — reflecting — of the other person's verbal and non-verbal behaviour. It's important to remember that this isn't overt mimicry; quite the opposite. When done well, the other person will feel a sense of connection with you without being conscious of you mirroring their behaviour.

Again, mirroring and matching happen very naturally when people are in rapport. Just watch the people around you in social situations; people stood at the bar reflecting each other's stance or a couple of friends sat together, both with their hands clasped and legs crossed. Notice what happens when you're next out with a friend, how you unconsciously and naturally match and mirror each other.

On a more conscious level, we can establish rapport verbally, too. Consider small talk with another person for example, where we try to find some common ground as a topic of conversation to create a connection — the weather, if they have any children, where they grew up, what plans they have for the weekend, etc.

We might also mirror and match on a verbal level during a phone conversation with a prospective learner. Doing so can hugely increase the chances of converting that potential learner to a client. For example, the caller might be distracted by their children playing or their dog barking, or they might mention that they work at a business which you know well, or live on a road in which you've taught a couple of other people to drive. Bringing these snippets of information into the topic of conversation can really enhance your sense of connection.

During driving lessons, all three elements of communication are there: words, the tone of voice and body language. It's essential that you can use all three elements effectively to establish and maintain rapport. Let's now take a look at four non-verbal levels on which you can mirror and match your learners to increase rapport.

Body language

People naturally make varying levels of eye contact; some are comfortable with it, and others aren't. There are also cultural differences you should be aware of when it comes to eye contact. Visit **http://gedclai.re/eyecontact** or scan the QR code to learn more.

What's important is that you match your learner; there's no easier way to break rapport with someone who naturally makes quite a lot of eye contact than for you to talk to them while looking elsewhere. Similarly, if you're working with someone who seems uncomfortable with eye contact, you can match this by perhaps looking at a visual aid or something outside the car when you're having a discussion.

You can match people's facial expressions, too, if a learner shows a worried expression and you subtly show a similar expression, they're likely to feel acknowledged and understood, creating a stronger feeling of trust. In a sense, you need to try and feel what they're feeling. It's also possible to mirror and match your learner's gestures. For example, if you're working with someone who gestures a lot while they're speaking — hopefully, while safely parked — you could match their hand gestures when it comes to your turn to speak.

Voice

Matching the tone, pitch[‡], volume and speed of the learner's voice, as well as matching their rate of breathing, is another way in which you can increase rapport. If a learner is quiet and timid when you first meet, a loud, confident voice from you may make the learner more withdrawn. But by subtly matching the learner's voice pace and volume, to begin with, you can then slowly try to lead them to a more positive place by gradually raising the volume and confidence of your voice.

Likewise, if a learner is annoyed, ranting, speaking loudly and at a fast pace, using your best soothing, slow-paced voice may only serve to irritate them more. Instead, try subtly matching their tone, pitch and volume until you feel you can start leading them with a calmer quieter tone of your own. The ultimate test of rapport is if you're successful in leading the learner to a state that's conducive to learning.

[‡] In matching the learner's voice pitch, this doesn't mean that male instructors should start speaking at the same pitch as a 17-year-old girl or that female instructors should lower their voice several octaves when teaching men to drive; subtlety is the key!

Language

To enhance rapport, we should use our learners' words, particularly when reflecting on what they're saying if we need to clarify something. Instructors use all sorts of jargon and technical terms, often without realising that the learner might not fully understand what they mean.

- "Find your bite."
- "Peep and creep."
- "Pause at your point of turn."
- "Full lock to the right."
- "Remember your all-round, effective observations."

Any terminology that you intend to use should be clearly explained to the learner on its first usage. If a learner comes up with their own terminology, use that with them. For example, if they refer to all-round observations as an "owl check", then referring to the "owl check" in future will show you've listened. This will strengthen your rapport.

> Shortly after I qualified as an ADI, I was working with a learner called Emily. During our third driving lesson, together, I pulled Emily up to discuss her road position once again, an issue she'd been having every now and again since lesson one.
>
> **Me:** "I've noticed that we've started driving a little too close to the kerb again, can you feel the car dropping down all the drain covers?"
>
> **Emily:** "Sometimes, yes."
>
> **Me:** "Why did we say it was important to keep a metre away from the kerb when we're driving?"
>
> **Emily:** "To keep away from all the debris and so people don't get confused and think we're parking or turning left?"

> **Me:** "Yes, that's it! Have you noticed we've been driving too close, or do you feel like we're in the correct road position?"
>
> **Emily:** "I thought I was a metre away."
>
> **Me:** "Hmm, okay. Could you show me with your hands roughly how big you think a metre is?"
>
> **Emily:** [Holding her hands apart about 30cm] "About that much?"
>
> **Me:** "Ah okay, that might be the issue then, a metre is actually about three times that distance. [Extending my arm] It's roughly the length of my arm, maybe a tiny bit more."
>
> **Emily:** "Oh. Why don't you just say an arm's length then? I'm absolutely rubbish with measurements, I could never understand them at school!"
>
> **Me:** "Well I'll use an arm's length in future if that would work better for you?"
>
> **Emily:** "Yes, I think I can remember that better."

Using words, phrases and terminology the learner is more likely to be familiar with builds rapport and will ensure a fuller understanding. If a learner prefers using feet and yards to centimetres and metres, you'd be wise to change your terminology to match theirs. If a learner struggles with the concept of turning "offside to offside" or "nearside to nearside" at crossroad junctions, find something they can relate to instead, such as "driver to driver" / "passenger to passenger", or "after the car" / "before the car" or "behind" / "in front". Use whatever works for *them!*

Beliefs and values

Matching and mirroring a learner's beliefs and values can create a tremendous sense of rapport. This is easily achieved if you agree with their beliefs and values in the first place, but it can be much more challenging if those beliefs and values aren't conducive to becoming a safe and responsible driver.

Learner drivers come to us with a variety of values and beliefs which have been shaped since birth — many will match those held by their parents. Some of these values and beliefs may not serve them well, however, and could even lead to them ending up in serious trouble with the law or another road user. *Chapter 7: Addressing Limiting Beliefs* and *Chapter 8: Dealing with Negative Attitudes* are dedicated to addressing limiting beliefs and challenging poor driver attitude, but the starting point with either of those objectives is gaining rapport.

- "All white van drivers are idiots."
- "The guy behind is so impatient."
- "I hate cyclists."
- "Drivers over 70 should be taken off the roads."
- "There's no way the speed limit on here should be 20mph."
- "I've learned to multitask really well, so I don't see why talking on a mobile phone should be banned."

How could you show rapport when a learner says one of the above, even though you don't agree with what they've said? Assuming you don't concur with what they've said, the temptation will often be to just dismiss their statement, or tell them they're wrong. Rest assured, this is the quickest and easiest way to break rapport and make learning much more challenging. As difficult as this may seem, you need to start with understanding and empathy. That's not to say you must agree with it — just understand it. Here are some alternative responses that will help to show understanding and empathy with the learner's perspective:

- "That's quite a common belief" or, "A lot of people think that."
- "I can understand why you might believe that …"
- "Yes, it can be frustrating to get caught up behind a cyclist …"
- "That's interesting …"
- "Yes, it's quiet along here today …"
- "I've often thought I could multitask quite well too …"

After the opening statement to show understanding, you can then work your way around to challenging their belief or attitude, as described in *Chapter 7: Addressing Limiting Beliefs* and *Chapter 8: Dealing with Negative Attitudes*. The purpose of showing understanding is to open channels for negotiation, not to show agreement with what they said. If you dismiss their statement out of hand, your learner's internal belief system will slam the door in the face of anything else you say on the matter.

Starting with understanding gives you a better chance of leading your learner driver to a safer way of thinking.

Key skill 2: Active listening

When you communicate, you need to be aware of the words you use, your tonality and your body language. But as communication is a two-way process, when other people are communicating with you, make sure you listen. No, we mean *really* listen, not just to what they say, but also to their tonality and body language. That way, you're more likely to understand the other person and respond appropriately.

Listening sounds like a simple skill, but it's not as easy as it sounds. Remember what Confucius allegedly said? "I hear and I forget." So to be good at listening and to retain the information we're hearing, we need to practise. How easy is it to tell when someone you're talking to isn't listening? You notice their eyes glazing over as they mentally "zone out". You can see that they're distracted, you can sense that they're waiting for their turn, interrupting you or turning the conversation into what experiences they've had. You may feel like there's no point in carrying on talking, that you should talk to them at a different time. It may make you feel like you're not important, that what you're saying doesn't matter to them.

As the instructor, you can't allow yourself to lose focus on what your learner is saying. You shouldn't be forming your next question or counterargument. You shouldn't allow yourself to become distracted. Doing so will contribute to a lack of understanding, frustration and a breakdown of rapport. By being a great listener, you'll hear real views, get information from your learner you might not have been expecting, and get a much deeper understanding of what your learner is thinking. A high level of self-awareness is needed to become an active listener. Understanding the total message being sent by your learner is more important than just hearing the words.

Here are some tips to help you to become an active listener:

Be present and pay attention

When your learner driver is talking to you, give them your full and undivided attention. As tempting as it may be to check the time or to look outside, you must resist the temptation and focus on your learner. While they speak, stay quiet and take the time to notice all three elements of their communication: their words, their tone and their body language. Jiggle around the letters of LISTEN, and you get SILENT. Being silent — including silencing your mind — allows you to listen intently.

Show that you're listening

To demonstrate that you're listening, you need to be acutely aware of your own verbal and non-verbal communication. You can show that you're listening verbally by making listening noises — "mm", "uh huh", "yes", "I see". Non-verbal listening cues include your facial expressions, your head position — slightly tilted to one side generally shows you're friendly and receptive — and nodding or shaking your head to indicate empathy with, or understanding of, what the speaker is saying.

Also, be aware of your body posture. If you turn your body towards the other person while they're speaking, they'll feel a closer sense of connection and a feeling that you're listening and are interested in what they're saying. Notice the position of your arms; you might naturally find it comfortable to sit with your arms folded, but consider how this might be interpreted by the person speaking — you could easily come across as defensive, nervous or arrogant.

Time your feedback and respond appropriately

While listening, there will be times when you disagree with what the learner is saying, or you want to add something. It's likely that your inner voice will be urging you to interrupt and have your say or correct the other person. But wait, remember, this is your *learner's* turn to speak. That's not to say you must agree with what they are saying — just respect their opinion and give them time and space to express it. This will make your learners feel valued and respected. Once they've finished speaking, you can ask further questions to clarify the learner's views or to share your own thoughts or opinions. As hard as it might seem the first few times you do this, try it; it really does help to enhance the relationship between instructor and learner.

Example: Ben has just approached a meeting situation in which the parked vehicles are on the right-hand side of the road. He braked very heavily for a car which was already committed to coming through.

Ben: "Woah! What an absolute idiot! Can't he see the cars were on his side of the road? It's not like he could b****y miss them! Idiot!"

ADI: "I totally see where you're coming from, Ben — it is better to give way when the parked cars are on your side of the road. Why do you think he might have pushed through before us?"

Ben: "Because he's an arrogant prick, bullying me because I'm a learner."

ADI: "I can totally understand why you're angry, Ben. He might well be an arrogant prick, but we can't know that for sure. What if he'd just received a phone call from the hospital because his wife has had a serious accident? What if he's

	worried he's going get sacked because he's been stuck in traffic and is likely to be late for work again? What if he's absolutely DESPERATE for the loo?"
Ben:	"Hmm, well I guess … But he's still a prick."
ADI:	"What if you're in any of those situations, what would you do?"
Ben:	"Haha, yeah. I'd probably try to get through first, as well."
ADI:	"Okay, and you're not a prick, are you?!"
Ben:	"Not normally!"
ADI:	"Good, so how could we maybe deal with a situation like that better next time?"

Reflect, clarify and summarise

During a conversation, we don't always accurately hear what the speaker said or meant. We tend to make unconscious assumptions and judgements about the message they're conveying. This is because we have our own mental filters and beliefs which affect the way we might interpret a message. It's important, therefore, that we focus on understanding the true meaning of the message by reflecting — paraphrasing — clarifying and summarising.

When a learner explains something, it may be difficult or take them a long time for them to express themselves fully. They may be explaining:

- what they want to get from the lesson/the course
- an area they feel they're struggling with
- something they need clarification on
- an idea they've generated which could resolve a previous issue

Reflecting back to the learner using their words will not only enhance rapport but also ensure you've understood them properly.

Example: Amy has issues with turning right into side roads. She tends to have an occasional habit of cutting the corner.

ADI: "Okay, tell me how you felt we dealt with that last junction, Amy?"

Amy: "I don't know ... I just can't seem to get this turning point thing right. I know I need to start steering when the car is level with the middle line of the road on the right, but it's hard to tell when it's there ... Especially when I'm trying to do everything else at the same time ... Then I don't get it right, and I cut the corner again. It's all so confusing! And that guy shouting at me didn't help either!"

ADI: "Yes, I can totally understand why you might be confused — it's a lot to remember, isn't it? So, what you're saying is that you'd like a good way of judging exactly when you've reached the turning point, so that you can get it correct and stay on our own side of the road?"

Amy: "Yes — like a way to get it right every time."

All too often, we listen at a very cosmetic level. By listening deeply and attentively, we can pick out the most important points and the true meaning the learner is trying to convey.

We can also reflect back things we notice from the speaker's body language, or things we feel intuitively. We can't possibly know for sure what's going on for our learner, so it's important to check that our interpretation of what they may be thinking or feeling is accurate. You can reflect back and clarify by saying things like:

- "I sense that ..."
- "I notice that ..."
- "I'm get the feeling that ..."
- "Would I be right in thinking ...?"

DON'T finish your learner's sentences

We think this one is obvious — if you've ever been the victim of this, you'll be only too aware of how irritating it can be to have your sentences finished.

Give your learner time and space to think and to reflect. Some learners will take a little longer to think things through and to respond than others, particularly if they have a preference towards a reflective learning style. We explore learning styles in more detail in *Chapter 6*.

DON'T interrupt

Another irritating habit is interrupting the other person with counterarguments or statements of one-upmanship — let the person speaking finish what they have to say!

- "He's not an idiot, he was already committed to coming through the gap. We should have given way!"
- "Wait, you think that's bad? When I was driving yesterday ..."

DON'T plan what to say or ask next

This one is hard; we find ourselves falling into this trap occasionally. While someone is talking to you or answering your question, it's easy for your mental focus to shift onto what you're going to reply or ask next. But when you do this, you're not truly listening to the speaker. While the mental chatter is going on inside your mind, you could be missing several other important pieces of information.

DON'T be distracted

Possibly the easiest way to show your learner that you're not listening is to look at something or someone else while they're talking to you.

> If Claire comes into the living room while I'm watching the football to ask me an important question and I continue to watch the match while replying, I'm in big trouble!

While your learner is talking to you at the roadside, be present with them. Quieten and ignore any inner dialogue so that your full focus is on the learner. Be sure to make eye contact with them occasionally. If you start chatting inwardly, look past them at what's going on outside, or start checking your watch or your phone, you could not only miss out on essential elements of their message, but the learner will feel a sense of disconnect. They're likely to feel that you're not interested or don't value what they think or have to say.

DON'T fidget

Pen-clicking, doodling, foot-jerking, finger-drumming and playing with jewellery may go unnoticed for you, but for someone who's talking, it can be hugely distracting and very annoying.

Key skill 3: Asking questions

Lou Holtz said, "I never learn anything talking. I only learn things asking questions."[70] Being client-centred means that questions will form an essential part of your toolbox. We often come across lots of confusion when it comes to questioning techniques. Here are a few examples of the types of things PDIs and ADIs say to us in relation to questions:

"I've heard you should never ask closed questions."

Never say never! Closed questions definitely have a place in driver training, especially when on the move.

"To be client-centred, you have to ask the learner questions all the time."

This is quite a common misunderstanding. Imagine for a moment that you were working with an extremely introverted learner driver who would much rather you took the lead; would it be client-centred for you to bombard them with questions? Or might it be better to work in the way the learner would prefer? As we discussed earlier, you need to match the expectations and needs of the learner. At times, this may mean you need to give direct help rather than ask questions.

"Asking your learners questions on the move is distracting — I never do it."

Yes, some types of questions can be extremely distracting when asked on the move, especially when asked at the wrong time, such as when emerging from a busy junction. Open questions, which typically demand more focus and attention than other types of questions, fall into this category. It's also advisable to keep the number of questions asked on the move to a minimum, especially in the early stages of learning, when your learners need to focus their attention on controlling the car.

"I've given up asking questions — my learners either don't know the answer or don't respond."

If your learners don't know the answer or don't respond to your question, it might not be because they didn't know the answer. It could be because they didn't hear you; they weren't sure if you were making a statement or asking a question; they weren't listening because they were distracted or focusing on something else; or they didn't understand the question.

Make sure it's clear you're asking a question by ending your question with an upward inflection. ADIs with a more monotonous voice often don't do this, which means the learner driver isn't sure if the instructor was asking them something or just making a statement. On the opposite end of the scale, some ADIs have developed an unconscious high-rising terminal, which results in every sentence sounding like it's a question.[71] It's much harder, therefore, for the learner to notice what a question is and isn't.

It's also important to consider the timing of your questions. Asking questions at the wrong time, such as when your learner is concentrating on finding a safe gap while waiting to emerge from a busy T-junction, will also often result in no response. If your learner does hear the question and you're sure it's a question they should be able to answer, chances are you're not asking the *right* question. Don't necessarily give up at this point — consider rephrasing it or asking a more focused question instead. They may not be sure how to articulate the answer.

Of course, a learner can respond with "I don't know" for various reasons — perhaps you're asking them a factual question to which they genuinely don't know the answer, and therefore need some more input from you, or perhaps they can't be bothered to think for themselves and would rather you give them the answer, or maybe they're afraid of giving the "wrong" answer.

If you're asking a more insightful coaching question about the learner's thoughts or feelings, it may be that they simply need a little longer to answer — you might be surprised to learn that if you remain silent for a little longer, they often come up with an answer. When asked correctly, questions can be enormously powerful, so please don't give up, it's all just down to practice.

"My learners are paying me to get them up to test standard, not constantly bombard them with questions."

Although it's perfectly possible to get someone up to test standard by giving them direct instruction, constantly bombarding a learner with questions isn't what we're suggesting — we've even heard some examiners refer to this as "death by Q&A". Questions have a time and a place. Remember, your aim should be to promote a long-lasting change in understanding and behaviour, not just to get them through the driving test. You can best achieve this goal by encouraging your learners to think, explore, notice, explain and discuss things through the proper use of questions.

It's really important that your learners understand why you're asking questions and what the long-term benefits are, to them, of using this engaging approach. We discuss how you can do this effectively in the section titled, "The active learning agreement" in *Chapter 5: What Does a Client-Centred Lesson Look Like?*

Types of questions and when to use them

> *"It is not the answer that enlightens, but the question."*
> — *Eugene Ionesco*[72]

The key to being a successful, client-centred ADI isn't in your ability to give the right answers, it's in your ability to ask the right questions.

There are many kinds of questions you can ask when providing driver training. These include closed questions, leading questions, open questions, TED questions, suggestive questions and a range of other non-directive questions.

Closed questions

A closed question is a directive question, in that it can be answered with either a single word or short phrase. This includes yes or no answers. They're very useful in that they're easy for the learner to answer; they're quick to answer; they give you facts, and the driving instructor keeps control of the conversation. Some closed questions can be useful when asked at the right time. They can test knowledge or get an insight into what the learner thinks is correct. Due to the nature of the driver training environment, closed questions can be an excellent tool while on the move, especially at times when you need a quick response.

- "Are we in the correct gear?"
- "Is it safe to go?"

- "Do we need the handbrake?"
- "Is this a 30mph or 40mph limit?"

However, some closed questions offer little value, such as:

- "Have you set up your mirrors correctly?"
- "Do you know what an open junction is?"

Most of the time, these questions will just generate a yes or no response, leaving you unsure as to whether the learner really has the best view of the road through the driving mirrors, or can define the characteristics of an open junction. In both these cases, you'd need to explore the learner's knowledge and understanding further. Asking an open question or TED question in the first instance would probably have been more appropriate and less time-consuming.

Closed questions can be useful in promoting further discussion, so shouldn't necessarily be disregarded. For example, when the learner is carrying out their cockpit drill, you could start by asking a closed question to start a conversation, then follow with a more open line of questioning:

ADI: "Are you feeling comfortable in your seat?" **(closed question)**

Rufus: "Yes, I think so." **(hesitant reply, therefore needing further discussion)**

ADI: "So what is it you're looking for when setting your seat up?" **(open question)**

Rufus: "That I can press the clutch down fully without stretching my leg too much." **(correct but partial response)**

ADI: "Okay, great. And what about the back of the seat — what is it you're looking for when adjusting that?" **(another open question)**

Leading questions

Leading questions are also directive questions. They can direct the learner to the correct answer or response. By their very nature, leading questions are designed to make the learner think or act in a specific way. These are, in effect, disguised commands or instructions.

Due to their closed, directive nature, leading questions can be very useful in the in-car environment when you need a quick, short verbal response (question and answer) or if you want to direct an action (question and action).

- "Where do we need to look before moving off?"
- "Which mirrors will we check?"
- "When will we signal for this junction?"
- "When will we press the clutch down?"
- "Which gear will we need now?"

The disadvantage of using leading questions is that they don't demand much thought from the learner. Also, they don't give us any idea of the depth of the learner's understanding. Whenever a leading question is asked to prompt an action, it would be important to follow it up with some further analysis, using open questions.

Open questions

Open questions are non-directive in nature. They're the opposite of closed questions, in that open questions seek longer answers. Open questions are useful in that they encourage the learner to think and reflect. They also give you an idea of the learner's depth of understanding, how the learner is thinking and feeling, and they hand control of the conversation over to the learner. Open questions generally begin with words such as what, why, which, when, who, where and how. In that way, they're like leading questions; however, unlike directive leading questions, there's no obvious answer to a non-directive open question.

As shown earlier, open questions can be used as a follow-on from closed questions to develop a discussion. They can also work well after having asked a leading question when you've checked that the learner knows what to do first.

- "**Why** would it be so important to observe effectively before moving away?"
- "**Where** is it best to position our car on approach to a right-hand bend?"
- "**Which** road users could benefit from our signal?"
- "**Who** else?"
- "**When** might it be appropriate to sound the horn?"
- "In **what** situation might a signal be beneficial to pass a line of parked vehicles?"
- "**How** do you judge if you have enough time and space to cross the path of an oncoming vehicle?"

TED questions

This is one of our favourite non-directive styles of instruction. Although described as questions, TED questions are more like an instruction to give more information and are similar to open questions in their nature.

- **T** stands for **T**ell
- **E** stands for **E**xplain
- **D** stands for **D**escribe

TED questions are a great way of encouraging your learner to name mistakes or issues, analyse the causes and effects, and then develop a strategy for next time they meet a similar situation again.

- "**Tell** me what you noticed about our speed at that last junction."
- "**Explain** the potential risks of approaching a junction that quickly."
- "**Describe** to me how you'll deal with it differently next time."

TED questions can also be used when you'd like your learner to elaborate further on something; "Tell me more about that"; "Explain that a little further" or "Describe to me specifically how you'll do it."

Suggestive questions

Sometimes a good coach will offer options or suggestions, especially if the learner is feeling exasperated and out of ideas. This is a way of finding out what will work best for the learner.

- "Let's have a think about what would work best for you. Would you like me to give you a demonstration so you can see what to do first and then you can have a go, perhaps?"
- "How about we choose a wider road until you feel confident turning around, and we can then work towards trying to turn around on gradually narrower roads?"

Suggestions can also be made if the learner is unaware of a solution.

Simon: "Hmm, I think I needed a lower gear for that junction."
ADI: "Anything else?"
Simon: "Hmm, no. I don't think so?"
ADI: "How about your speed, would we have had more control at a slower speed, say a walking pace?"
Simon: "Ah yes, probably. I think I need to do that too."

Other non-directive questions

Other non-directive styles of questions include:

- **Chunking/Funnel questions** — we can seek more or less detail by chunking/funnelling up or down
- **Empowering questions** — these are helpful for helping someone overcome limiting beliefs
- **Probing questions** — specific questions which dig for more detail

- **Emotion questions** — questions which explore how someone is feeling

Although non-directive questions can be split into many different types, they're all very similar in nature, and it's often unhelpful and unnecessary for an ADI to spend time working out what kind of question to ask. To keep it simple, non-directive coaching style questions are the questions you ask that you don't necessarily know the answer to. Whereas more simplistic styles of question tend to focus on facts, knowledge and understanding, coaching questions tend to be more introspective, delving into the learner's feelings, emotions and thoughts.

- "How did you feel about that last roundabout?"
- "You look a bit tense, is there something worrying you?"
- "Okay, so you felt anxious at the right turn, which parts specifically made you feel anxious?"
- "What would make it easier for you to deal with next time?"
- "What would you prefer to work on now?"

Until the instructor understands how the learner is feeling and how that affects their behaviour, it could be counterproductive to just carry on regardless.

Example: Sarah has shown signs of anxiety when turning right at traffic lights.

ADI: "I know you don't like these right turns, but you did really well there. Let's do a few more, so you get more used to them."

Sarah: "Okay then."

ADI: "There's no need to worry, I'll help you with them, especially the busy ones. They can be a bit tricky, sometimes can't they?"

Sarah: "Yes they can."

ADI: "Okay let's go to the next traffic lights and turn right again."

Although it's apparent from the above discussion that the instructor is trying to reassure Sarah, it doesn't address the real issues. Asking questions would have provided a better insight into what Sarah was thinking and feeling.

Pulling it all together

The style of question you use will depend on the situation, the purpose of the question, and your learner. You wouldn't just repeatedly use one type of question — you'd use a variety throughout a conversation.

ADI: "Okay Becky, could you please pull up on the left in a suitable place?"

Becky: [Begins to pull over without signalling, but there's a car following]

ADI: "Do we need a signal here Becky — for that car behind?" **(leading question)**

Becky: "Oh yes! Sorry." [signals left and pulls up on the left]

ADI: "Good. Why was it important for us to signal to pull up?" **(open question)**

Becky: "Because there was that man behind and it might have caught him by surprise if I just stopped in front of him!"

ADI: "Yes, exactly. That's the first time you've done that for a while — would you like me to remind you about possibly signalling next time to stop, or can you remember that for yourself?" **(closed question)**

Becky: "No, it's okay, I can remember. I was distracted by thinking about that last turn I did."

ADI: "Yes, I sensed that. That's why we've pulled up actually — how did you feel about that last right turn?" **(open question)**

Becky: "I hated it, I just felt really rushed."

ADI: "Yes, I get that — when I was learning to drive, I hated dealing with busy junctions, too! **(showing understanding and empathy)** What specifically makes you feel rushed and what is it you hate about them?" **(chunking down for more detail)**

Becky: "I just get really panicky when cars are coming."

ADI: "Ah, so the panic is triggered by cars coming from the junction opposite? **(reflecting back)** Out of 10 then, how panicky did you feel at that junction?" **(using the learner's word "panicky" and creating a scale — see Chapter 6: Learning Styles for information on scaling)**

Becky: "It was definitely a 10!"

ADI: "What would have made it less than a 10?" **(encouraging the learner to self-analyse)**

Becky: "If it had been quieter without any cars coming opposite."

ADI: "So when cars are coming, what specifically makes you panic?" **(chunking down)**

Becky: "I'm not quite sure where to stop, you know, where to wait in the junction."

ADI: "Okay. Well I have some aerial images of junctions, shall we look at those, and we can work out where you'd wait?" **(suggestive questions)**

Becky: "Yeah, that would be good."

ADI: "Okay, and then would you like to try some quieter ones with little traffic while we can work out what position we would wait in? We can even pull up before each one to discuss it first if you prefer?" **(suggestive questions)**

Becky: "Yes, please."

Timing is critical

Whatever question is most relevant to the situation, it's also important to time the question appropriately. To manage risk effectively, asking, "When is it safe to turn?" will be a useful question to find out when your learner is planning to make a turn. If they say, "In front of that bus" which is closing in fast, you can prevent a dangerous turn by telling them to wait until after the bus. It's good to find out what's going on in a learner's mind *before* they make a risky move rather than afterwards.

It's also important not to distract the learner with poorly timed questions. Asking them where they should have positioned at that last junction while they're approaching a fast-flowing roundabout is probably going to end in disaster. Save asking any open questions for when your learner has time to listen, think and answer.

Key skill 4: Feedback

It's important that a learner driver is encouraged to give feedback to their instructor on how they feel they're progressing. It's also important that the learner receives regular feedback from their instructor.

Feedback is especially important when a learning opportunity presents itself or when a learner has done something well. From a client-centred perspective, it's essential that the learner is encouraged to self-reflect and self-evaluate — to notice what happened, to become aware of their strengths and weaknesses, and to come up with possible solutions. This helps the learner to take more responsibility for their learning. If they work things out for themselves, this can deepen their understanding and assist them to retain valuable skills more effectively.

Some learners relish the opportunity to share their thoughts about how they're doing and enjoy working out things for themselves. Conversely, some learners feel very uncomfortable assessing their own performance and would much rather take a passive role, receiving feedback from their instructor. Feedback from the instructor, when given correctly, will motivate the learner and positively reinforce their improvement. Feedback can come in many forms, from a smile, nod, thumbs up or a "well done" to a short conversation on the move or an extended discussion at the roadside; your job is to decide what type of feedback is most appropriate at that moment.

The instructor can also encourage the learner to self-evaluate. This can take place either on the move or at the roadside, depending on the road and traffic conditions and the complexity of the task they're dealing with at the time. For more information on self-reflection, refer to *Chapter 2: Coaching*.

The four essential elements of giving effective feedback

> I've lost count of the number of times I've observed a driving lesson where the learner driver gets something right when the situation is repeated, and the instructor gives little or no positive feedback. This occasionally results in the learner asking, *"Was that okay?"* to elicit some positive reinforcement from their instructor.

Success, praise and positive reinforcement motivate people, so once your learner has completed an action successfully, praise them for it! There are four key elements to giving feedback after mistakes have successfully been corrected.

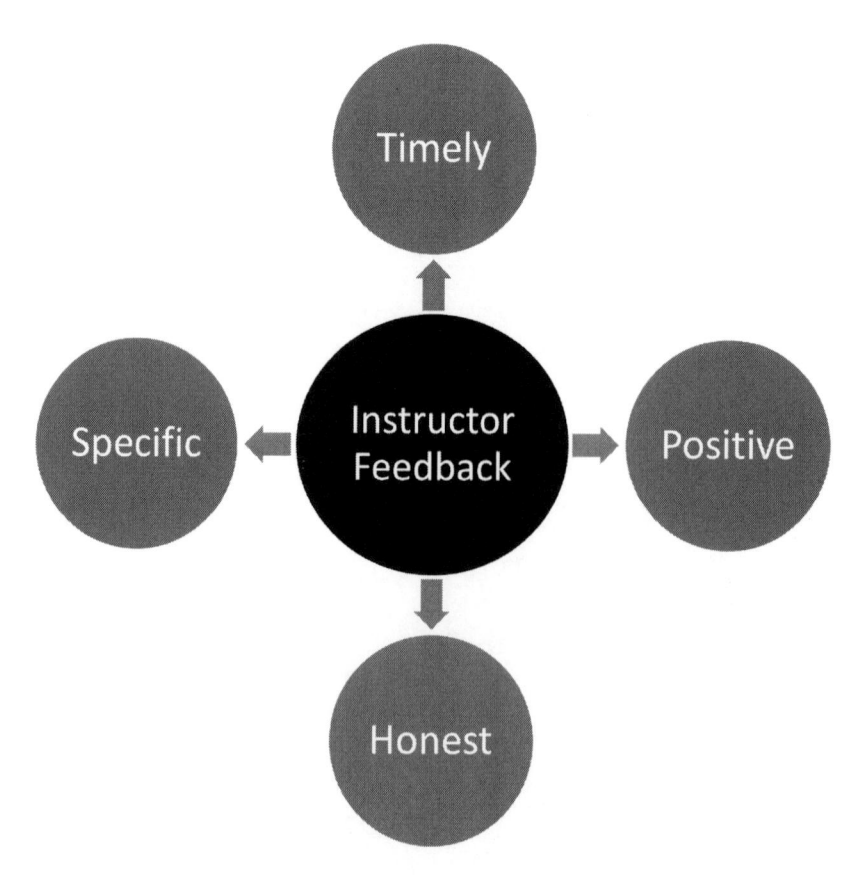

- Timely
- Specific
- Positive
- Honest

(Instructor Feedback)

1. Timely

Feedback should preferably be provided and elicited at the earliest possible opportunity. Delay almost always lessens the impact of the feedback, regardless of whether it's positive or 'constructive'.

Timely feedback *to* the learner:

Sometimes, you might be able to pick up on verbal or non-verbal cues which let you know a mistake is about to be made. For example, you ask your learner to take the second road on the right, and their finger reaches for the indicator stalk well before they've even reached the first junction. Immediate feedback — in some form — at this point may be safer and more appropriate than discussing it a few minutes later, e.g. "WAIT — don't signal just yet."

Similarly, if your learner successfully carries out a task they've done incorrectly or struggled with before, immediate positive feedback will have a much greater impact than giving it at the end of the lesson.

Timely feedback *from* the learner:

Although end-of-lesson self-evaluations are important, so too is self-evaluation during the lesson, especially after having made a mistake or correcting an earlier error. If for example, your learner winces as they go around a corner slightly too fast, you really need to be asking them for feedback at the earliest opportunity. In effect, we should be encouraging awareness and responsibility every step of the way.

- "I noticed you winced as we went around that corner?"
- "How do you feel we dealt with that last junction?"
- "How did you feel about your speed at that junction?"
- "On a scale of 1 to 10, where 1 is terrible, and 10 is perfect, how would you rate the way we handled that junction?"

- "If we were to go around again to that junction, what would you do differently next time?"

2. Positive

Whenever possible, try to ensure that you present your feedback *positively*. Examiners are encouraged to do this at the end of the driving test, too. Instead of saying, "I'm sorry to say you've failed," they instead rephrase the failure element in a more positive frame: "I'm sorry to say you haven't passed/haven't been successful on this occasion." This is because they're expected to convey the message sympathetically.

Positive feedback *to* the learner:

Try to use positive words where possible. When the learner has corrected an earlier error, for example, it can be better to say, "Well done for *checking* your mirrors — can you see how much *safer* that is?", than to say, "Well done for *not forgetting* your mirrors — can you see how *dangerous* it can be to miss your mirror checks?"

When used correctly, the "feedback sandwich technique" can be helpful.

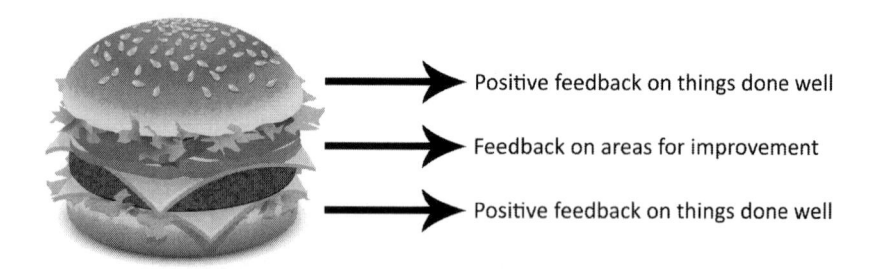

Positive feedback on things done well

Feedback on areas for improvement

Positive feedback on things done well

Feedback Sandwich[73]

Although the sandwich technique looks simple enough, it's important that the sandwich filling is constructive and positively phrased, especially when it comes to highlighting areas that need improvement. Please don't confuse this feedback model with the "sh*t sandwich" model of

The 5 Key Skills Of A Client-Centred Instructor   127

giving feedback, which is saying something nice before and after saying something bad, like in this illustration!

I like your hair
Your face is ugly
But your dress is nice

When given correctly, feedback given using the sandwich technique is **positive** and **focused on solutions**.

ADI: "Your mirror use is coming along really nicely now, Darren, and the timing of your signal was spot on there. Also, well done for bringing your speed down to a walking pace — that was the perfect speed for the corner. The icing on the cake would have been if we'd have selected first gear for that junction, rather than the second, as it was a bit tight, wasn't it?"

Darren: "Yeah, I realised that after I'd turned the corner."

ADI: "You actually managed to control it quite well because the car didn't stall. What problems could we have caused by stalling in the junction, do you think?"

Darren: "Well, the guy behind could have rammed us, or swerved. He wouldn't have expected me to stop on the road there."

ADI: "Exactly, yes. Like I said, though, the rest of your approach was great, so let's perhaps revisit that corner, and we can nail the gear part this time, okay?"

Darren: "Yeah, okay."

Notice that being positive doesn't mean we dismiss the risks of that error — they still need bringing to the learner's attention. But the learner is likely to be more motivated to get it right next time if feedback is given in the above constructive manner, rather than being reprimanded for forgetting to change into first gear.

Positive feedback *from* the learner:

We feel that enhanced learning takes place when feedback comes *from* the learner. This generates greater levels of awareness and responsibility, which is so important if we're to develop good, safe drivers. So instead of giving positive feedback on what went well and giving the learner the positive steps to correct it next time, we should try to encourage our learners to become more self-aware, to take ownership of the successes and the areas for improvement, and to handle generating a solution. Our job is to elicit positive feedback from the learner on their achievements and positive steps to correct it.

- "What do you think went well?"
- "What was good about …?"
- "What parts of it do you think we could improve on?"
- "What improvements could we make?"
- "How could we make it even better next time?"

3. Honest

Feedback should always be honest, whether it comes from you or your learner. Otherwise, what's the point?

Honest feedback *to* the learner:

Telling a learner that they did something well just to make them feel better after making several serious or dangerous mistakes isn't going to lead to success in the long term. They can usually tell when you're lying, so always be honest but respectful. Remember, they probably didn't do it wrong on purpose; focus on what parts did go well, no matter how small, and then talk about where improvements could be made.

Conversely, when someone genuinely does do well, it's best to avoid the over-use of superlatives such as "brilliant", "excellent", "fantastic", "amazing" and "superb". This is particularly the case if the thing that you're praising is something rather insignificant.

- "Well done Jim, that was a **fabulous** gear change!"
- "Wow, Pete, I have to say — that blind spot check was **phenomenal!**"
- "That was an **beautiful** mirror check, Melissa — well done!"

This isn't to say that we shouldn't be giving praise where it's due, of course — used every now and again, when genuinely called for, superlatives can have a positive effect on your learner's confidence — but over-use will reduce the impact of the praise when you need it most. You must be honest too; if your learner improved slightly, but it's still not 100% perfect, it's more honest to say that it was "better" than "excellent".

Honest feedback *from* the learner:

Let's face it, we can all find it hard to be constructive and honest about our own performance. From the learner who thinks that they're marvellous to the learner who beats themselves up all the time, your role is to help them generate an honest and unbiased appraisal of how they're doing.

We've lost count of the number of times we've heard learners and PDIs say things like:

- "Yes, I know I do that wrong sometimes — but I won't do that on my test."
- "I don't normally do that, though."
- "I know you're saying I'm not ready for my test next week, but I know I can do it!"
- "Oh, my God, that was horrendous!"
- "I'm so rubbish at this."
- "That was so awful — I don't know why I bother."

Asking questions which hone in on specific parts of their performance, which they may not be aware of, can help your learner with appraising themselves more honestly. For example, you could say:

- "OK, you said you don't normally do that. Being honest for a moment, how many times in the last couple of lessons have I needed to remind you about it?"
- "So you say it was horrendous/rubbish/awful. Which parts of it *did* go well? Was it all wrong, or just a couple of bits?"
- "Imagine a scale from 1 to 10, where 1 is you haven't got a chance of passing in a million years, and 10 is you'll pass your driving test with no faults at all. If you booked a test for three weeks' time, where would you place your chances of passing on the scale?"

This last example will usually, although not always, generate a response of less than 10, which enables you to point out that there's still plenty of room for improvement, backing up your advice to postpone the test. We take an in-depth look at the "scaling" method in *Chapter 6: Learning Styles*.

4. Specific

Both the instructor and the learner need to be conscious that when giving positive or negative feedback, it's important to be specific, rather than to make generalisations.

Specific feedback *to* the learner:

Consider the following pieces of feedback:

- "Well done!"
- "I think you've done really well."
- "Let's do that reverse park again because it wasn't as good as it could have been."

A lot of the time, the learner may be none the wiser about what specifically the feedback was targeted at: "*What* did I do well?" or "*Which part* of my reverse park exercise wasn't as good as it could have been?" So, when giving feedback, **be specific**.

- "Well done for bringing your clutch up before turning that time, Matt[§] — that was much better."
- "I think you've definitely improved with your early observation on approach to roundabouts and the timing of your signals now, Becca."
- "That right turn was so much better that time, Gemma — you judged the turning point really well!"
- "Let's do that reverse park manoeuvre again — I think we could do with working a little more on your all-round observations and awareness whilst reversing."

[§] Use the learner's name from time to time when giving feedback as it can really amplify the impact of your message.

Specific feedback *from* the learner:

By taking time out at the roadside to encourage the learner to evaluate their performance so far, it enables you both to assess how well the original learning goals have been achieved and, where necessary, adapt or set new learning goals for the lesson time remaining. But the key here is to get specific.

- "How did you feel about your speed on approach to that junction?"
- "How aware were you of what was in your right blind spot before we moved away that time?"
- "Which parts of the manoeuvre did you actually deal with really well, and which parts need some work?"

Generalisations about overall performance can be useful at times, such as when reviewing the entire lesson, but improvements can only come about when you start getting specific about what needs work.

Key skill 5: Intuition

The final key skill of a client-centred instructor is the ability to pay attention to, and act on, intuition.

The Oxford English Dictionary defines intuition as, "The ability to understand something instinctively, without the need for conscious reasoning."[74] In simple terms, intuition is knowing, without knowing how you know. As ADIs, it's our intuition that sometimes prevents safety-critical incidents, or helps us anticipate what other road users are about to do. A typical question from a learner with an intuitive instructor is, "How did you know he was going to do that?"

If you examine a situation carefully, sometimes our intuition can be explained easily and logically — all the signs and clues were there. We could anticipate the actions of other road users based on previous experience.

Equally, we sometimes intuitively know what our learners are thinking or about to do. We pick up on signals they give off with their body language or facial expressions. One example might be when we've asked our learner to turn left, and they position their fingers under the indicator stalk while they look for the next road on the right. Within a second of spotting this, we can say, "It's the road on the *left* we're taking, Jon, not the right."

Another example might be when we approach a large roundabout and ask a learner to take the fourth exit. On approach, we get the sense that they're not comfortable with the idea. The clues that the learner is uncomfortable are there on an unconscious level: the eyes widening slightly, the increase in tension with the hands and arms, the deeper intake of breath, the pale facial complexion, etc. At other times, the instructor may just have a "gut feeling" that something isn't quite right. Paying attention to our intuition can enable us to explore the learner's thoughts, feelings and beliefs.

ADI: "I've noticed that we seem to be driving unusually slow today, Chris. I know it's your driving test in 45 minutes, but this just doesn't seem to be 'you'. Is there any particular reason? Has someone said something to you?"

Chris: "Yeah, my Dad — he said to make sure I remember to keep it slow and drive extra carefully."

Another example:

ADI: "You don't seem yourself today, Amanda — is there something worrying you?"
Amanda: "Not really."
ADI: "Oh okay — it's just that you seem a little distracted, like your mind is on other things?"
Amanda: "Well, yes, I suppose it is a bit. I'm anxious about my exam results; I really need to get in at Leeds Uni."

Intuition on the road develops through years of driving and instructing, and from observing the actions of other road users. Intuition with other people develops through being present, actively listening, and having a genuine empathy with them. As Julie Starr said:

> *"Based on years of experience and technical skill, what looks like magic is simply wisdom in action."*[75]

In a sense, our experience and skill give us the opportunity to use our intuition to appear to be almost psychic.

Points for reflection

- With which of your learners do you have a natural rapport? Which of the rapport-building techniques we've discussed in this chapter could help you to connect better?
- Are you truly an active listener, or do you tend to finish off other people's sentences? Perhaps you're easily distracted, fidget, or are planning what to say next? During your next few driving lessons, pay attention to how well you're truly listening to your learners.
- How good is your questioning style? Do you phrase your questions well, or do you sometimes get a blank look of confusion from your learner? Do you time your questions well or do you frequently find yourself saying things like, "Oh it's okay, I'll let you deal with this situation first"?
- How good are you at giving and eliciting constructively phrased, positive, honest, specific and timely feedback from your learners? How could you improve?
- How intuitive are you? Do you tend to trust or ignore your sense of intuition?

CHAPTER 5

WHAT DOES A CLIENT-CENTRED LESSON LOOK LIKE?

"What matters is not what we teach; it's what they learn, and the probability of real learning is far higher when the students have a lot to say about both the content and the process."[76]

Alfie Kohn

Watch Video Message: Ged & Claire Introduce Chapter 5

http://gedclai.re/chapter5

The active learning agreement

Many new drivers will start their driving lessons with the expectation that their driving instructor will be wholly responsible for the learning process, the content of each lesson, for correcting mistakes and for managing risk on the road. By this point of the book, you should hopefully recognise that this probably isn't the most efficient way to help your learners develop into safe, responsible drivers.

Therefore, before adopting a client-centred approach with your learners, it's vital that your learner driver understands and accepts the benefits of taking a more active role in their learning. If you don't explain the benefits of such an approach, you may come across to the learner as being lazy, unplanned or unprofessional. A good sign that this might be happening is that your learners repeatedly answer, "I don't know" to a lot of your questions. They may even say, "You're the instructor — you tell me!" or, "Aren't I paying you to *teach* me?"

By taking a couple of minutes before, or at the start of, the first driving lesson to explain your approach and the benefits of active learning, your learner is given the opportunity to accept or embrace the challenge of being more in control of their learning. Of course, your learner may reject the concept of active learning and express their desire for you to lead and manage the learning process altogether. Either way, you'll know what the learner wants from their learning experience, and you can focus on delivering training to suit their learning preferences.

ADI: "Okay Caitlyn, I just want to take a minute to explain how I like to teach and why I work that way. Is that okay?"
Caitlyn: "Yeah, sure."

ADI: "Great. Well, lots of learners come for driving lessons fully expecting me to tell them exactly what to do, when to do it and why to do it, without them having much input at all. Although that approach *can* work, I tend to find that it's not the best way. If I take on all the responsibility now, you may not feel totally equipped or prepared to drive on the roads by yourself after you pass. You could easily 'forget' what to do at times, or you may meet situations you haven't encountered before and struggle to deal with them. You could even get yourself into situations where you make the wrong decisions."

Caitlyn: "Oh, God. I don't want to be like that!"

ADI: "Good, me neither! So, for that reason, I prefer to involve all my learner drivers in the learning process much more. I'll encourage you to think about new situations and, together, we'll consider how best to tackle them. I'll be asking you lots of questions to get you thinking, and I'll encourage you to reflect and learn from situations, opportunities and mistakes along the way."

Caitlyn: "Yeah, of course. I get that. I'll probably do loads of stuff wrong!"

ADI: "And that's fine! Mistakes are an essential part of learning. I'm not here to leave you to do everything yourself, of course. I'm here to help you through the course as efficiently as I can and to make sure you're ready for driving on your own. The more you get involved in the learning, the better you'll be able to problem-solve and deal with new situations after you pass your test! How does that sound to you, Caitlyn?"

Caitlyn: "Yeah, sounds good."

You could also give some more detail on how the learner will be actively involved in the process.

ADI: "I'll be asking you what you think you're doing well with and what you want to improve on further because it really helps if I know what you're thinking and if there's anything you're worried about.

>"I'll ask for your input on what you want to work on — this may be something listed on my syllabus, or perhaps something you feel you'd like to spend more time on.
>
>"I'll encourage you to learn from mistakes and challenge you to work out how to do things better next time — you're much less likely to make the same mistakes again if you've come up with the solutions yourself."

And you could summarise the benefits.

ADI: "You'll become more responsible for your decisions, those decisions will be safer, and you'll have greater confidence in your driving. It's likely you'll learn quicker and possibly take fewer lessons and feel better prepared for driving on your own."

Finally, but *most importantly*, your learners need to buy-in or agree to this approach.

- "Is that okay with you?"
- "How does that sound?"
- "Will that work well for you, do you think?"

From our experience, most learners will be enthusiastic about the client-centred approach, but there will be a small number of learners that evidently won't be comfortable with the idea. Watch your learner's body language as you explain your approach, listen for any signs of, "Ooh, I don't like the sound of this — this isn't what I was hoping would happen" in their tone or their words. If you sense anything that suggests they're not buying into that approach, you could say something like:

ADI: "I sense you're not comfortable with that? If it's not for you and you prefer the traditional way of being taught and me leading your learning, then that's fine too! We'll use whichever approach you prefer, and I'll be aiming to help you become the best driver you can possibly be. Okay?"

We have a handout you can give to your learners explaining the active learning approach. We also have one you can give to their parents, explaining how learners today are more actively involved in the learning process than perhaps when they learned to drive. You can download these handouts from **http://gedclai.re/activelearning** or by scanning this QR code.

The structure of a client-centred lesson

A client-centred lesson follows a simple cycle, which is structured in the same way as an instructor-led lesson, but with emphasis on the client (learner) having more input into the lesson's direction and content.

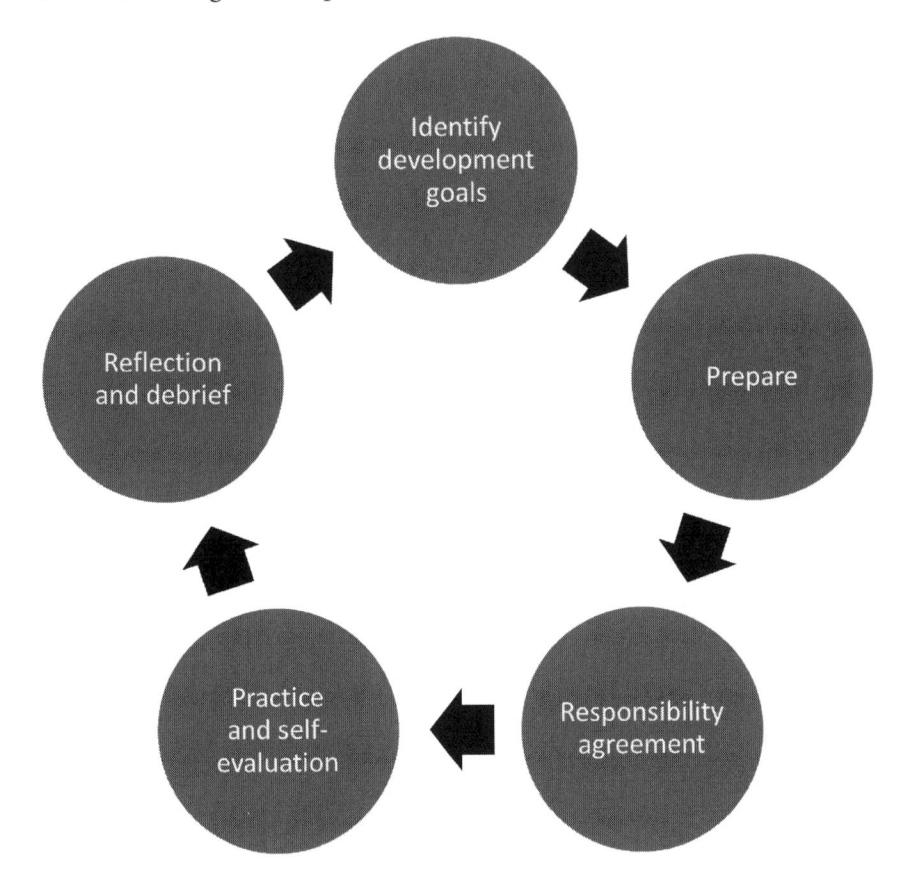

- Identify development goals
- Prepare
- Responsibility agreement
- Practice and self-evaluation
- Reflection and debrief

Step 1: Identify development goals

In any given lesson, the learning cycle starts with you and your learner working together to determine your learner's development goals. What your learner *wants* to do and what your learner *needs* to do might be very different, of course; that's why this part of the lesson is so crucial.

You're there to help provide a framework. You should be able to develop your learner's awareness of the need to learn about something new, or any areas for improvement; you can achieve this by encouraging your learner to analyse their current performance and to consider the level of performance they'd like to achieve. It's likely that the lesson goals will already have been established at the end of the previous lesson, but it's still beneficial to review them at the start of the lesson, to check if any changes are necessary.

- "How do you feel last week's lesson went?"
- "What do you think went well?"
- "What would you have liked to have done better?"
- "So based on that, what do you think you'd most benefit from working on today?"
- "Anything else?"

The lesson goals should be SMART (or PRISM) — see *Chapter 2: Coaching*. In the example below, we will focus on setting SMART goals.

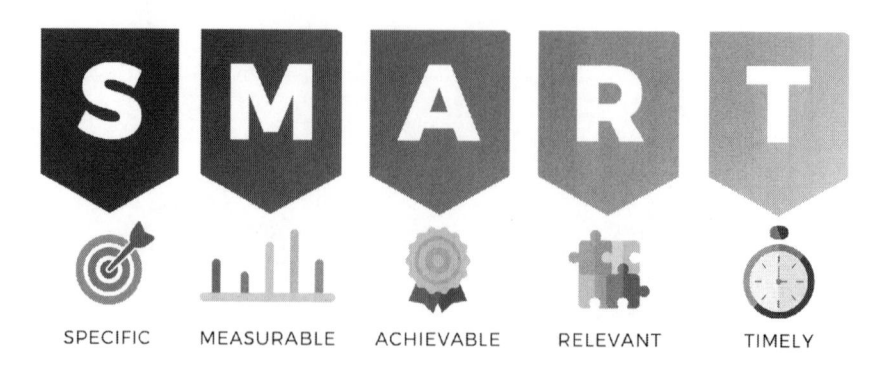

SPECIFIC   MEASURABLE   ACHIEVABLE   RELEVANT   TIMELY

SMART: Specific

Goals within each lesson ideally need to be specific to enable both the instructor and the learner to realise when they've been achieved.

ADI: "So can you remember from last week what you said you wanted to achieve during today's lesson?"

Joanna: "Yeah, I really want to get better at turning right at the big traffic lights."

A goal such as this one can be made more precise.

ADI: "Okay, and what specifically would you like to be able to do better?"

Joanna: "Understanding where to wait."

Sometimes the goals might relate specifically to performance, such as being able to do or be better, at something. At other times, the goals might relate to emotions, like being able to feel better about a task; more confident, more comfortable, less panicky or less anxious. In the example above, having dug a little deeper into the specific goals the learner has, we now know which specific elements of "turning right at big traffic lights" the learner wants to improve on.

If your learner comes up with lots of different things that they want to cover, it may be necessary for you to reflect back and summarise their goals and, where appropriate, suggest a structure for the lesson:

- "So, what you're saying is that you'd like to …?"
- "Which one would you like to work on first?"
- "How about we start with [skill], and then move on to cover [skill]?"
- "There's quite a lot there, which ones are your priority for this lesson?"

SMART: Measurable

The learner needs to know when they've achieved their goal. Being able to measure progress is essential to help maintain focus and experience the exhilaration of achievement.

ADI: "How will you feel when you understand where to wait?"
Joanna: "I'll feel a lot better, more secure I suppose."
ADI: "Okay, so you'll feel more secure."

So now we know what it will *feel* like to Joanna when she has achieved these goals. Remember, it's a process and dialogue, so it's important to keep the conversation flowing naturally. Don't forget to use the learner's words when summarising back, even if those words aren't the ones you would have used; this is essential if you want to maintain good rapport.

Although measurement can be done through how the learner feels about the situation, it can be helpful to use a more tangible measurement. Scaling can be an effective technique for this (you can read more about scaling in *Chapter 6: Learning Styles*). Helping your learner to explore where they are now and their current level of capability raises their levels of self-awareness. You could ask about their current level of ability and the skills they need to have to achieve their goals. You might also find out what they're thinking and feeling right now.

ADI: "So before we tackle these right turns at traffic lights then, Joanna, let's see where you're at now. You said you'll feel 'secure' when you understand where to wait. How secure do you feel now on a scale of 1 to 10 with 1 being totally insecure and 10 being totally secure?"
Joanna: "About a 4 at the moment."
ADI: "And why's that?"
Joanna: "Because they're so complicated, sometimes I have to go in further and sometimes I have to stop straight and other times at an angle."
ADI: "OK, well we'll work hard on that today then and reassess your 'secure score' at the end of the lesson!"

So now we know what it looks like to our learner; she's described how she feels whenever she needs to turn right. We're looking through our learner's eyes and using her words. Each learner will have different issues in different situations. By asking questions and being a good listener, you'll find out what your learner thinks and what concerns them.

The goal is now measurable because the learner can revisit her "secureness" scale at the end of the lesson and score her level of achievement.

SMART: Achievable

Goals should always be achievable. That isn't to say that we should set our sights low – far from it. We should be aiming to stretch and challenge our learners, but not to destroy their confidence and motivation for learning.

There are two aspects to setting achievable goals. Firstly, the goals should be achievable within the time available, so don't be over-ambitious and try to master several large topics within a single driving lesson. Failing to achieve all the agreed goals can be very demoralising for your learner.

Secondly, the goals set should be achievable for that learner in terms of their current ability and skillset. It's clear that Joanna's goal in the example above is achievable. But let's imagine a learner who is in the very early stages of learning for this next example.

In his 2 hours experience so far, Isaac has been practising moving off and stopping and has successfully changed up into second gear.

ADI: "Okay Isaac, so we've gone over what we covered in last lesson and set a plan for today. Are you still happy to work on those areas?"
Isaac: "Erm ... I guess so"
ADI: "Hmm, I get the sense you're not on board with this, Isaac. Is there something else you'd prefer to cover instead?"
Isaac: "Yeah, can we do some driving on the dual carriageway?"

How achievable do you think Isaac's goal is? Bear in mind that the fastest speed he has driven at is 15mph in second gear. In this case, you would need to coach Isaac around to a more achievable goal.

ADI: "That's a really good 'big' goal to aim for. Let's just think about that dual carriageway for a moment though. What's the speed limit on there?"

Isaac: "70mph I think"

ADI: "Yes, exactly. Now what's the maximum speed we've driven at so far, and in which gear?"

Isaac: "Not sure what speed … I've been in second gear though"

ADI: "You have, yes. Your top speed was around 15mph. Now on the dual carriageway, you'll need a few extra skills, such as firm acceleration, being able to quickly and smoothly change up through the gears to sixth gear, merge with faster moving traffic … things like that. How much of that have we covered up to now?"

Isaac: "We haven't done any of that yet"

ADI: "No, not quite yet. The risk is far greater on faster moving roads, particularly if you're only confident driving slowly. So how about we work towards that bigger goal of going on the dual carriageway by working up to third gear today and trying driving on some slightly busier roads?"

Isaac: "Ah right yes OK. That sounds like a good plan"

Notice that the instructor doesn't scoff or laugh at Isaac's ambitious goal. Instead, he respects Isaac's choice, helps Isaac to become more self-aware of his current skill level and makes him aware of the extra risks of driving on dual carriageways.

Ultimately, you need to be able to coach your learners to set *achievable* but *challenging* goals for themselves. That may mean breaking down over-ambitious goals into micro-goals which are more achievable in the short term, but are goals that the learner is still happy to work towards.

SMART: Relevant

Having **relevant** goals to work towards is also important. For example, if your learner has a desire to drive on dual carriageways at the earliest opportunity, each micro-goal should relate to this larger one.

> **Isaac:** "Can we do some reversing today?"
>
> **ADI:** "We can if you like, yes, but you did say you wanted to work towards driving on dual carriageways. How helpful will it be for us to learn reversing right now, if you aspire to drive on dual carriageways soon?"
>
> **Isaac:** "Umm well I don't suppose I'll be reversing on dual carriageways, will I?"
>
> **ADI:** "Hopefully not, no! It's up to you though, Isaac – we can work on some reversing or we can work towards some higher speed driving. Which would you prefer?"
>
> **Isaac:** "No, let's stick with working on getting faster. I can do some reversing another time"

Learner drivers will often want to cover topics which you know aren't relevant to the goal they *need* to achieve. For example, you'll undoubtedly come across learners who want you to conduct a mock test with them, when it's clear to you that they're a long way off the standard required to pass it. Would a mock test be the most helpful thing you could do? Similarly, if you have learners who are struggling to pass the theory test, it might be more relevant to take some time during the driving lesson to develop some theory knowledge in car, rather than spend the whole duration of the lesson working towards the practical driving test.

SMART: Timely

To help focus efforts, it can be helpful to specify a time period within which we aim to achieve the goals. Smaller goals can be converted into micro-goals that can be achieved within a lesson, for example, half the lesson on roundabouts and then move on to doing a reverse park. Larger goals might be achieved over a longer period and within several lessons, for example, "to become confident on faster, busier roads".

> **ADI:** "So we have two hours today, how much of the lesson do you want to spend on these right turns at traffic lights?"
>
> **Joanna:** "Can we do them until I feel better? I don't mind if we spend all lesson on them, I just want to feel better about them, especially that really busy one near my college that I'll have to do a lot when I've passed."
>
> **ADI:** "Of course, we'll do that one as many times as you want."

Step 2: Prepare

The amount of discussion required in preparing for the lesson would mainly depend on whether your learner is revisiting a previously learned skill or topic, or working on something completely new.

If you're going over something that was covered previously, you might just ask a few questions to establish what your learner remembers. You can them help them "fill in the gaps" in their knowledge and understanding. By exploring any issues fully before re-practising, you will increase the likelihood of them achieving success on this lesson.

If learning something new, you may need to explore the new topic with your learner using whatever means is appropriate, whether that be via a briefing, a mind map, or something else. Some learners may even prefer, or benefit from, bypassing a lengthy discussion and instead learn through experience — depending on the subject matter. In some situations, it might be better to leave this discussion until later in the lesson when you have reached a suitable training area.

Client-centred questions you could ask at this stage of the lesson include:

- "Have you seen this done before?"
- "Talk me through how you think we might go about …"
- "What skills do you think we'll need?"

- "What potential problems could we come across?"
- "Would you be happy for me to give you some suggestions?"

Step 3: Responsibility agreement

Once goals are decided, you and your learner need to agree on the balance of responsibility. How much input do they want and need? For example, your learner might be happy to take responsibility for topics they mastered last week but would rather you took control in any new situations they encounter.

Example: Early stages learner, Diana, has started to deal with traffic light junctions.

ADI: "We agreed last week that you're really great now at dealing with give way and stop junctions, both approaching and emerging, didn't we?"

Diana: "Yes."

ADI: "So are you happy to do those by yourself this lesson then, Diana? I can just watch and only step in when I need to or when you ask, if you like?"

Diana: "Yeah, I should be okay with those."

ADI: "Great! Well whenever we approach any traffic light junctions, I'll give you lots of help to start with, until you feel more comfortable with dealing with them." As you get better and want to take more responsibility for them yourself, I'll back off and start handing more control over to you. Is that okay with you?"

Diana: "Yep. Sounds good."

ADI: "Well, as usual, if there's anything else you feel you'd like help with, just let me know! As you know, I do have my dual controls down here — which I'll only use as a last resort — but if I do use them, I'll let you know, and we'll pull up and talk about it."

Example: John, a full licence holder, lacks confidence when joining fast-flowing dual carriageways and motorways.

ADI: "Okay then, John, so with you having held a licence for a while now, I'll leave you in charge of keeping us safe. I'll only step in if I need to or if you ask for it — would that be okay with you?"

John: "Yes, sure. It might take me a minute or two to get used to your car, but I should be okay other than that."

ADI: "So, how much help would you like from me on the slip roads when we're joining the dual carriageways or motorways?"

John: "Well, could I show you how I would do them first, and then you tell me how I can make them better?"

ADI: "Yes, sure — let's look at how you deal with them first. Of course, if I feel there's any need to intervene verbally or physically, it will only be because of a safety issue, which we can discuss afterwards. Is that okay?"

John: "Yes, that's fine."

Step 4: Practice and self-evaluation

The balance of responsibility and level of input agreed upon at the start of the lesson may alter as the lesson progresses, so you need to be regularly checking on how much instructor input both you and your learner feel is necessary. Factors influencing your level of input will be based on the internal and external environment, the level of risk and the time available. Practice areas should be suitable and appropriate for your learner's experience and ability. Where applicable, your learner should be encouraged to determine the route and/or choose adequate training areas. There should also be plenty of opportunities for your learner to develop their skills and, where necessary, repeat specific sections of the route to validate learning.

Mistakes made by your learner should be promptly identified or, especially in the case of a safety-critical incident, prevented altogether. Where possible, your learner should be encouraged to take responsibility for identifying any mistakes or weaknesses. By reflecting on the situation, they should be able to highlight any errors they noticed or things with which they felt uncomfortable. The root cause of the mistakes should be discussed and the effects on us, the car, or any other road users — potential or actual — thoroughly explored. You should decide together how the error could be fixed, and then agree on how much responsibility for this lies with you, the instructor, and how much is left to them, the learner, when they encounter the same (or a similar) situation again.

Ideally, your learner should be fully engaged in the lesson, be encouraged to self-evaluate and be actively involved in the decision-making process. The amount a learner will want to participate in making decisions and self-evaluation will vary from learner to learner. It's believed that the more active the learner is in the lesson process, the better they'll learn, and the more aware and responsible they'll become. However, to remain client-centred it's important to use a blend of teaching and coaching techniques which suit the learner. Self-reflective questions you could ask during this part of the lesson might include:

- "How do you feel that went?"
- "More specifically, how do you feel we dealt with …?"
- "What did you notice about …?"
- "What could we have improved on …?"
- "What do you think might have caused that?"
- "What was going through your mind when/just before …?"
- "If we were to go back to that situation again, how would you handle it differently next time?"

Remember, for optimal learning and to promote lasting change, it's essential that you create opportunities for the learner to correct their earlier mistakes. Where necessary, try to revisit the same situation again — or at the very least, something similar — then give as much or as little help as the learner needs to ensure success next time.

Step 5: Reflection and debrief

The final stage of a client-centred lesson is at the end, when your learner is invited to reflect on the whole lesson. It might start with a discussion about the initial goals and to what degree those goals were met. Your learner should be encouraged to explore what specifically went well, where improvements were made and what parts of the lesson they enjoyed. They should also be asked what specific improvements could be made, what didn't go so well and what parts of the lesson they found challenging. Based on these reflections, specific goals for the next lesson can be set.

All this information can be recorded on a reflective log, ready for the start of the next lesson.

Reflective logs

Okay, so now we've looked at the structure of a client-centred driving lesson as a whole, we're going to spend some more time exploring the final part of the lesson — the time where we encourage the learner to self-reflect and self-evaluate.

Most driving instructors keep some form of training record for each learner. At our driving school, for example, instructors have a 'client record' for each learner, which gives the instructor and learner a brief overview of which skills and topics have been covered to date, and to what standard. In addition to the client record, each learner has a reflective log. So depending on what you currently use, a reflective log can be used in addition to, or in place of, your current record system.

A reflective log is essentially a record of the learner's learning experiences, thoughts, feelings and reflections. It should be thought of as a critical assessment of how the learner is progressing. Despite the word critical, this shouldn't be thought of as a negative evaluation, quite the contrary. It should be an honest and positively framed appraisal of what areas are

What Does A Client-Centred Lesson Look Like?

going well, where improvements can be made, together with a plan for moving forward — the goals or next steps.

Reflective logs, or journals, are nothing new; they've been used successfully for many years in other industries and educational establishments, including some primary and secondary schools. Therefore, it's entirely possible that your learners will be very familiar with the process, even if it might feel alien to you at first.

Some ADIs will advocate using a reflective log as an additional resource for their learners to complete and keep. For others, the reflective log can be used in place of a lesson record.

> From starting out as an ADI in the late 1990s, I've always kept lesson records in A4 landscape format. They looked like this (I could fit 13 lesson records to a double-sided A4 sheet of paper):
>
> | **Lesson Record** | | | Name: | |
> |---|---|---|---|---|
> | Date | Topics Covered | Strengths | Areas for Improvement | Next Lesson |
> | | | | | |
>
> Keeping records like this enabled me to keep track of not just what we covered and when, but precisely how well my learners carried out those tasks and where they needed to improve. Together, we would then plan what to include next lesson — although admittedly I often led the learner to this decision. I later replaced this lesson record with a reflective log.

A reflective log will help your learner take more responsibility for the direction and content of their lessons. It can also improve flow throughout their course of lessons — as they become accustomed to using a log, you may find they progress quicker as they develop the skill of self-reflection. As a bonus, you get an insight into your learner's thought processes.

Completing the reflective log

A reflective log is essentially the same format as a lesson record but now phrased with more client-focused headings and extra space for more information, where required.

REFLECTIVE LOG			Name:	
Date	Today's Goals	What Went Well	Areas for Improvement	Goals for Next Session
Before Next Session, I Will...			Other	

Today's goals

List the original goals and anything else that came up during the lesson.

- "What did we set out to achieve on today's lesson?"
- "What topics have we covered today?"
- "What particular skills have we worked on improving today?"
- "What changes did we make to our original lesson plan?"

Make sure you list *specific* goals here, rather than general content. For example, "Roundabouts" is not a goal, it's simply the topic covered. A goal might be, "To feel more confident joining roundabouts". Writing specific goals will enable you and your learner to recall, at the start of the next lesson, exactly what aspects of "roundabouts" you worked on.

What went well

Make sure this section is completed. Some ADIs and their learners tend to focus too much on the negative, but the "what went well" section is critical to maintaining motivation and seeing positive movement towards the end goal.

- "Which parts of today's lesson went well?"
- "What were the positive elements of the lesson?"
- "What improvements do you feel you've made?"
- "Anything else?"*

Areas for improvement

Note any areas where your learner might need to pay particular attention. Some instructors might use the term "areas of weakness" here, but we prefer "areas for improvement," as the language is more positive and suggests that we're focussed on looking for solutions.

- "What parts of the lesson didn't go so well?"
- "Which particular parts/topics did you struggle with or find most challenging?"
- "What do you feel you need more help with?"
- "What improvements do you think we need to make?"
- "Anything else?"

Goals for next session**

Remember, this isn't necessarily about you allowing your learner a free rein of what they want to cover; as the ADI, you're there to provide structure, so feel free to make suggestions based on your thoughts, perceptions and experience. If your learner has a few areas for improvement listed, it would be normal for those areas to form at least part of the goals for next lesson (or "training session").

---

* The "Anything else?" question will help you understand when the learner has finished reflecting in the *What Went Well* and *Areas for Improvement* sections. When they have nothing else left, you could add in some of your own feedback that you think they'll find useful.

** We prefer to use the term "training session" over the term "driving lesson" for our paperwork, as this terminology encompasses all types of driver training, and not just learner driver tuition.

- "So based on those areas for improvement, what skills/topics do you think we need to focus on next lesson?"
- "Might it be a good idea to do some more work on …?"
- "What do you say about perhaps going over …?"
- "How do you feel about moving on to …?"
- "I was thinking it could be a good idea to spend some time working on [skill], how does that sound?"
- "Anything else you'd like to practise?"

Before next session, I will …

It can be an excellent idea to get your learner to commit to a home learning task, as this will only serve to accelerate their learning process. Your learner might choose to:

- read a handout or section of a book
- watch a relevant video
- make notes on the day's lesson or mentally prepare for the next lesson
- create a mind map about what they've learned or in preparation for next lesson
- complete some mock theory tests
- book their theory/practical test
- observe someone else's driving in particular situations
- practice a skill or topic in-car with a friend or relative

If your learner needs some encouragement in this area, you might make some suggestions to help them.

- "Would you like a handout on *[skill/topic]* to read before next lesson?"
- "What could you be reading between now and next lesson to give you a head start?"

- "There's a great video on YouTube explaining how to deal with *[skill/topic]*. Could you perhaps watch that over the weekend, and we can chat about it on our next lesson?"
- "What key areas will you work on when out practising with Mum or Dad?"
- "Could you commit to booking your theory test before we next meet?"

Other

This section can be used to note anything else of relevance, such as "advised to put test back a couple of weeks" or "block booking payment due next week".

Q: When should the log be completed, and by whom?

Ideally, your learner should fill in the log at the end of their driving lesson. We say *ideally* because sometimes the learner won't want to do it, and instead would rather the instructor take notes. If you're truly client-centred, you'll leave it up to the learner to decide who writes it. It's most beneficial for the learner to write the log themselves so that they don't censor their thoughts and feelings. However, if the record is an accurate and honest reflection of the learner's thoughts and feelings, it shouldn't matter too much who does the writing.

Some learners need time to reflect on their progress and are better at expressing their thoughts verbally than in writing. If that's the case, you can just summarise what they've said and enter it onto the log yourself; this can also save a lot of time.

If you're completing the log, we'd recommend that you still write in the first person — as if the learner has written it. Be careful not to alter the learner's terminology or wording. It's important that what's written on the log comes from them, with a small amount of input from you, as their instructor.

It's best if the reflective log is completed in-car, as you can ensure that it's completed thoroughly. Expecting a learner to go into their house, school, college or work and finish their reflective log, surrounded by a myriad of other distractions, usually results in them "forgetting" to do it!

Q: Doesn't it take too long to complete? Learners want to be driving, not writing.

We think it's fair to say that most conscientious ADIs have been completing some form of lesson record at the end of each lesson for some time; whether that be giving a score for each skill on the training log, or writing some notes on progress during a specific lesson. Yes, it's true that some ADIs choose to complete lesson records after the lesson is over and the learner has gone, but the end of session debrief is such an important and integral part of the lesson that ADIs shouldn't feel obliged to exclude record completion from the lesson time.

Make it a regular part of your lesson and your learners will accept it. In every educational setting, lessons have a start (recap), middle (learning) and an end (recap/debrief), so why should driving lessons be any different? Completion of a reflective log is likely to take no more than a few minutes.

Q: My learner is always eager to get out of the car at the end of the lesson. How can I keep their attention?

We've all been there — as soon as the learner pulls up outside their house, their hand is on the car door handle and they're readying themselves to jump out. Their attention is on the missed text messages or calls on their mobile phone. They're mentally "elsewhere" — certainly not in the right frame of mind to complete any paperwork. Fortunately, there's an easy solution to this problem; pull up a couple of streets away from your learner's drop-off point and complete the reflective log there. Their full attention will still be on the lesson, as there's still more driving to do. Once the log is complete, they can drive home!

Q: Where can I get one of these reflective logs?

Here are four reflective log options:

1. Some instructors initially supply each of their learners with a starter pack, which might include a branded pen, terms and conditions, Highway Code, referral vouchers, etc. Adding an inexpensive blank notepad to this pack, labelled *Reflective Learning Record*, is one idea. Who keeps the learning record is entirely up to you, although in our experience, teenagers and young adults can be quite forgetful. If you intend to leave the learning record with your learner, you'll need a plan in place for when they forget it, or it gets "eaten by the dog".

2. The DVSA have conveniently supplied a sample reflective log in sections 3.23 and 4.30 of their ADI1 Standard Operating Procedure.[77] You could print that off or maybe even develop your own, based on the headings used on the DVSA version.

3. Download and use our version of the reflective log, pictured earlier in this chapter. Simply scan this QR code or visit **http://gedclai.re/reflectivelogs** to download it. It's double-sided and A4-sized to fit conveniently in a binder or plastic wallet, and you can record up to six driving lessons on each sheet.

4. If you have access to an iPad, check out the Robosoul Reflective Logs app designed by Neil Snow and Neil Beaver.[78] At the time of writing, the app is available for £2.99 from the iTunes App Store.

    Using the app has the added benefit of you being able to email completed logs to your students from within the app, keeping them up to date and enabling them to build a personal record of their progress.

It's useful for both you and your learner to each have a copy of the reflective log. With the paper format reflective logs, you could achieve this by asking your learner to take a photo of the log on their mobile phone at the end of the lesson. That way, they can remember what was written on it before their next lesson — especially important if they have committed to a few home learning tasks.

Q: I have my Part 3 test or Standards Check soon. Will the examiner want to see me using a reflective log?

Not necessarily. Section 4.15 of the ADI1 Standard Operating Procedure states that:

> *If the ADI offers to supply training documents (such as the reflective log) you should discuss the content with them but if they do not bring such papers this will not invalidate the standards check.*[79]

If you and your learners do use reflective logs successfully, we would recommend taking your learner's log into the test centre to show the examiner before the lesson commences. It all contributes to giving the examiner a great first impression. We believe it can make a big difference to the examiner's initial perception of your skills before they even get into the car if they can already see your excellent lesson records.

Some ADIs have concerns about the time taken to fill in the reflective log at the end of their Part 3 test or Standards Check. If you can relate to this, we'd recommend that you at least have the reflective log in front of you and discuss the contents verbally. You can explain that it will be completed in writing while the examiner is in the test centre finishing their assessment.

Using a reflective log as a PDI or ADI to reflect on your performance

Reflective logs can also be a brilliant tool for your own development as a driving instructor. There's no right or wrong way for you to self-reflect but if you want to improve your skills, knowledge and service as an ADI, it's worth considering writing things down. Your reflective log is your tool for learning and growth; you don't have to share any of its contents with anyone else, so feel free to express your thoughts, feelings, questions and experiences openly. Note down your strengths, successes, "aha" moments and ideas. Admit your uncertainties, insecurities, anxieties, gaps in knowledge and mistakes. It's important to explore these fully so that you can learn from them.

A reflective log can take the form of a notepad or journal, sheets of paper within a folder or binder, or in digital format on a mobile device or computer. It can be structured — as in our example of the learner's reflective log — or unstructured, where you might express yourself freely in sentence and paragraph form. Some people like to write their reflections in a diary. Again, there are many ways to achieve the same outcome; choose whichever way works best for you.

Using the Part 3 test or Standards Check marking sheet to reflect on your performance

The Part 3 test or Standards Check marking form provides you with a ready-made tool for self-reflection. If you have a planned or unplanned gap between lessons, take a marking form out and score yourself against the assessment criteria. Use the guidelines in the ADI1 to help you figure out which score to award yourself on each competency.

Note the competencies in which you haven't scored a '3' — how could you improve in this area next time? What resources do you need, if any? Who or what could help you improve further?

Points for reflection

- How much involvement do your learners currently have in your lesson's direction and content? How do you think you could involve them more?
- How well do your learners understand the benefits of "active learning"? If you get little engagement from most of your learners, what can you improve on to shift the balance so that they participate more in their learning?
- What student records do you currently use? How interactive is the layout of those records? How well do they fit into a more client-centred approach?
- Currently, how involved are your learners in reflecting and contributing to the completion of their lesson record? When thinking about the end of lesson debrief, who does most of the talking?
- If your learner is quite an interactive type of person, but you recognise you're doing most of the talking, how could you get them more involved? What home-learning activities do you currently encourage? What other options might you add?

CHAPTER 6

LEARNING STYLES

"When you allow students to envision their own learning and create a style that really works for them, what you're doing is creating lifelong learners."[80]

Jeanne Halderson

Watch Video Message: Ged & Claire Introduce Chapter 6

http://gedclai.re/chapter6

Theories and models

The term "learning style" refers to how an individual learns best. The theory behind learning styles is that we're all intrinsically different and therefore we all learn differently, using a combination of various methods and techniques. Many different theories and models claim to account for the way in which we learn, most of which stem from research development in the 1970s. Two of the most popular learning style theories, which some driving instructors have found useful, are Peter Honey and Alan Mumford's learning styles, and Neil Fleming's VARK (Visual, Aural (Auditory), Read/write and Kinaesthetic) model).[81,82] You may already be familiar with one or both of these models but if not, you can find lots of information about them online.

Fortunately, you don't need to take the time to find out whether the learner sat next to you is an activist, reflector, theorist or pragmatist, just as you don't need to categorise your learner as a visual, aural, read/write or kinaesthetic learner. All you should do is recognise that all your learners will learn differently. In recent years, some educationalists and researchers have even questioned the benefits of teaching learners in the way they learn best, known as "meshing", suggesting that an over-reliance on offering education specific to those preferences could even be counterproductive.

In their 2009 review, *Learning Styles: Concepts and Evidence,* by Pashler et al., they state: "Although the literature on learning styles is enormous, very few studies have even used an experimental methodology capable of testing the validity of learning styles applied to education. Moreover, of those that did use an appropriate method, several found results that flatly contradict the popular meshing hypothesis. We conclude, therefore, that at present there's no adequate evidence base to justify incorporating learning styles assessments into general educational practice."

For a somewhat controversial view on whether learning styles even exist, visit **http://gedclai.re/learningstyles** or scan the QR code. While the debate rolls on, here's our take on it...

We're all unique

- Some people need lots of information before trying something; others are very practical and prefer to learn through experience.
- Some people are happy to learn the theory and take the time to self-reflect; others are impatient with lengthy discussions and being asked questions.
- Some people are very logical — they like set routines and step-by-step guides; others like to work things out as they go along in a way that works best for them.
- Some people are open-minded about trying new methods, whereas others prefer sticking to tried-and-tested approaches.
- Some people will like it when you use driving apps on tablets; others hate technology and will mentally switch off whenever you bring your tablet out.

We're all different in the way we learn. While the above examples describe opposites, people may fall somewhere in between, too.

Learning preferences are contextual

It's important to recognise that our learning preferences can change depending on what we're learning (the context), and where we're learning it (the environment). As an example, if you're learning how to use a new mobile phone which is like your old one, you could independently experiment until you figure out how to use all the new features. If you dropped your phone and cracked the screen, you might search for a YouTube video explaining how to repair that particular phone, rather than experiment yourself and risk making the problem worse.

If you were learning how to fly a helicopter from scratch, then learning through experimentation or a YouTube video wouldn't be enough, and would most certainly end in carnage! You'd need to know what everything in the cockpit does first and receive a full rundown of each control. You'd then perhaps like to watch lots of flight demonstrations and receive systematic instruction with detailed commentary. Not only is the context different, but the environment and level of risk are, too.

Your choice of learning strategy will depend on many factors, especially on how confident you were in being able to carry out the task, based on prior experience in similar situations. When learning to drive a car, there is, of course, a certain degree of risk involved, which is managed by the instructor. The instructor offers a safety net for the learner and as such, this opens up the opportunities for the learner to acquire knowledge, understanding and experience through a variety of ways.

There are many ways in which a learner driver could begin to learn a new skill. Consider a reversing manoeuvre, for example. They could:

- **read** a section of a relevant book which explains the manoeuvre
- **watch a YouTube video** about the manoeuvre
- **listen to a briefing** given by the instructor
- **complete a mind map** of the manoeuvre — including what's involved and what the risks might be
- **watch a demonstration** given by the instructor
- **practise** the manoeuvre under full guidance of the instructor
- **learn through experimentation** — have a go independently and see how it turns out

As a truly client-centred instructor, you need to consider how each learner learns best. You can support your learner's process of learning in the best way possible by adapting your techniques and strategies and observing the outcomes. Sometimes, it will be best to stick with what's working, but at other times, it might be better to try different approaches to stretch the learner further to achieve even better results.

Be aware of your own learning preferences

As well as recognising and adapting to each of your learner's learning preferences, it's important to notice your own. The reason for this is because we're likely to unconsciously impose our preferred learning methods on the learner. For example, if you're the type of person that likes to see a detailed picture and know the ins and outs of everything before you have a go, it's likely you'll teach in this way, too. Alternatively, if you prefer to learn new things by just getting stuck in and having a go, it's likely you'll want your learners to learn like this as well.

By being aware of your own learning preferences, you can notice times when you might be imposing your preferred methods of learning on your learners, and when that style isn't working for them.

Seek feedback

If you're paying attention to your learner's body language, you'll get an idea as to whether your methods are working for them. If they're gazing out of the window, yawning, rolling their eyes or seem anxious to get on the move, chances are you're not connecting with them in the way they prefer. On the other hand, if they're making eye contact, nodding, smiling, asking questions and showing healthy levels of interaction, it's likely they're connecting well with your methods.

As uncomfortable as this might sound, it's always a good idea to ask for feedback on the teaching/coaching methods you're using.

- "Does it help when I demonstrate?"

- "I notice that sometimes you seem keen to get driving while I'm explaining something using my visual aid. Would you prefer me to explain it another way?"
- "How do you find you learn best?"
- "How can I maybe change my teaching methods to help you?"
- "Is there anything I could do differently?"
- "Is there a better way I could help you?"

Asking your learner for feedback gives them a chance to:

- tell you what methods they like and which methods they don't like
- become more active in their learning process
- experience an increase in rapport
- get the most from every lesson

Visual aids

Let's start with the driving instructor's primary tool: the visual aid. Here, we're using the term visual aid to describe a series of pictures or illustrations used to explain a specific skill or topic to a learner. When we both qualified as driving instructors in the 1990s, the visual aid of choice for many instructors was a notepad and a pen. Nowadays, visual aids come in many more polished forms such as:

- 2D and 3D colour illustrations
- Magnetic road boards
- Miniature toy cars
- Static and animated mobile apps for smartphones and tablets

Finding a visual aid you can use efficiently is a simple matter of preference, there's no right or wrong solution. Be open-minded and have a few options at your disposal — some learners might relate better to one type of visual aid than others, even though you might not particularly like it.

A picture paints a thousand words

Imagine we asked you for a favour: to pick our childminder up from the train station. We describe in words that she's in her sixties with dark brown hair and is about 5' 1". Would you be able to identify her? A longer verbal description may ensure greater success, but your mind's eye of what she looks like may be completely different to what she looks like. Now, how about we asked if you could pick our childminder up from the train station and we gave you a photo of her? Would we need to describe her in as much detail? Would we even need to describe her at all? How much more likely are you to successfully identify the correct person when you've seen a photograph over having been given a verbal description?

Human beings absorb visual information extremely well. Using pictures will often help eliminate any misunderstandings and will allow the learner to see what you're talking about. It will also enable the learner to free up brain power — instead of wasting resources on trying to imagine what you're describing, they can instead look at a picture and mentally focus on the point you're making or the question you're asking.

Deciding on when to use a visual aid will depend on your learner — some learners benefit from using them whereas some will prefer to work things out themselves without one. If you sense your learner "doesn't get it" or they close their eyes or look upwards — a typical eye movement from someone who's trying to picture what something looks like — then a visual aid can be helpful. Remember, the visual aid isn't just for you to use. Consider sharing it with your learners, especially those that prefer a more hands-on approach to learning. If you give your learner the visual aid and a pen or a couple of miniature cars, can they tell and show you how they think they should do a specific task? Can they describe to you what happened in an earlier situation and what they'll do differently next time? Getting the learner more involved will prevent them from mentally switching off, and it will afford you a valuable insight into what they're thinking.

Videos (including in-car camera systems)

Thanks to advances in technology in recent years, videos can be used in a similar way to visual aids. Most driving instructors now own a smartphone or tablet, so it's easy to show downloaded or online videos to learners. Here are some examples of how videos can be used in-car:[††]

- Reviewing video footage from a dashcam or other in-car camera system, discussing what happened, what they did well, what the learner may have missed, what else they could have anticipated/planned for, how they could handle it differently next time, etc.
- Watching a short video demonstration of how to correctly carry out a task or manoeuvre.
- Showing a road safety video to analyse the importance of carrying out an observation or action, especially if it's one that the learner tends to forget.
- Situational awareness and hazard perception training.

The real world

Often, using the real world can be the most efficient visual learning tool. For example, when discussing how to identify and safely deal with pedestrian crossings, pull up near one if it's safe and legal to do so. Rather than looking at a two-dimensional, top-down sketch of a crossing, the learner can now see the crossing and notice how pedestrians and other drivers deal with it. The same technique can be used when helping learners deal with lots of topics, including dealing with junctions or carrying out manoeuvres.

Sometimes, learners find roundabouts quite challenging, mainly when it comes to working out when to go. We've been known to walk with our learners to a nearby roundabout and take a few minutes to help them understand where they need to be observing (scanning) on approach,

---

[††] To stay on the correct side of the law, remember to ensure you only review video or use a mobile device whilst safely and legally parked, with the engine switched off.

and what clues they can get from the signals, speed and position of vehicles on the roundabout as to where they're going. The walks we take with our learners accelerate their learning and, in our opinion, are far more efficient and interactive than any visual aid or video.

Another way you could use the real world is to notice the actions of other roads users. If someone is following another vehicle too closely, speeding, driving while talking on a mobile phone or running a red light, for example, you can use the event as a great learning opportunity.

- "Tell me your thoughts on …"
- "Why do you think he/she …?"
- "What are the risks of …?"
- "What would have been a better/safer thing for them to have done?"
- "How would you react if you were a passenger in that car, and your friend was driving like that?"

Using the mistakes other road users make can also be valuable, particularly when your learner has made that same mistake earlier on in the lesson. For example, learners sometimes cut right corners when turning into side roads. If your learner is forced to brake as they're approaching a T-junction due to another driver cutting the corner, you can use this example to your advantage.

Handouts and books

Encouraging your learners to read sections of books or printed handouts in between lessons can be extremely beneficial to their learning as it can help consolidate information and better prepare your learner for the next lesson. For that reason, it's a good idea to have a selection of your most important books and visual aids in the car for use in your lessons. Just make sure you have some current editions and not some battered copy of the Highway Code from the 1970s!

Storytelling

Never underestimate the power of sharing personal anecdotes, local news stories and past learner experiences. We're huge advocates of this learning tool and use it daily.

Example: Sam has repeatedly forgotten to check the right door mirror before signalling to turn right.

ADI: "Remember to check that right door mirror!"
Sam: "Oh sorry, I forgot again!"
ADI: "It's important not to forget. Why did we say it was so important to check that before signalling?"
Sam: "In case something is overtaking me."
ADI: "That's right. And if there was something overtaking and you signalled, what could happen?"
Sam: "They might panic and swerve."
ADI: "Exactly, so come on, let's make sure you check it next time!"

Does this work? Is it enough to tell the learner to remember to check the right door mirror in future? Possibly. How about this next example?

ADI: "Remember to check that right door mirror, Sam!"
Sam: "Oh sorry, I forgot again!"
ADI: "Could you just pull up for two minutes — I just need to chat with you about something…
A good friend of mine, John, was out in his car last week. He's been driving even longer than me; he's a really experienced driver. Anyway, he went out on Tuesday morning to get a few bits of shopping from Tesco. As he was coming up to turn right into the car park, he signalled to let people know where he was going. Suddenly, John heard this awful yelp and a loud scraping sound. A motorbike slid along the road on his right-hand side, straight into the path of a van coming the other way. The motorcyclist who had been

	on the motorbike somersaulted along the road and just stopped before he too was hit by the van.
Sam:	"Oh my God, that's awful! Was he okay?"
ADI:	"It was horrendous. Fortunately, the motorcyclist only suffered a broken collarbone and some cuts and bruises, but can you imagine what would have happened if the van hadn't stopped in time, or had been travelling a few miles per hour faster?"
Sam:	"He could have died! Why did the motorcyclist crash though? Did your mate knock him off his bike?"
ADI:	"No, he didn't touch him. What happened was, the motorcyclist was just about to overtake John. Okay, it might not have been the safest place to overtake — these things happen. But John signalled to turn right, and the motorcyclist braked heavily in panic. He lost the back end of his bike, and … Well, he was very fortunate to survive, put it that way."
Sam:	"That's terrible. I bet your mate felt awful."
ADI:	"He did. But he also learned a precious lesson that day. Can you guess what it was?"
Sam:	"To check his mirrors first?"
ADI:	"Exactly. Before he ever puts a signal on, he now asks himself, 'Is it safe to give it?' Now we don't want you to have to go through a similarly awful experience, do we? So, every time you're going to signal right, what do you need to remember to do?"
Sam:	"To check my mirrors — especially that right one for any motorbikes."

Stories are much more memorable than potential "what if?" scenarios. It's worth remembering that stories like the above don't necessarily need to be 100% true or based on your own experience. Please don't worry if you don't have a mental bank full of true personal stories to use with your learners. The point is, whether factually true or not, stories, anecdotes and personal experiences give our brains a shortcut to understanding cause-and-effect relationships. So don't be afraid to use your imagination to create or elaborate on your own stories, or to share other people's stories as your own. It's all for the sake of enhancing learning, which can only be a good thing, right?

To read a great article about the science of storytelling, visit **http://gedclai.re/storytelling** or scan this QR code.

Discussions

Discussions are a great way of actively engaging your learner. Only when you explore what your learner is thinking, can you get an understanding of what they know and what they understand. All too often, instructors get sucked into the notion that the car needs to keep moving in order for the learner to learn and for them to get maximum value for money. This belief can be counterproductive. Without pulling up to discuss a specific issue, the learner is forced to do it repeatedly, potentially not improving, because they don't understand what exactly is going wrong.

Imagine for a moment you're back in maths class. Your teacher gives you a sum to do, and you get it wrong. She pushes forward regardless and provides you with another sum which you get wrong again. She gives you another one which you get wrong again, and so on. Would you want some time away from each sum to work out, with the teacher's help, what's going wrong and how to fix it? In the same way, our learners need time to work out, with our help, what exactly isn't going to plan, why it's not quite right and how to fix it next time. In the future, they're more likely to be successful, cutting out all the times they get it wrong and saving valuable lesson time. It can be helpful to think of stationary time as *learning time* and driving time as *practise time*.

Discussions can also be used to replace the traditional lesson "briefing". Nobody is a blank slate — all learners can relate back to some knowledge and understanding; it may have been gained during earlier driving lessons, while in the car as a passenger, from books/internet/TV, etc. Effective questioning can often encourage your learners to work out for themselves what needs to be done, when and why; this will significantly deepen their level of understanding as they'll remember their own words better than yours. It's the quality of question that counts. If you get a blank expression in response to your question, consider how you can simplify or close the question down to make it easier for them to answer. Refer back to *Chapter 4: The 5 Key Skills of a Client-Centred Instructor* for further guidance on questioning techniques.

Discussions are useful in many other situations, too. If you notice your learner is tired, unwell or upset, for example, take the opportunity to have a short discussion about how their physical or emotional state will affect their driving. This will help them to become more aware of the risks and potential consequences. Even more importantly, it will encourage them to take more personal responsibility for their driving choices when they're in different physical and emotional states after they've passed their driving test. We explore this in greater depth in *Appendix A: Useful Coaching Scenarios*.

Demonstrations

Demonstrations can create helpful shortcuts in learning. Without a demo, it can feel frustrating when your learner struggles to get something correct, despite your best efforts to explain what they should be doing.

When we see a task being performed, it gives us a clear picture of what to do and how to do it. It then becomes easier to replicate and perform the same task. Knowing when to do a demonstration can be hard to judge. Do you see what your learner can do first, or always demonstrate first? By asking the learner, "Would you like me to show you how to do this?" you'll find out if a demonstration will be helpful for your learner. A learner who feels confident and has a good understanding of the task will probably feel happy to give it a go without a demonstration. On the other hand, a learner who's lacking in confidence or doesn't fully understand what to do is more likely to accept a demonstration.

> Have you ever had to explain to a non-computer-literate person how to do a basic computer task such as sending an email? Perhaps you've been that person! I've tried to do this with my mum over the phone. It's time-consuming and frustrating at both ends. However, when we both sat in front of the computer and I showed her what to do, we had more success. She then had a go at sending an email, and she did it much quicker.

Demonstrations should always be **engaging** and **interactive**. The learner should be actively involved as you demonstrate — this will enhance their understanding much further than if you just talk *at* them for several minutes. Ask the learner questions, see if they can guess what comes next, check their understanding, and ask what questions they have.

Talk through

Although coaching and self-discovery are an excellent way to learn, they're not always the most desirable methods for you and/or your learner. Some situations may call for good verbal intervention on your part; this might be because the learner needs or wants you to give them lots of help, or because the potential risks of that situation mean you need to do so.

As the instructor, you can offer support in many forms. A learner who prefers more of a coaching approach and is happy to work things out themselves will probably need less talk through, but will still need support and encouragement through questions and reflecting back. A learner who prefers a more direct, instructor-led approach will often require a higher level of talk through. Whether your learner prefers an instructor-led approach or more of a learner-led approach, you'll need to pitch your level of support according to their ability.

Learning Styles

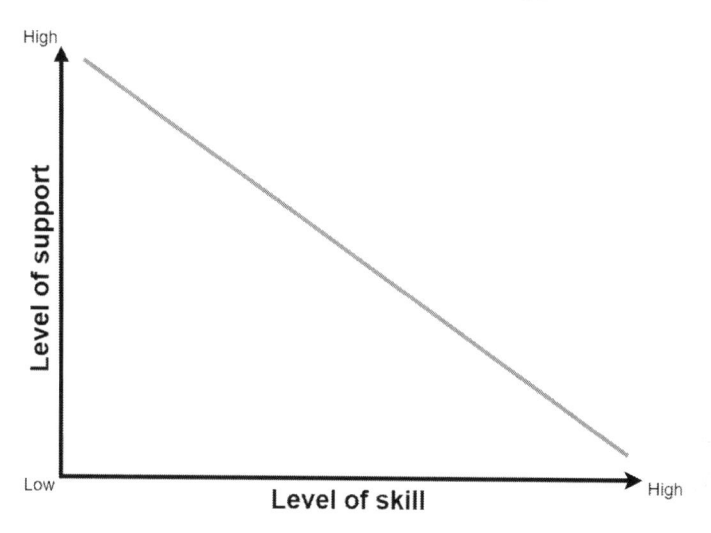

Low level of skill → High-level support
High level of skill → Low-level support

[Graph: Level of support (y-axis, Low to High) vs Level of skill (x-axis, Low to High), showing a downward sloping line from high-left to low-right]

If the level of support is too low when the learner's level of ability is low, the learner can lose confidence, and this will negatively affect their motivation. If the level of support is too high when the learner's ability is high, it can be frustrating for the learner, reduce their sense of personal responsibility and again, negatively affect their levels of motivation. The amount of support you give — which may well include talk through — becomes invaluable when your learner comes up to a situation they haven't previously met. Saying something like, "I'll help you with this mini-roundabout and we'll cover them in more detail on a later lesson" reassures the learner that you'll help and they're not expected to deal with it for themselves.

Also, remember that not all situations are equal. A learner driver won't always get something right because they've successfully managed it before. For example, this crossroads junction may be slightly different to the last one because the other drivers are doing something else or turning a different direction this time. Observe your learner for body language cues — panic, freezing, "glazing over" or unresponsiveness — and be ready to step in to assist.

Experiential learning

The concept of learning through experience, or "experiential learning" as it's commonly known, can sound quite daunting, especially in the context of learning to drive. After all, would it be advisable to allow a new driver to learn through experience, without any input from an instructor or accompanying driver?

- How many times would they crunch the gears before recognising they need to press the clutch pedal fully down first?
- How many other road users and obstructions would they have to hit before they understand the need to reduce their speed and plan further ahead?
- How many kerbs would they need to strike before they can learn how to judge a safe distance from the kerb when pulling up on the left?

The instructor or accompanying driver is ultimately responsible for the safety of the car, its occupants, other road users and property that could be affected by the learner's actions. However, it's still possible to allow a certain degree of experiential learning within a controlled and safe environment. Experiencing effects and consequences within safe boundaries can be very powerful, although in themselves, these effects may not achieve maximum learning. In such cases, the instructor's role would be to encourage the learner driver to reflect, self-evaluate and come up with strategies for handling similar situations in the future.

Imagine that your learner continually tries to approach junctions too fast. You're always telling him to brake more firmly, get the speed down to a jogging pace/below 10mph, etc. You ask him to turn left at a junction that's very open in view, but the corner itself is very sharp and the new road very narrow. There are no other road users around. You have two options:

1. Instruct him to brake more firmly, reducing the speed to a walking pace and select first gear. After entering the road safely, you can then tell him the reasons why you intervened and discuss the potential consequences of cornering so fast.
2. Allow him to take the corner at a speed he feels is appropriate, even if this is a bit faster than you'd like. You're acutely aware that he's likely to swing the car's position wide as he turns into the junction and so it's liable to cause him to panic a little.

Having made a careful risk assessment of the whole scene — not just the road layout and presence of other road users, but also the learner's level of experience, their levels of resilience and confidence, and the likelihood of them damaging your car — you could take option 2 on this occasion.‡‡ By exploring how it felt and what control he had on the junction, your learner will learn how speed affects other aspects of the turn. By discussing potential consequences such as how much time he would have had to respond to a pedestrian crossing the road, if there had been oil on the road, or if he'd been travelling 10mph faster, the realisation of the consequences of his speed will be more hard-hitting than if you'd intervened.

Experiential learning can also be useful for smaller tasks. For example, allowing your learner to experience a stall can help your learner to understand the biting point much more efficiently. Again, we must stress that this should only be allowed in a safe environment. Another example could be when carrying out the turn-in-the-road exercise. Encourage your learner to keep moving slowly towards the kerb until the tyre very gently touches the edge of the kerb; this will help them develop spatial awareness and an understanding of how far forwards or backwards they can take the car before it's likely to strike the kerb.

---

‡‡ Be careful of employing option 2 during your Part 3 test or Standards Check. Although you may well be 100% aware of what's happening and understand the benefits of experiential learning, the examiner may not view it in quite the same way. In our experience, they usually prefer to see you managing risk proactively rather than retrospectively.

Role reversal

Role reversal is another way of encouraging your learner drivers to analyse and work things out for themselves. It can be done effectively with the learner either in the passenger seat or the driving seat. Placing the learner in the role of instructor is extremely empowering for them. It also encourages them to discover answers for themselves and to unlock any knowledge and understanding they may already have, which was previously outside of conscious awareness.

When the learner is invited to take on the role of instructor, they increase trust in their own decisions and judgement. Done correctly, it can create a safe environment where the learner can learn from trial and error. However, this technique doesn't work for everybody, and although some learners will accept the challenge eagerly, some may feel too self-conscious.

Example: Jake has reached the stage where he is ready to learn how to reverse park.

ADI:		"Okay Jake, you seem to have picked up your other manoeuvres really well, so how do you feel about this one?"
Jake:		"Pretty good. I've never tried it, but it can't be too hard."
ADI:		"That's what I like to hear! Have you seen other people carry out this exercise before?"
Jake:		"Yeah, quite a few times on my road."
ADI:		"Okay, well how about you play the role of instructor for a moment and I'll be the learner? Here's the visual aid and pen. Explain to me how we're going to carry out this manoeuvre."

Role reversal can also be useful when a learner is struggling to master something when they're at the wheel. For example, confidence issues often play a huge part in judging safe gaps at roundabouts, or when turning right across oncoming traffic. By swapping seats, you take responsibility for everything apart from the judgement element, which the learner has control over; this is an excellent way to build up your learner's ability to choose a safe gap to emerge or turn. If they get it wrong a few times at first, of course, it doesn't matter — they may say it's safe to go, but you can hold back if it isn't. Once their confidence in judging safe gaps grows, it will make the world of difference when they get back into the driving seat.

Role reversal can also be useful to encourage self-analysis. Sometimes, learners find it difficult to analyse and critique their own performance. By reversing the roles, they often find it much easier to explain their thoughts.

> **ADI:** "Okay, Emily, let's try something for a moment. Imagine you're the instructor and I'm the learner. Explain to me what happened at that last crossroads and what I need to do next time to get it better. Here are the visual aid and pen if you want to use them to help explain where I need to improve."

Although it might sound ridiculous at first, the role reversal technique can really help learners who struggle to self-analyse. Often, if the learner takes a moment to look at things from a different perspective, such as from the instructor's point of view, it becomes much easier to understand what went wrong and how to put it right.

Commentary driving

Commentary driving enables you, the instructor, to gain valuable insight into your learner's thoughts and feelings. It's also a fantastic method of helping your learners develop their planning, awareness and anticipation skills. It helps them to reduce issues caused by inattentional and change blindness and is invaluable, for young drivers, in developing risk assessment skills which are commonly lacking in the adolescent brain. We discussed these crash causation factors in more detail in *Chapter 1: Why Drivers Crash.*

When practiced and mastered, commentary driving increases the driver's levels of **concentration**, **observation** and **anticipation**. In turn, this enables the driver to give more **space** to hazards and other road users, which then affords them more **time** to deal with situations around them.

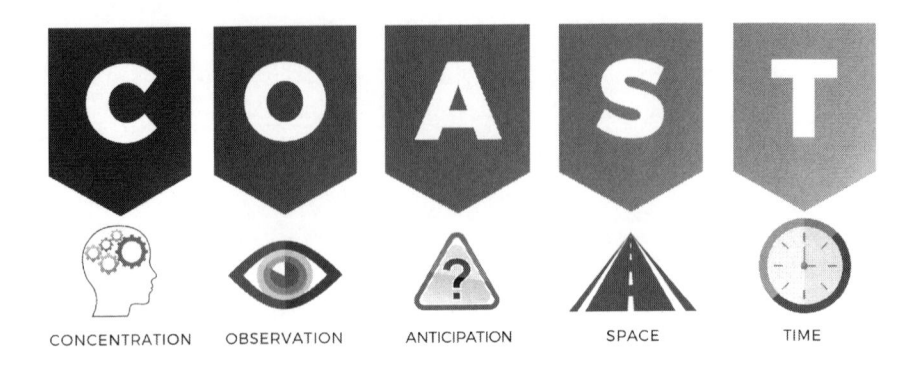

CONCENTRATION   OBSERVATION   ANTICIPATION   SPACE   TIME

The primary skill learned by giving a good commentary is effective eye scanning into the near, mid- and far distance, and the rear-view mirrors. Chris Gilbert, a specialist in advanced driver training with a wealth of experience in police advanced driver training, refers to our natural focal point, which he describes as akin to driving with our eyes "on dipped beam".[83] He believes a running commentary can help lift the driver's vision to a high visual horizon, well beyond the natural focal point. He uses the expression "eyes on main beam" to emphasise the importance of looking and scanning much further ahead than is natural. By driving with eyes on main beam, the driver can assess earlier, act sooner and have smoother use of the controls and fewer applications of the brakes.

For complete all-round awareness, it's important to scan from side to side, as well from near distance to far distance. In this sense, we're trying to encourage "funnel vision" rather than "tunnel vision".

We can split commentary driving into two types:

1. **Hazard commentary driving** — the simplest form, where the driver comments on all the potential hazards they can see.

2. **Instructional commentary driving** — a more complex form of commentary, where the driver adds more depth and detail to what they can perceive, commenting on all the potential hazards, what could happen and what action they'd take.

When introducing commentary driving to a learner driver, it's always a good idea to demonstrate it first and to keep it simple! The point of giving a commentary drive isn't to show off, but to show a novice driver just how far ahead you're scanning and planning.

Explain to your learner that you're always looking into the far distance first. Say what you see there and work backwards, mentioning any relevant hazards behind you (such as cars following closely, motorcyclists, etc.) before scanning well ahead into the far distance again, eyes on main beam. By routinely scanning the far distance, you'll often already have commented on hazards in the mid- and near distance. A hazard may only need a further mention as you get closer if its status changes in any way.

Some learners will relish giving a commentary drive, particularly those who enjoy talking. For those learners who are very quiet and introverted, asking them to give a commentary will often be their worst nightmare and will fill them with dread. Remember — be client-centred! You can get around this by asking quieter learners questions instead, which may only need a one- or two-word response. Here are some examples:

- "What's the furthest hazard you can see?"
- "What about now?"
- "What other hazards can you see?"
- "Is the driver behind following at a safe distance?"
- "What do we need to plan for further up the road?"

Commentary driving can even be split down into smaller tasks to help develop a specific skill. For example, a reasonably experienced learner who regularly fails to see signs would benefit from simply identifying all the signs they see for the next few minutes.

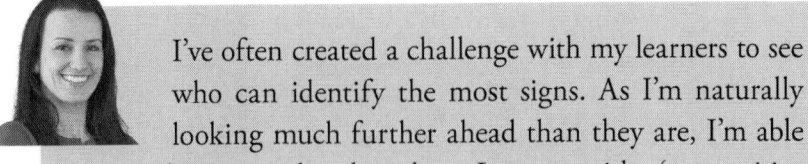

I've often created a challenge with my learners to see who can identify the most signs. As I'm naturally looking much further ahead than they are, I'm able to spot the signs earlier than them. Learners with a 'competitive streak' then start looking further ahead to try and beat me; I occasionally let them win to give them that motivational boost! Identifying a sign or hazard after a bend encourages the learner to look through bends — between gaps in trees or over the hedge-line. This challenge increases their awareness of where to expect signs, such as when areas become increasingly more built up, or at junctions. It also encourages them to identify locations where they may not have realised signs are placed — central islands and traffic bollards, for example.

You could set similar challenges to find changes in road markings, spot pedestrians early, scan junctions and identify approaching vehicles.

The GROW model

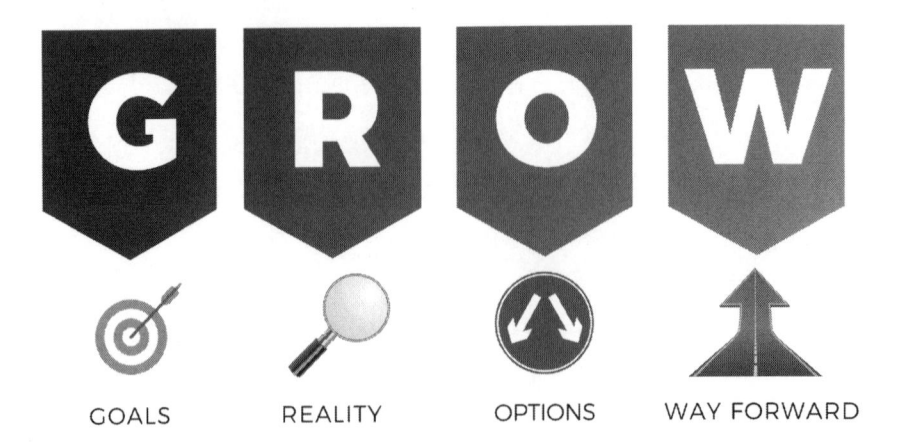

GOALS REALITY OPTIONS WAY FORWARD

Developed by Sir John Whitmore and his team in the 1980s, the GROW model is a process for goal setting or problem-solving.[84] The GROW process promotes conversation which can help the learner change and adapt the way they think and act. Predominately used in business and personal coaching, it can easily be used in driver training. The GROW process follows the sequence:

Goals: What do you want to achieve?

Reality: Where are you now? What might be stopping you from moving forward?

Options: What options are available to help you move closer to your goal?

Way Forward: What will you do and when?

Although GROW is a process, you don't necessarily have to follow it in any set sequence. You may need to revisit specific parts throughout a lesson. This is especially true when problem-solving. With that in mind, goals may change throughout the lesson based on how your learner is coping with the original goals set. As problems arise, new goals to overcome these problems can be dealt with using GROW. If a learner is finding difficulty in achieving a specific goal, it may have to be simplified or broken down into more manageable micro-goals.

When it comes to problem-solving, such as when your learner encounters a situation they've not dealt with before or when they make a mistake, the GROW model can be helpful. The learner becomes more aware of what they want to achieve and where they are currently in relation to that goal. Using GROW increases their sense of ownership of the issue and encourages them to take responsibility for generating solutions.

GROW: Goals

If the learner has had input in selecting their goals, whether it be goals for the lesson or goals following a problem, they'll be more committed to achieving them.

Following a problem, exploring what happened (the reality) will help the learner set their own goals for a successful outcome next time.

Here are some example questions you could ask to establish your learner's goals following the identification of a problem:

- "What would you like to happen next time we do that?"
- "If we did that again, what would you like to be different?"
- "What do you want to achieve when we come across that again?"
- "If it was done perfectly, what would it look like?"
- "What skills would you like to practise?"
- "Which parts do you want to improve?"

GROW: Reality

Here, you need to encourage the learner driver to examine their current situation; their reality. Where are they right now? Some example questions you might ask are:

- "What happened?"
- "How do you feel about …?"
- "What effect did that have on you?"
- "What's concerning you?"
- "What problems did we have?"
- "How did it affect others?"

GROW: Options

In this stage of the GROW process, you can encourage your learner to think of solutions. They may come up with some fantastic options that you wouldn't have thought of yourself. As the instructor, you still need to be prepared with some ideas of your own, just in case your learner struggles to think of anything.

Learning Styles

Your learner might come up with some options that you know won't fix the issue, or may not relate to the problem at all, but don't discard those options. This will only serve to demoralise the learner and break rapport. Instead, you could try gently 'steering' them in the right direction with a question. To illustrate this, here's an example in which the learner driver turned left into a side road and clipped the kerb with their back wheel:

ADI: "What could we do next time so we don't clip the kerb, Lena?"
Lena: "Well I suppose I could go slower or maybe steer later?"
ADI: "Those are two possible options, yes. And how did you feel about our position leading up to the turn?"
Lena: "Maybe I was a bit close. Should I have been further away?"
ADI: "Maybe it would have helped, yes. So, you've come up with three options: go slower, steer later or position a bit further away from the kerb on approach ..."

In this example, the learner is encouraged to come up with options for correcting an error. Letting her come up with possible solutions strengthens her problem-solving skills.

Every so often, learners might come up with options which they can better relate to, which you can then use on lessons with other learner drivers. For example, if someone had problems with harsh braking and you asked them to come up with a solution, they might say something like, "I could imagine a ripe tomato on top of my brake pedal and press it gently so it doesn't splat the tomato." Finding out the weird and wonderful ways in which people think is a great way to add to your teaching strategies toolkit!

Here are some other questions you could ask a learner to generate options and solutions:

- "What could help you get it better next time?"
- "What are your options?"
- "How could we go about achieving it?"

- "What specific skills have we already learned which we could apply in that situation?"
- "What could you do to overcome the *[learning issue/obstacle]?*"
- "What else could you try?"

GROW: Way forward

Now it's time for your learner to decide on what option, or options, she wants to take to achieve her goals; this helps her to take responsibility and commit to a plan of action.

ADI: "... so, Lena, which option do you want to try first?"
Lena: "I think I'll try slower first and see if I can steer a bit later or maybe not as much."
ADI: "Okay, great — shall we try that and see what happens?"

Here are some other questions you could ask the learner regarding their way forward:

- "What are your next steps?"
- "What are we going to do first?"
- "What help would you like from me?"
- "Can you see any problems with doing that?"

Your learners should be encouraged to plan and work things out for themselves. You can offer additional help, if needed, by giving your guidance and support. If the 'way forward' they have taken doesn't achieve the desired outcome, that option can be eliminated, and the learner encouraged to problem-solve again. Finding ways that *don't* work are just as important for problem-solving as finding the ways that *do* work.

The GROW model is also a method which can help you structure a short goal-setting session at the start of a driving lesson, too. It doesn't take long, and once your learners get used to the process, they'll often come to you with a plan already in mind.

It might be that your learner has a few ideas of what they want to achieve during their lesson. Any goals to be set during the lesson can only be determined after exploring the reality of where they are now, and what skills they already have. As with the 'achievable' section of the SMART model (which we discussed in *Chapter 5: What Does a Client-Centred Lesson Look Like?*), you might have a learner who suggests practising a lesson topic well beyond their current level of ability. This is where some tact, diplomacy and some excellent coaching skills will come in handy.

The GROW model can also be particularly useful in the 'self-evaluation' and 'reflection and debrief' stages of the lesson, e.g. when encouraging a learner to identify suitable goals for the next lesson or commit to some home learning tasks.

Mind mapping

Many driving instructors find mind maps confusing and worry about the "right way" of doing them. If you're one of these people, then you needn't worry — we'll help you to understand how other instructors are using them, which will hopefully inspire you to try using them too!

A mind map is simply a visual diagram, used to expand thoughts and ideas around a central, usually new, topic. Unlike lesson briefings, which can often be regarded as a *passive* learning tool, mind maps are an *active* learning tool, in that they require the learner to be *actively* involved in the learning process.

A mind map can help you and your learner to explore their current knowledge about the topic you're going to cover. The experience of being a passenger and a pedestrian will have provided them with some knowledge that they can use as a driver. You could ask the learner to write down anything they know and need to know about the topic and then explore each idea or thought in turn. Each point on the mind map should ideally only consist of a single keyword, short phrase or image. As the learner generates their ideas and solutions, they take ownership of them. Instead of having to remember what they're told, they'll find it easier to recall information when they've come up with the keywords themselves.

The realisation and insight the learner gains from making a mind map allow for much more responsibility. Human beings tend to do things when they have their own reasons for doing so. In some cases, *telling* someone what to do simply results in them wanting to do the opposite — I'm sure those of you with teenage children or those of you who remember being a teenager can relate!

Mind mapping - A case study

Lou Walsh is just one of many ADIs who makes use of mind maps a lot in her driving lessons. Lou has been kind enough to write a systematic guide on how she develops them with her learners.

When creating a mind map with my learners, I keep to the following steps or fundamental principles:

Step 1. Start with a central topic and a defining question

Step 2. Ask questions that develop conversation and open up the discussion

Step 3. Add your points *only after* a pupil has finished adding his or hers

Step 4. Lead into solutions and enhance the pupil's problem-solving skills

Step 5. Review the mind map and use it to develop future goals

If you find a mind map hasn't been as successful as you'd hoped, the chances are it's due to a lack of one or more of the above principles.

Below, you can see a mind map created with one of my pupils, following those principles. You can watch the video of the mind map being created during the actual lesson by scanning this QR code or by visiting **http://gedclai.re/mindmap1**

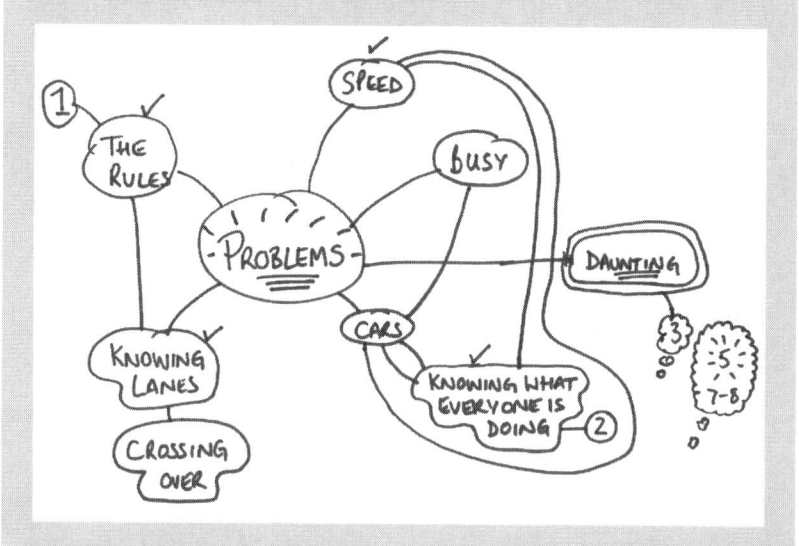

You can also watch a second video showing how I refer back to the original mind map during a follow-on lesson by visiting **http://gedclai.re/mindmap2** or by scanning this QR code. Keep the above steps in mind as you watch the two clips.

Here are some suggestions to help you through each of the steps:

Step 1. Start with a central topic and a defining question

Introduce the topic by writing a single word or phrase in the centre of a page or whiteboard — there are many iPad apps you could also use — and then pose a question to start the brain working. Questions I like to ask my pupils include:

- "I'm going to say one word to you. Tell me the first thing that comes into your head: roundabouts!" [this forms the central word of the mind map]
- [With "bay park" as the central phrase] "So we've agreed that we're going to look at bay parking today. When you think about parking in a car park, what problems do you think you may have to deal with?"
- [With "driving test" as the central phrase] "So, you feel ready to book your driving test. Let's look at what you expect to happen on the day and use this to make a plan to work on as we build up to that date."

Step 2. Ask questions that develop conversation and open up the discussion

Be led by the pupil and take cues from what they say. Rather than jumping in with your own ideas, sit back and give your learners time to generate thoughts and links. Paraphrasing and repeating back work well too. You'll see me use these techniques in the videos. Sometimes the most powerful questions are the simplest.

- "That's interesting, tell me more about that."
- "Anything else you can think of?"
- "What do you already know about that?"

Step 3. Add your points *only after* the pupil has finished adding theirs

When you're sure that the learner has exhausted his or her thoughts, then you can step in to add additional concepts. By jumping in too early, you limit your learner's potential to explore his or her understanding wholly or to allow their brains enough time to develop links and generate new ideas. When you give a pupil time to do this, you're creating a learning environment and allowing the learner to expand his or her active learning skills. I may introduce a missing link by saying something like:

- "Can I add a point that I think would be useful for us to consider?"

Step 4. Lead into solutions and enhance the pupil's problem-solving skills

It's vital that once the visual brainstorm is complete, that you move on to the solutions — the more a learner is encouraged to find his or her answers, the more likely these will be remembered and implemented. I find it useful to move a mind map onto the solution stage by saying something like:

- "So, let's take this point on the mind map. What could we do to make that less of an issue?"
- "You mentioned that this point is a problem. Can you think of any solutions we could try?"

Step 5. Review the mind map and use it to develop future goals

For a mind map to be complete, it should be examined in a way that can lead on to future goals; this is best done at the end of the session or when all solutions have been given a chance to be put into practice. It gives a great way of rounding off a lesson, finding out what's working and looking ahead to future drives. I find questions like this useful:

> - "So, let's relook at our mind map solutions. Which ones worked for you?"
> - "Out of all those things we put into practice today are there any areas where you feel you'd like to gain more experience?"

Lou Walsh and her husband, Blaine, have a great website for PDIs and ADIs which you can see by visiting **http://gedclai.re/walsh** or by scanning this QR code.

The role model technique

The role model technique involves asking the learner to imagine someone who can do a task exceptionally well, such as a relative, friend or colleague. It could even be a public figure who they don't know personally. Asking a learner to imagine someone who possesses the qualities or skills which the learner wishes to acquire can encourage them to work through tasks or issues for themselves.

- "Who do you know who can do this bay park really well?"
- "What would your dad do now if he'd misjudged the gap?"
- "How would Anna deal with it?"
- "How would Frank advise you to go about it?"
- "What do you think your brother would do now if he was in this situation?"
- "If you were Sue, what would you do next?"

Yes, we know the role model technique might sound crazy, but it often works really well! Try it! This approach can be useful when you're working with a learner who seems resistant to coming up with their own solutions. Maybe they're not confident enough to make their suggestions in case they get it "wrong". Crediting the advice or recommendation to their role model means that if it doesn't work, they don't take it personally.

The role model technique can also be helpful when helping someone to overcome limiting personal issues or beliefs they want to defeat.

- "If your mum was here now, what would she say to you?"
- "What would Chris say or how would he react if he heard you say that?"

Befriending thinking

Most people are great at advising other people, but not so great at working out solutions to their own problems. Sound familiar? Well, this is where befriending thinking comes in.

Like the role model method, befriending thinking involves asking the learner to imagine someone else having a similar problem or limiting belief as them. What would the learner say to that person to help them work through it? It doesn't matter whether the individual they imagine actually has the same issue or not — it's just something the learner is playing with in their mind.

It can be really surprising to see just how many solutions and strategies the learner can come up with!

- "Who do you know who struggles with changing lanes? What advice would you give them if they were unsure of when to change lanes?"
- "If Hannah asked for your help in this situation, what advice would you give her?"
- "If your friend, Alex, struggled with this, what could you suggest that would help her?"
- "If your friend panicked in a similar situation, what would you tell her to do to help her keep calm?"

Perceptual positions

Perceptual positions is a technique to help your learners see, hear and feel things from another person's perspective. Lots of instructors use this to some degree, but it can be made much more efficient by asking your learner to actually *become* the other person in their mind, rather than just getting them to consider what the other person thought or might think. There are three perspectives from which we can view a driving situation:

- **Self** — from our own perspective
- **Other** — from the perspective of the other road user(s) involved or affected
- **Observer** — from a neutral observer's perspective

The perceptual positions technique comes in handy when your learner would benefit from understanding how their actions could affect other road users.

Example: You've asked your learner, Natalie, to move off from the side of the road. Cars are approaching from behind, and there's a gap in the traffic flow behind coming up. Natalie has seen the oncoming traffic and signals right.

ADI: "Cancel the signal please, Natalie."
Natalie: "Oh." [cancels signal]
ADI: "Did you notice the cars coming up from behind?"
Natalie: "Yes, I wasn't going to go, I was just letting them know I'd be moving off in a minute."
ADI: "Okay, but what do you think they thought when they saw your signal?"
Natalie: "Oh, I suppose they may think I'm going to try and move off before them. I wasn't going to, though."
ADI: "No, I know you weren't. And I know you'd seen them. But when should we signal if cars are passing?"
Natalie: "After they've gone past?"

ADI:	"Yes, if you still feel it will benefit someone. And why is it important not to signal too early? How might the other driver react if they're about to pass us?"
Natalie:	"Hmm, I think you said they might swerve or panic if they think I'm going to move off in front of them?"

This approach seems practical because Natalie is encouraged to think about how her actions might have affected other drivers. However, we can make it even *more* useful by placing her in the position of the other driver.

ADI:	"Cancel the signal please, Natalie."
Natalie:	"Oh." [cancels signal]
ADI:	"Have you any idea why I asked you to cancel the signal?"
Natalie:	"No! I thought you asked me to move off, so I was just letting people know what I was doing."
ADI:	"Ah yes, I see. Okay, I want you to imagine you're driving along this road ahead of us."
Natalie:	"Okay ..."
ADI:	"You start to get nearer to a car parked at the side of the road. As you get closer and are about to pass it — say, within a few car lengths — you see the car's right indicator come on. What's the first thing that goes through your mind?"
Natalie:	"He's going to pull out."
ADI:	"Yes! And what are you going to do now if you think he's going to pull out in front of you?"
Natalie:	"I'm going to brake or maybe swerve out in case he hits me ... Ah [penny drops], that's what I did to those other drivers isn't it?"

Now Natalie has "experienced" the situation from the other driver's perspective, she's more likely to remember the correct action — more so than if she'd purely looked at the situation from her own point of view.

There are many ways to encourage self-reflection and self-evaluation, including raising awareness, developing responsibility and using reflective logs — see *Chapter 2: Coaching* and *Chapter 5: What Does a Client-Centred Lesson Look Like?*

We utilise a few more tools from our 'training toolbox' which we'll share with you now. Although we've given titles to these tools, it's not always helpful to name these methods during your lessons — just make them flow as a part of your everyday work.

Gibbs' reflective cycle

When a learner driver makes a mistake, they need to go through a three-step process to correct it effectively.

1. **Identification** (using the skills of **self-awareness** to recognise what happened, what went well, what didn't go so well)
2. **Analysis** (to **self-reflect** and understand what caused it to happen and why it's wrong/dangerous to make that mistake)
3. **Remedy** (to **self-develop** by coming up with solutions for next time so it doesn't happen again)

As we discussed in *Chapter 4: The 5 Key Skills of a Client-Centred Instructor*, specifically *Key Skill 4: Feedback*, it's important that feedback is *elicited* from the learner for maximum learning. A straightforward way to do this is to follow the Gibbs' reflective cycle, illustrated opposite.[85] Created by Graham Gibbs in 1988, the reflective cycle was developed as a method to structure a discussion on Kolb's experiential learning cycle — see *Chapter 2: Coaching*.

In brief, the reflective cycle is all about encouraging your learners to:

- become more self-aware of their thoughts, feelings and actions
- identify their own strengths and areas for improvement
- analyse why any errors might have occurred, and in doing so, consider how their ideas and feelings might have played a part
- take responsibility for coming up with possible solutions

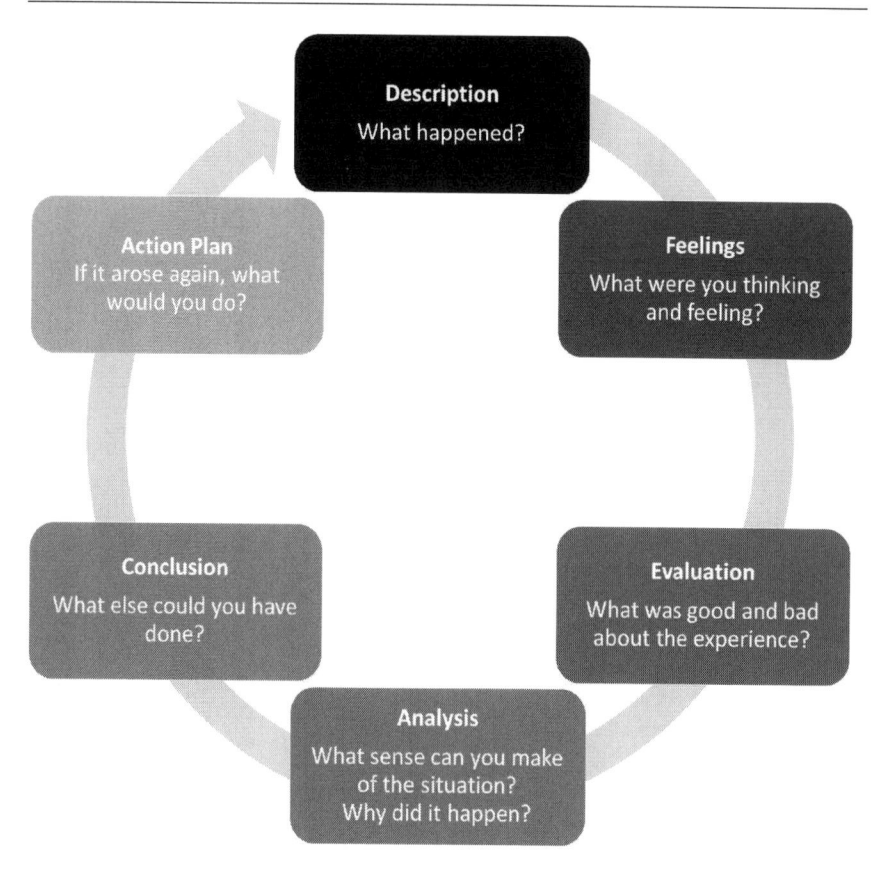

```
                    Description
                    What happened?

   Action Plan                        Feelings
If it arose again, what           What were you thinking
    would you do?                     and feeling?

    Conclusion                       Evaluation
What else could you have      What was good and bad
         done?                   about the experience?

                     Analysis
                What sense can you make
                    of the situation?
                   Why did it happen?
```

Scaling

Scaling is one of the best, most practical, solution-focused self-evaluation tools you can use as a driving instructor. This is probably our favourite tool of all.

By using a scale of 1 to 10 — and defining its extremes — the learner can evaluate their own performance, confidence, skill level and emotions about their desired outcome or state. Like Gibbs' reflective cycle, the main purpose of the scaling exercise is to develop the skills of **self-awareness**, **self-reflection** and **self-development**.

Applicable in a wide range of situations, scaling can also be used to help a driver assess their levels of satisfaction or to clarify their next step.

To use scaling effectively, simply follow our five-step SCALE system:

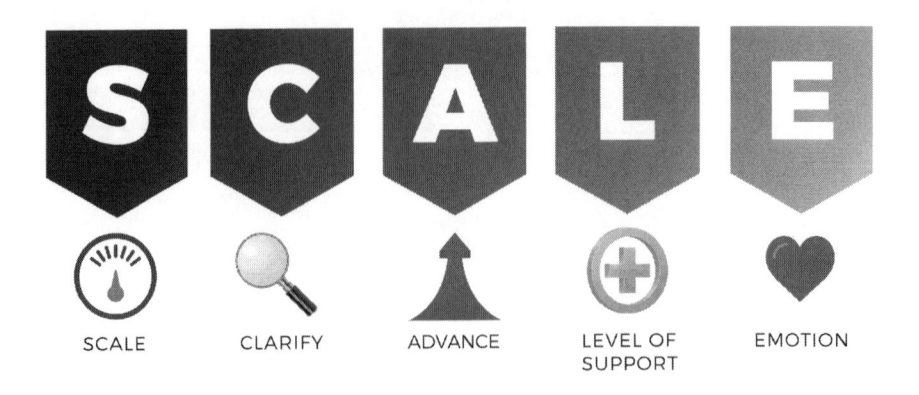

| SCALE | CLARIFY | ADVANCE | LEVEL OF SUPPORT | EMOTION |

SCALE / SCORE - Define the scale and its extremes.

- "So, on a scale of 1 to 10 — where 1 is a poor, dangerous manoeuvre, with no observations, poor control and accuracy; and 10 is the perfect manoeuvre, with total awareness of what was around you, excellent control and precision — where would you rate your performance for that first attempt?"

CLARIFY - Without judgment, encourage your learner to explain their decision.

- "Okay, a 3. So, what made you decide on a 3? What was good about your observations/clutch control/steering/accuracy? What wasn't as good as you'd have liked?"

ADVANCE - Where would your learner like to be?

- "That's good. So, what score are you going to aim to achieve next time?" or "Where could we make improvements?" or "What specifically will you do next time to make it even better?"

LEVEL OF SUPPORT - Find out if your learner needs any input or support from you.

- "What parts would you like my help with next time?"

EMOTION - Consider encouraging your learner to emotionally connect with their desired outcome.

- "How will you know when you've reached *[learner's desired number]* on the scale? How will you feel once we've mastered it?"

Score significance

No two scoring scales are the same, as the numbers will mean different things to different people. When scaling performance on a task, for example, one learner driver may consider a 7 to be test standard, with 8, 9 and 10 only achievable after they've been driving for some time on their own. To someone else, a 10 may be test standard. In this respect, the score the learner gives isn't that significant; it's the *advancement* part that's most important — working out the steps to becoming even better next time. The power of the scaling technique comes from the questions you ask rather than in the score the learner gives.

There's something important you need to know at this point: **It's essential that you never undermine the learner's response to the scaling question or tell them it's wrong.** If you do, the next time you use scaling with that learner, they will either be too afraid to give an answer at all, or they'll respond with the score they think *you* would give, rather than the score they would give.

"But wait — what if the learner doesn't do well, but scores themselves as a 10?" we hear you ask. To be honest, in our experience this is fairly unlikely. But even if they did, you *must* hold back from blurting out something like, "Haha! What planet are you on?! You think THAT was a 10? It was more like a 6!" A score of 10 could indicate any number of things: a misunderstanding of the scaling exercise, a lack of understanding of what a top-level performance looks like, or perhaps even over-confidence in their own ability. Conversely, if a learner who performs well scores themselves low down on the scale, it could be because they have a very low level of self-confidence.

In *Chapter 2: Coaching,* one of the nine fundamental principles of coaching we described was experiencing unconditional positive regard for your learners. Accept their response with a smile, respect their judgement and be inquisitive as to what led them to choose that number. Essentially, you want your learner to offer evidence to back up their answer.

In the case where a learner scores a reasonably good performance very low on the scale and appears to be a little deflated with their progress, a good way to encourage a more realistic self-evaluation would be to ask them what was good about their performance or to name three things that went well. Another method is to break the overall performance scale down into smaller elements and scale those individually.

Example: Alyssa forgot to change down into second gear for a left-hand turn and the car almost stalled. The rest of the manoeuvre went well. She has rated her overall performance at a 2 on the scale.

ADI: "Okay, a 2. Let's break it down then. How would you rate your mirror use where 1 is you didn't check your mirrors at all before signalling and turning, and 10 is you checked the correct mirrors promptly and knew what was behind you and to your left before you signalled and turned?"

Alyssa: "I did them okay, I knew that driver was a bit close … Maybe an 8 then for my mirrors."

ADI: "Great. What about your signal and road position?"

Alyssa: "I did those bits okay, I think?"

ADI: "Yes, they were spot on, weren't they? How about your awareness of what was on the new road? Even though the car struggled a bit in the gear you were in, how much time did you have to look at the new road? 1 means you didn't

	get a chance at all to see what was there, and 10 means you had an opportunity to look, knew what was there and could have stopped if you'd needed to?"
Alyssa:	"Hmm, maybe an 8 again? I knew that lady wanted to cross and she saw me and waited."
ADI:	"Okay, that's great! So, which parts of that turn perhaps didn't go as well as you'd have hoped?"
Alyssa:	"Well it nearly stalled on the corner because I was in third gear!"
ADI:	"Yes, excellent spot. So, based on the fact that was the only part that didn't go so well, would you still say a 2 is a fair assessment overall?"
Alyssa:	"Hmmm yes, perhaps a 2's a bit harsh. It was more like a 5, I guess. If I get that gear right next time, I'll be happy."

In this example, the instructor was able to build Alyssa's confidence by encouraging her to focus on the many positive elements. Simply telling Alyssa that her initial score was "wrong" would haven't been as effective.

Similarly, if you feel a learner has completely over-estimated their performance or is overconfident in their ability, you need to challenge it tactfully by redirecting their focus to the parts that weren't as good as they could have been.

Example: Patrick has scored his performance as a 9 for a junction he just whizzed round at high speed without looking into the junction first.

ADI:	"Okay, a 9. How about the speed into the junction, Patrick? What would you give yourself out of 10 for that, where 1 isn't in control and it would have been difficult to stop if needed, and 10 is where it was perfectly paced so you could have easily braked if someone had already stepped out into the road we turned into?"
Patrick:	"Hmm, that was probably more like a 5. Maybe a tiny bit too fast?"
ADI:	"Yes, I'd agree. And how about your awareness of what was happening on the road? 1 being 'I didn't really get a chance to look to see if there was anything there I needed to stop

for', and 10 being 'I knew what was on the road and was 100% sure it was clear to drive into?"

Patrick: "Ah, I think I forgot to look until I started turning actually... Maybe a 4?"

Once your learner has brought their score up or down to a more appropriate level, you can then help them look for opportunities to improve next time.

"I don't know"

Sometimes, when scaling performance, you may get the "I don't know" response; this can happen because the learner doesn't understand the reason why you're asking ("You're the instructor —tell me!") or worse, they may think you're trying to trick them. In this case, it's important that you've explained the benefits of self-evaluation to your learner, as this will usually stop this from happening. Refer back to the section titled, "The active learning agreement" in *Chapter 5: What Does a Client-Centred Lesson Look Like?*

An "I don't know" response could also arise if the learner considers you as the "expert", and they don't want to look stupid by giving a "wrong" answer. This shouldn't be the case if you've gained a good rapport with your learner, since you'll have created a trusting environment in which they feel free to express themselves without having their responses ridiculed or corrected.

Another common reason that someone might reply, "I don't know" is simply because they can't be bothered to think. Again, make sure your learner understands the benefits of self-reflection and self-evaluation. Assuming they do, a question like, "And if you did know?" or, "If you could give me a rough number, what would it be?" can often bring out an answer.

Scaling emotions

If you find someone is particularly resistant or struggles to scale their performance, it can be useful to ask them to scale their *feelings* instead, as you can't possibly have an answer to that. Only the learner knows what they're thinking and feeling. For example, "How did you think you did on that last roundabout, out of 10?" might be met with, "I don't know, what do you reckon?" So instead, you could change it to, "How comfortable did you feel at that last roundabout on a scale of 1 to 10?" They'll often find this question much easier to answer.

Following up with, "Okay, great. So why was it a 4?" can give you a fantastic insight into what bits they find challenging, such as "I really don't like having to change lanes; I'm worried that cars will come around on the left." This insight then gives you a chance to discuss these issues with your learner. Asking them to scale themselves on later roundabouts makes them more aware of how they're feeling and more importantly, how they're progressing.

Scaling is an amazingly versatile tool — we're always experimenting with it to measure things like confidence, anxiety, calmness, commitment and understanding. There are many ways of scaling, too. You don't always have to use a numerical scale, for example, you could use a colour wheel or chart. Some learners can better relate their feelings to a colour than to a number. Encourage your learners to choose the colour that most relates to how they feel and to identify the colour they would like to be. Then, as with a numerical scale, work out together how they can get there. We've also seen instructors using a picture of a ladder and asking the learner to point at the rung they're on in relation to where they feel they are. The key is to be client-centred and use a scaling method to which your learner can relate.

In a nutshell ...

The only thing you need to know is that the person sat next to you is *unique*. They'll respond well to some approaches and not very well to others. Your job is to simply spot what's resonating with them and what isn't, and then to do more of what's working and less of what isn't. Try different methods and techniques, notice how your learners are responding and enjoy the process of discovering how they respond best. It may be that they'd benefit from you using an approach other than the one they prefer.

Get curious and experiment!

Points for reflection

- Consider how you learn best. Do you like to have a full understanding of what is expected of you before having a go, or do you prefer to get stuck in and learn through experience? Notice how your answer to that question may change, depending on the situation and the level of risk involved.
- Think about two or three of your learner drivers. How do they differ in the ways they like to learn? How easily are you able to adapt to different learners' learning preferences?
- Do you find it helps to work in the way they prefer to learn, or do you find that better learning is achieved when you use a variety of learning methods?
- Which techniques do you currently use with success? On which techniques do you feel you could improve? Which techniques haven't you used before which you might try now?

CHAPTER 7

ADDRESSING LIMITING BELIEFS

"When we truly realize everything we experience — our perceptions, our feelings, our problems, whatever we call 'reality' or 'the way it is' — is really only a product of our own thinking, everything then changes for us. Our experience of life changes."[86]

Jack Pransky

Watch Video Message: Ged & Claire Introduce Chapter 7
http://gedclai.re/chapter7

What is a "belief"?

The Oxford English Dictionary defines a belief as "An acceptance that something exists or is true, especially one without proof."[87] Beliefs are judgements and evaluations we make which can influence our feelings and actions, either positively (empowering beliefs) or negatively (limiting beliefs). Beliefs have the power to influence our decisions, actions and outcomes. Typically, positive beliefs will bring about a positive result, and negative beliefs will lead to a negative result; beliefs can determine our success or lack thereof.

Our beliefs are formed through a variety of stimuli.

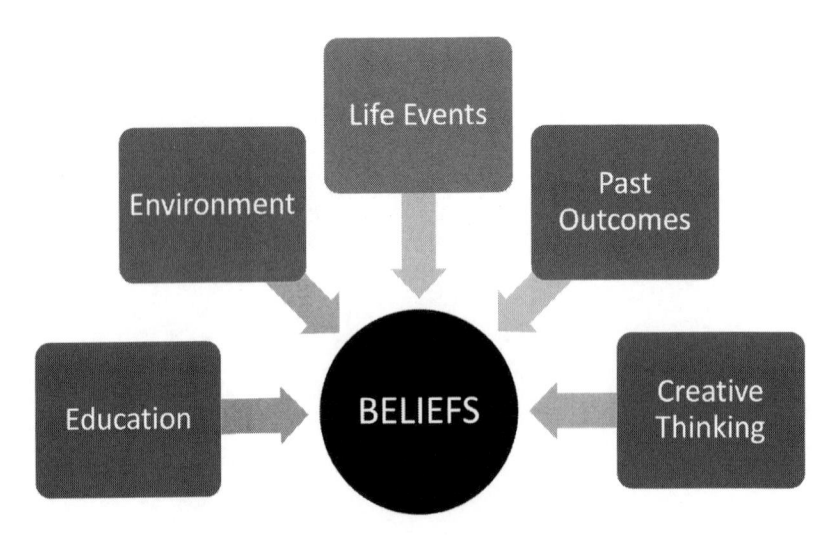

- **Education**: School, college and university — "Bullying is wrong", "You must work hard to be successful", "You must have respect for your teachers", "You'll get a good job if you get good results", etc.

Addressing Limiting Beliefs

- **Environment**: News and media, family and friends. For teenagers and young adults in particular, friends can have a *huge* influence on the beliefs they form.
- **Life events**: Some life events can give us new ideas and input into our lives and give us new beliefs into what's possible or not possible.
- **Past outcomes**: The past doesn't equal the future, but it can influence it tremendously. A belief that "I'm rubbish at tests" can adversely affect the outcome of future tests.
- **Creative thinking**: Our subconscious minds can't differentiate between vivid imagination and real life.[88] Our experience of the world is created in our minds and isn't a reflection of reality but an interpretation of it. After a driving test fail, we've heard comments such as, "He was a horrible examiner" or "He had it in for me from the start — I could tell he didn't like me." Most of the time, the reality was that it was a completely fair test with the examiner doing their job.

Performance-interfering thoughts (PITs)

I'm sure you've had learners who have stalled at traffic lights with another car behind. And then comes the inevitable honk of the horn from the driver behind. Typically, you may have been tempted to say something like:

- "Don't worry, just get started up again."
- "It's okay, she'll have to wait, take your time."
- "He was a learner once, don't let him panic you."
- "Just ignore the idiot behind, and let's get the engine started."

But, if we're to resolve such an issue so that it never happens again, we need to know what specifically caused the learner to stall. It might have simply been that the clutch was brought up too quickly. Maybe the learner needed to give a little bit more gas, or they were in the wrong gear. It could be that the handbrake wasn't released or fully released in time. Such things are only natural while learning to drive; it takes time to get coordination consistently perfect. Even after more than 20 years behind the wheel, we still stall occasionally.

Perhaps, however, the root cause was much deeper than that. Maybe what caused the coordination issue was what was going through the learner's mind. For example, imagine the learner's thought process was like this:

> *"The driver behind is really close …*
> *He's obviously frustrated at being stuck behind me …*
> *He'll want me to move off quickly …*
> *I hope I don't stall …*
> *I'm rubbish at moving away quickly …*
> *He'll get furious at me if I stall …*
> *And my instructor will think I'm useless!"*

How do you think such thoughts, or limiting beliefs, will affect the learner's actions? What the learner was thinking and the emotions these thoughts produced had a much bigger part to play in the stall than the environmental issue of bringing the clutch up too fast. Reminding your learner to bring the clutch up slower next time, or squeeze the gas pedal more firmly, is unlikely to resolve the issue in the long term because the root cause hasn't been addressed.

What the learner *thought* about the situation affected how they *felt* emotionally. Their thoughts and emotions then resulted in the *physical* response of bringing the clutch up too quickly and stalling the car. The above examples are all known as performance-interfering thoughts (PITs). The learner driver is mind reading, predicting, labelling, personalising and using negative language. These are all limiting beliefs or faulty thinking patterns — beliefs and patterns we need to challenge if we're to break the cycle and stop the issue from happening again.

Faulty thinking patterns

A learner's negative thoughts and beliefs can be categorised into different limited thinking patterns. Here are some examples, based on the work of Aaron Beck in the 1960s.[89]

All or nothing thinking

The learner's experiences are perfect or terrible; also called black-and-white thinking as there are no shades of grey. Example: *"That was absolutely rubbish."*

Polarised thinking

The learner's experiences go from great to bad and are over-dramatised, almost like a rollercoaster — up, then down, up, then down. Example: *"I think I did perfect on my manoeuvres but then messed up the roundabout altogether!"*

Focusing on negatives

The learner discusses their experience in negative terms rather than more empowering or positive terms, such as "I need to …" or "It would be better if …". Example: *"I brought my clutch up too fast."*

Mind reading

The learner makes assumptions about another person's thoughts or behaviour without having any supporting evidence. Example: *"She thinks I'm useless."*

Predicting

The learner jumps to conclusions and imagines a particular outcome, when in fact, other potential outcomes are possible. Example: *"I'm never going to be able to do this."*

Catastrophising

The learner assumes the worst, making more of an event or situation without sufficient evidence to back up their claims. Example: *"When I pass my test, there's no way I'm going on motorways. I'll end up crashing and killing myself."*

Blaming

The learner lays the blame for adverse outcomes at the feet of another person; no responsibility is taken for his/her part in the incident or situation. Example: *"It was his fault!"*

Emotional reasoning

The learner makes conclusions based on emotions, rather than facts. Example: *"I feel so fed up that I'm sure this lesson won't go well."*

Labelling

The learner brands themselves with a label, rather than a description of their behaviour, usually because of one instance. Example: *"I'm so stupid."*

Low frustration tolerance

The learner can't be bothered to finish a task, or they become impatient with a situation, even though it's in their best interests to follow it through. Example: *"I can't be bothered to study for my theory test, it's so boring!"*

Magnification

The learner focuses in and magnifies the importance or aspect of an event or experience. Example (after a minor error): *"Oh my God, I've got my test tomorrow … What hope is there for me?"*

Minimisation

The learner minimises the importance or significance of an event or experience. Example: *"I was only slightly over the speed limit, it doesn't matter."*

Overgeneralisation

The learner makes sweeping negative conclusions based on a single instance or lack of evidence. Example: *"My manoeuvres are awful."*

The ABC model

We've found that Albert Ellis' ABC Technique of Irrational Beliefs extremely helpful when it comes to understanding beliefs and how they affect our emotions or consequences.[90]

A	B	C
Activating Event / Situation	**B**elief / Thought	**C**onsequence / Emotion

In the ABC model illustrated above, you'll see that it's not the situation or event that causes the consequence or emotion; instead, it's the interpretation of the event or situation that causes the emotional response. Take someone with a spider phobia, for example. As soon as that person sees a spider, they appear to have an immediate physical and emotional response. But it's not the spider that causes this reaction — it's the person's thoughts *about* the spider. If their thoughts were that spiders were lovely little harmless creatures, then the outcome would be much different.

This model is quite empowering when you think about it since it means *we have control over the outcome.* Consider two different people who fail their driving test. Both were fully prepared by their driving instructor and were, in the instructor's opinion, at the standard required to pass the driving test comfortably.

Driving test candidate 1

The examples below illustrate two extremes, but they do show that it's not the event that leads to the outcome, it's how the individual interprets or thinks about that event. It's the person that gives the situation meaning, which in turn affects them emotionally.

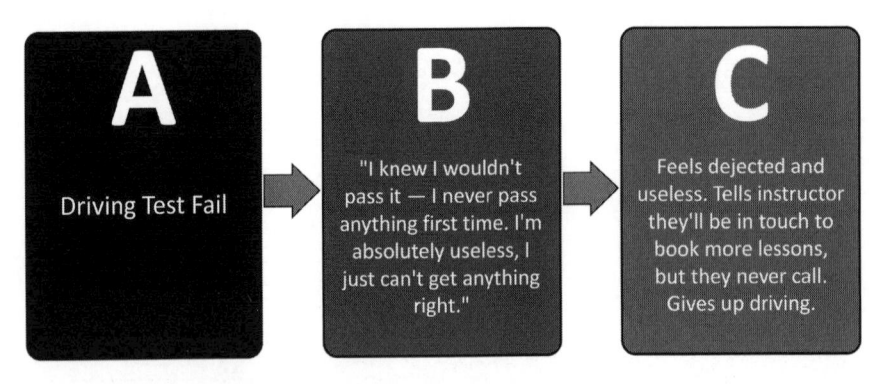

A — Driving Test Fail

B — "I knew I wouldn't pass it — I never pass anything first time. I'm absolutely useless, I just can't get anything right."

C — Feels dejected and useless. Tells instructor they'll be in touch to book more lessons, but they never call. Gives up driving.

Driving test candidate 2

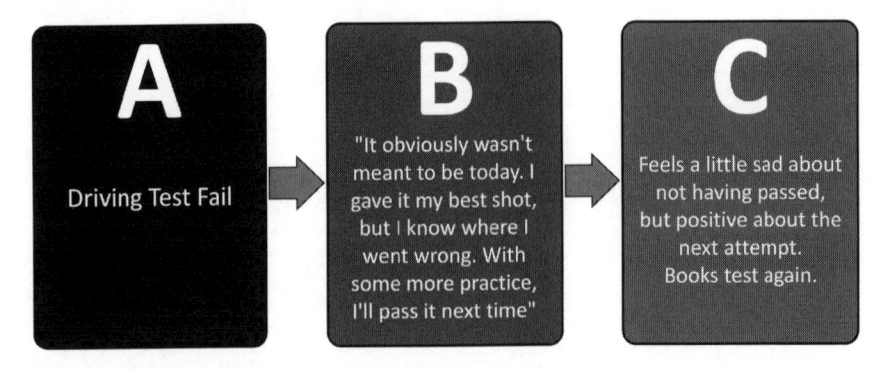

A — Driving Test Fail

B — "It obviously wasn't meant to be today. I gave it my best shot, but I know where I went wrong. With some more practice, I'll pass it next time"

C — Feels a little sad about not having passed, but positive about the next attempt. Books test again.

Addressing Limiting Beliefs

In some cases, the outcome further reinforces the belief. For example, a learner driver may have had trouble joining a roundabout (A). Their new belief is that roundabouts are hard (B). They may experience increased levels of anxiety approaching any roundabouts in the future (C). They may panic which may result in them freezing and not slowing down to join, or they may overreact and stop dead, even if it was possible to keep going and join the roundabout. Now the limiting belief that "roundabouts are hard" is proven and so the cycle goes on.

Negative thought cycle

Negative thought cycles can develop at any time. Some learners are particularly vulnerable to them on approach their driving test, when doubts about their ability to pass begin to creep in.

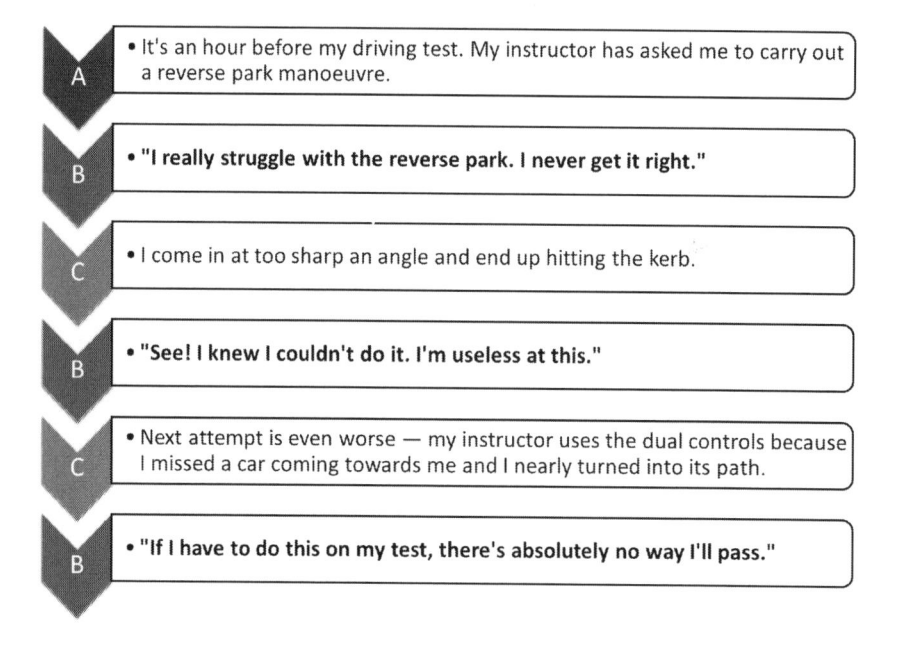

- **A**: It's an hour before my driving test. My instructor has asked me to carry out a reverse park manoeuvre.
- **B**: "I really struggle with the reverse park. I never get it right."
- **C**: I come in at too sharp an angle and end up hitting the kerb.
- **B**: "See! I knew I couldn't do it. I'm useless at this."
- **C**: Next attempt is even worse — my instructor uses the dual controls because I missed a car coming towards me and I nearly turned into its path.
- **B**: "If I have to do this on my test, there's absolutely no way I'll pass."

Guess what the likely outcome will be on the driving test? You've probably seen first-hand, with your learners, just how destructive negative thoughts can be, and how learners can easily find themselves in a negative thought cycle.

The Belief Window

When we hold a belief, our brains consistently look for evidence to support it. Hyrum W. Smith referred to this invisible brain mechanism as the "Belief Window": "You cannot actually see your Belief Window because it's invisible, but we all have one. It's figuratively attached to your head and hangs in front of your face. Every time you move, that window goes with you. You look at the world through it, and what you see is filtered back to you through it."[91]

If a new driver comes to you for lessons with the belief that he's stupid, incompetent and a slow learner, for example, he'll unconsciously seek out evidence to support this view. Every mistake or piece of negative feedback reinforces that belief.

We naturally filter out events that contradict our beliefs. So for the learner driver in the above example, any positive action they make and any positive feedback from you tends to go unrecognised. Learners with negative self-beliefs may sigh a lot when things go wrong, chastise or berate themselves, or even have an emotional outburst. They may cancel lessons altogether, believing that it's just not worth trying any more.

Before 1954, the entire world had a belief that the human being couldn't run a mile in less than four minutes. Then a 25-year-old medical student came along and ran a mile in 3 minutes and 59.4 seconds. Roger Bannister was the first of many. As soon as it was proven that the 4-minute mile *could* be broken, people's beliefs changed. Amazingly, Roger Bannister's record was shattered just a month later, and since then, hundreds more athletes have also run a mile in under four minutes.

So, if we become aware of our Belief Window, can we change what we see through it? And more importantly, if we know of our learners' Belief Window, can we change what they see through theirs?

Is it possible to change our learners' limiting beliefs and negative thought patterns? Thankfully, the answer is "yes". Well, sometimes, at least!

The impact of our beliefs

Before we look at how to challenge limiting beliefs, or PITs, we need to understand the impact that they have.

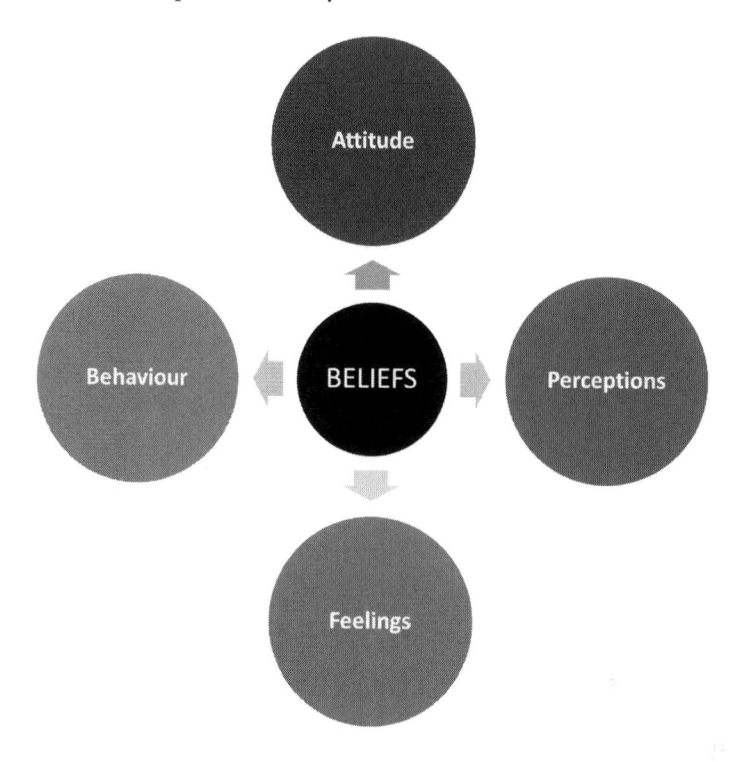

Our beliefs drive our attitude, perceptions, feelings and behaviours. If we have negative or limiting beliefs about ourselves or the situation we're in, then our attitudes, perceptions, feelings and behaviour will align with those thoughts. For example, imagine a learner driver goes in for their driving test with the following set of PITs: "I'm not ready for my test … Nobody ever passes first time … The examiner won't like me … My nerves are bound to get the better of me." By holding such PITs, this is what's likely to happen after making a small mistake on the test:

Perceptions — They may think "Oh my God, the examiner must think I'm an idiot … He's not even talking to me … That must mean I've definitely failed now."

Feelings — They feel sad, disappointed, upset and angry at themselves.

Attitude — They inwardly ask, "What's the point of carrying on?" and have a defeatist attitude.

Behaviour — All of the above manifests in their behaviour. Their driving worsens, they begin to break the speed limit to get back to the test centre as quickly as possible to get it over with. They become focused on the road ahead and stop using their mirrors.

During the debrief, the examiner explains that although he has noted the first minor error, the learner failed the test because of all the mistakes that came after that point. The whole experience reinforces the learner's original thoughts and beliefs and they've inadvertently proven themselves right. Often, negative beliefs will result in adverse outcomes. Some might call this a "self-fulfilling prophecy". Of course, the opposite is also true; positive beliefs can result in positive outcomes. So instead of performance-interfering thoughts, we need to focus on generating performance-enhancing thoughts.

Performance-enhancing thoughts (PETs)

> I first learned the specifics about PITs and PETs while on a training course presented by Professor Jonathan Passmore back in 2009.[92] I remember him saying the phrase, "Get out of your PIT and get a PET." This really resonated with me and stuck in my mind, because the point is this: exchanging PITs for PETs is entirely possible. Change the way you think, and you can alter an outcome from a negative one to a positive one.

PETs are often referred to as "empowering beliefs" as they can give us the fuel we need to succeed. Empowering beliefs shouldn't be confused with over-optimistic positive thinking. For example, "I'll take my driving test after just five hours of lessons and will pass with ease" is incredibly over-optimistic and is likely to result in failure. Instead, empowering beliefs, or PETs, are positive, powerful, realistic, constructive and success-oriented in nature. PETs are about seeking excellence, rather than perfection.

- "I have absolute control over my thoughts and feelings, and I'll be calm and confident on test day."
- "Although that manoeuvre didn't go as well as I'd planned, I've learned where I need to improve and therefore I can do it much better next time."
- "I wasn't successful on my driving test today, but the examiner's feedback was positive for the most part, and I know where I made some mistakes. I'll learn from it and pass next time."

Some limiting beliefs are easier to challenge than others, but there are quite a few ways in which you can help your learners to think differently. We won't pretend this is easy, though. Some people almost seem to have negativity coursing through their veins; they may even come from a family of negative thinkers. Some people truly are "mood hoovers" — they suck the life and soul out of everything and everyone in their path with their negativity.[93] Don't give up, though; it's amazing how your positivity can be transferred to your learners. When it works, it can create massive transformational change!

Cognitive behavioural coaching

Cognitive behavioural coaching (CBC) came about through the development of cognitive behavioural therapy (CBT) in the 1960s by Aaron Beck and Albert Ellis.[94, 95] CBC focuses on the beliefs and thoughts we have, how they influence our actions, and how to develop and try out new ideas and thoughts to bring about a positive change. Put more succinctly by Helen Whitten: "The focus in CBC is developing constructive thoughts and behaviours to support action towards the identified goals."[96]

Earlier, we looked at the ABC model of emotions; this can be expanded upon to create the ABCDE model used in CBC.

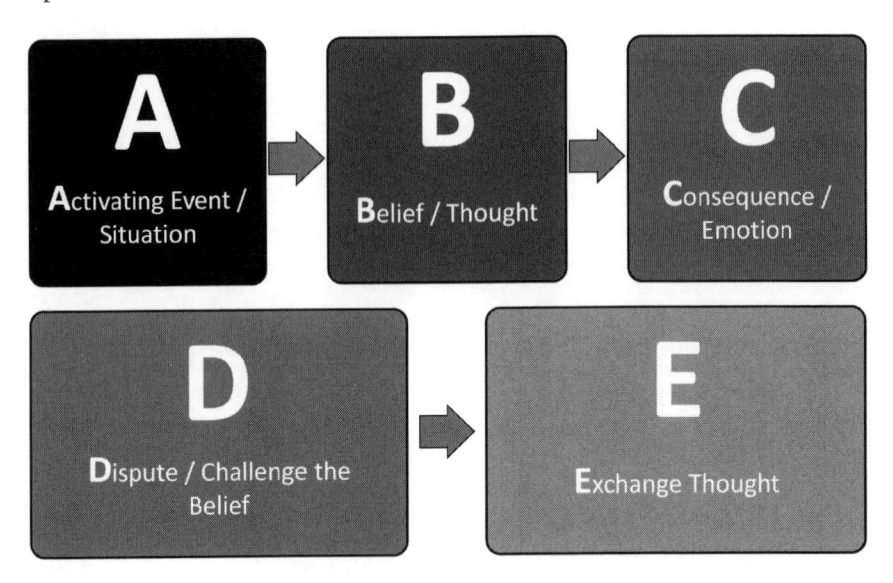

```
┌─────────────────┐      ┌─────────────────┐      ┌─────────────────┐
│        A        │  →   │        B        │  →   │        C        │
│ Activating Event│      │ Belief / Thought│      │  Consequence /  │
│   / Situation   │      │                 │      │     Emotion     │
└─────────────────┘      └─────────────────┘      └─────────────────┘

┌─────────────────┐      ┌─────────────────────────────────────────┐
│        D        │  →   │                   E                     │
│ Dispute /       │      │           Exchange Thought              │
│ Challenge the   │      │                                         │
│ Belief          │      │                                         │
└─────────────────┘      └─────────────────────────────────────────┘
```

Here is how the ABCDE model works in practice:

A. The learner experiences an event or situation, which then **activates**...
B. a **belief** or thought about the activating event, which then ...
C. manifests in emotions or **consequence**.
D. We non-judgementally challenge or **dispute** the belief so that ...
E. the learner can **exchange** the negative/limiting thought (PIT) for a positive and more constructive thought (PET), which will benefit them and prevent the same negative consequence from arising again.

By using the ABCDE paradigm, we can help transform negative thinking into positive thinking. Consequently, our learners will feel and behave much more positively; their attitudes and beliefs are also affected, which will help them not only during their driving lessons but well beyond test

Addressing Limiting Beliefs

day. Now, we do recognise that not all beliefs can be changed and that we're not miracle workers, but there will be some beliefs we *can* change, so it's worth trying. Challenging our learners' negative thoughts and feelings should be an integral part of their learning; after all, our aim is to promote safe driving for life, isn't it?

Using another ABCDE to challenge limiting beliefs

A **Acknowledge** the trigger event or situation.
B **Build** a picture of what the learner was thinking or saying to themselves at that moment.
C **Create** a connection between the thoughts and the emotion or outcome.
D **Dispute** the limiting thoughts/beliefs.
E **Establish** a more suitable exchange thought or PET.

Once you've found the situation in which your learner's thoughts may or may not have had an influence, start by encouraging them to identify internal dialogue.

- "What were you thinking just before …?"
- "What are you saying to yourself when …?"
- "What tends to run through your mind when …?"

Listen to their reply carefully and pay attention to any non-verbal cues which might show how they feel when they recall the incident. Find which thoughts are performance-interfering and which, if any, are performance-enhancing. You need to understand any negative or faulty thinking patterns before you can challenge them. In *Chapter 2: Coaching*, in our nine fundamental principles of coaching, we outlined the importance of experiencing unconditional positive regard for your learner and believing in their ability to succeed. To transform a learner's PITs into PETs, we need to enter *their* world and accept what *their* truth is. Here are some examples of ways in which some instructors typically respond when a learner expresses a negative thought pattern or belief:

- "Why on earth would you think that?"
- "That's not true at all!"
- "Well, I think you can do it."
- "That's a bit of a strange thing to think!"
- "But that doesn't make any sense! Why would you say stuff like that to yourself?"
- "Ah, don't worry about them — just focus on your own driving."

As tempting as it may be to respond in such a way, you need to forget about what you think. What you think about the situation is completely irrelevant; instead, your task is to help the learner make sense of what *they* are thinking and feeling, and help them to find a better way. Ultimately, you're looking for your learner to be able to answer the following four key questions which will challenge their belief:

1. Is their belief **realistic?**
2. Is their belief **logical?**
3. Is their belief **helpful?**
4. Is their belief 100% **true?**

Recognising that their belief isn't realistic, logical, helpful and/or true can generate an exchange of thought.

Useful coaching techniques to dispute limiting beliefs

Remember to be non-judgemental and listen carefully and actively for further or deeper limiting beliefs and thinking patterns. The purpose of using these techniques and questions is to challenge your learner's way of thinking and help them exchange their original thought or belief for a more empowering and constructive one. With a new positive belief, their view of what caused the problem in the first place will have changed. In the words of Dr Wayne Dyer, "When you change the way you look at things, the things you look at change."[97] Some of the

Addressing Limiting Beliefs

techniques outlined below are also explored in more detail in *Chapter 6: Learning Styles*. We've also filmed a video to demonstrate some of these techniques being used — the link to this video is on page 223.

Look for supporting evidence

Encourage your learner to give tangible evidence for their belief. Ask them questions to find out what leads them to believe what they believe.

Modelling

Ask the learner to think of someone that holds an opposite, empowering belief? How would *they* deal with the situation? How would *they* physically respond in that situation?

Befriending thinking

It's often easier to offer good advice to others than to ourselves — "If your friend held the same belief, how would you recommend they deal with it?"

Perceptual positions

A situation or event may appear very different, depending on one's point of view. Encourage your learner driver to look at the situation from other perspectives: self (first person), other (another person involved), and meta/observer (third person removed from the situation).

Visualisations

These can help when "rehearsing" new empowering beliefs, which assist in reinforcing them. Visualisation works so well because the subconscious mind can't distinguish between real memories and imagined ones.

De-labelling

Learners often negatively label themselves after a negative experience. Try to "de-label" the learner by rephrasing it to something more constructive. If they say that they're "rubbish", you could reply, "So what you're saying is that there are a few areas we can work on together?"

Demagnification

Learners sometimes focus on an exaggeration of the negative elements when reviewing an event or situation. Encourage your learner to find evidence to contradict that belief. For example, if they say, "I've been absolutely *awful* today!", you could demagnify it by encouraging them to list a few areas that they've actually improved upon since last week.

Thinking more coolly

Under times of extreme stress, anxiety or self-doubt, the learner may appear to be descending into a negative abyss, showing no signs of positivity in their non-verbal or verbal communication. Look to "break" the learner's negative state by asking them to take a breath and step back for a moment to rationalise their thought patterns.

Self-disclosure

It's nice to hear we're not alone in having a particular limiting belief. Sharing your own stories and explaining how you've overcome similar issues can really help your learner to recognise that how they are feeling is completely normal and that there is a light at the end of the tunnel!

Identifying reflex thoughts

Identifying reflex thoughts is particularly important in identifying specific limiting beliefs. Asking "What are you thinking now?", "What's going through your mind?" or, "How does it feel?" at the critical moment can reveal otherwise subconscious negative self-talk.

Become curious

Encourage your learner drivers to be more inquisitive about their limiting beliefs. Instead of automatically identifying with those beliefs, your learners should begin to question them. Through your coaching, you can help them to understand this process. To help put all of this into some context for you, we've filmed a couple of short videos for you.

The first video can be watched at **http://gedclai.re/stall1** or by scanning the QR code here. This video shows an example of how most driving instructors might deal with a learner stalling the car at a set of traffic lights. Notice that the instructor only addresses the "surface cause" (bringing the clutch up too quickly), and not the root cause (the PITs about the driver behind). Each time the learner expresses their PITs, the instructor brushes them off. This isn't because he isn't listening or doesn't care — it's because he either doesn't realise that the PITs are the root cause or because he doesn't know how to deal with them.

The second video can be watched by scanning this QR code or by visiting **http://gedclai.re/stall2**. In this video, we give an example of how an instructor could coach the learner around their PITs and help them to create some PETs. We highlight some of the negative thought patterns that the learner is expressing and show you how an instructor might challenge some of those unhelpful beliefs and thought patterns. At the same time, it's important to connect the learner to the desired emotion. Notice how changing the emotion can modify the thoughts and therefore the behaviour.

And if all else fails ...

Remember that you can't change people who don't want to change. You may find that naturally negative people want to stay that way. Recognise that every behaviour, no matter how destructive it might seem to you, has a positive intention. For some negative people, that might mean getting attention. After all, an "Oh, woe is me!" attitude will, to some degree, get attention from others. Such an attitude will result in others telling them that they're worthy and that they're amazing.

Unless you're a trained psychotherapist, keep in mind that as a driving instructor, you're hired by your learner to do a job — to take them from point A, not being able to drive, to point B, being able to drive. As challenging as this might seem at times, we need to make the best use of our coaching skills along the way. However, as we've said all along, you can't coach someone that doesn't want to be coached. So please don't beat yourself up over not being able to transform a "mood hoover" into a person who constantly exudes positivity and enthusiasm; let's face it, that's unlikely to happen.

We encourage you to help your learner drivers overcome their difficulties, but if it feels like you're coming up against a brick wall, accept that your best is good enough and that you're not the problem.

Points for reflection

- What types of limiting beliefs do your learners have? Have you tried to challenge these thought patterns in the past? If so, how successful was your intervention?
- Having read this chapter, what could you try using next time to help your learners turn their PITs into PETs?
- Think about one of your limiting beliefs or faulty thinking patterns. It could relate to any area of your life. Is the belief realistic, logical, helpful and true?
- Start to become more aware of your own thoughts and begin making a conscious effort to get rid of your PITs and transform them into PETs.

CHAPTER 8

DEALING WITH NEGATIVE ATTITUDES

"Have you ever noticed when you're driving that anyone who is driving slower than you is an idiot and anyone driving faster than you is a maniac?"[98]

George Carlin

| Watch Video Message: Ged & Claire Introduce Chapter 8 |
| http://gedclai.re/chapter8 |

What are attitudes and how are they expressed?

Hogg & Vaughan (2011) defined attitude as, "A relatively enduring organization of beliefs, feelings and behavioural tendencies towards socially significant objects, groups, events or symbols." [99] Put another way, our "attitude" can be considered as the way in which we represent our beliefs and values through our words and behaviour.

Here are some examples of what learner drivers, or newly qualified drivers, might say, internally or externally, to illustrate their attitude towards a situation or other road user:

- "Look at this idiot driving close behind. I feel like slamming my brakes on and teaching him a lesson!"
- "A 20mph limit on this road is stupid — no one goes that slow!"
- "Flippin' cyclists, they shouldn't be allowed on the road!"

Non-verbal expressions of attitude might include body language such as:

- Tutting
- Head-shaking
- Sighing
- Gritting teeth
- Flushed complexion
- Increased breathing rate
- Shoulder shrugging
- Throwing hands up in the air
- Giving a one- or two-fingered "salute" to another road user

The learner driver may also express their attitude through their driving behaviour. Some examples could include swinging back to the left sharply after barely passing a cyclist, accelerating harshly away from a junction or situation, or harsh use of the controls. Challenging negative driver attitudes will always be a difficult task for an instructor. It's not as easy as saying, "Woah! Hang on a minute — you shouldn't think like that; you should think like this ..." Because your learner's perception of the world is unique, their beliefs and attitudes are part of their world. Their beliefs are true for them and until we can acknowledge that fact, we won't be able to guide them towards a better way of thinking.

The Belief Window and driver attitude

Our views are reinforced by our Belief Window, which we described in more detail in *Chapter 7: Addressing Limiting Beliefs*. Inwardly, we look for information to support our beliefs. We're always looking through our Belief Window, which filters out events that contradict our belief and only notices the things that support it. Some stereotypical beliefs that drivers may hold about other road users:

- "Audi drivers are idiots and always tailgate."
- "BMW drivers never signal."
- "Cyclists always go through red lights and are a nuisance."
- "Women are rubbish at parking."
- "Young male drivers drive too fast and take far too many risks."
- "White van drivers are inconsiderate and ignorant."
- "Taxi drivers drive dangerously."
- "Motorcyclists are maniacs."

We wonder just how many of those you agree with? What other beliefs do you hold that may be different from those listed above? Our beliefs are upheld and enhanced by our Belief Window. If you subscribe to the beliefs above you'll unconsciously make a mental note of every Audi that might be following a little too closely; every time a BMW driver doesn't signal; every mistake a cyclist might make, etc. It's a little bit like when you decide to buy a new car. Suddenly everyone else has the same car as you! Or when you decided to train as a driving instructor — "Wow, look how many driving instructors there are in my area! I'm pretty sure there were never this many before!"

Our Belief Window filters out all the events that don't support our beliefs. For example, we don't notice the female driver that parks her car perfectly and accurately, first time; we don't notice the conscientious, young male driver who's driving safely and within the speed limit; we don't notice the white van driver who smiles and allows us to pull put in front of them into slow-moving traffic, etc. Every piece of filtered, supporting evidence reinforces our attitudes, and subconsciously triggers an inward negative feeling or outward negative emotion or behaviour. We may swear, tut, shake our head, criticise, scream, shout or even experience full-on road rage.

Not all unhelpful beliefs and attitudes will relate to other road users, either. Our learners may also hold some other views which you might want to challenge, such as:

- "I should be ready for my driving test after ten lessons."
- "I need to drive like this to pass my test, but once I pass, I can drive how I like."
- "You learn to drive *after* you've passed the driving test."
- "Passing the hazard perception test is purely down to luck."
- "It's easier to pass your test on a Friday afternoon."
- "Nobody passes their test first time."
- "Some examiners are racist/sexist/ageist/homophobic."
- "I've heard Mr X doesn't pass anyone."

Take a few moments to think about how your learner's Belief Window will only filter through experiences that support the above beliefs and will filter out those pieces of evidence that contradict them. Can you see how it becomes a vicious cycle? Our beliefs are responsible for driving our behaviour. How this behaviour is expressed shows the driver's attitudes in any given situation. Pay attention to how your learner shows any unhelpful, or even dangerous, behaviour towards another road user or situation. It may be verbal, non-verbal or a combination of both.

Where do our attitudes come from?

Attitudes are formed from a multitude of sources, including parents, friends, teachers/mentors, culture, education and experience. Opinions form at a very early age; children often form attitudes by observing and imitating the behaviours of others. The conduct of a parent while driving will play a significant role in the conduct their child displays once they reach driving age and embark on driving lessons.

As children become young adults, the behaviour and influence of their peers also have a significant impact on their actions and attitudes. If action isn't consistent with attitude, it's possible that this is a result of peer pressure. In other words, a young adult may not want to behave a certain way, but they do so to fit in with their peers.

- He chooses to speed because his friends think it's cool and it gives them a "buzz", even though internally, he feels it's wrong.
- She has that drink before driving her mates home, even though it doesn't sit comfortably with her. They kept insisting one is okay — they do it all the time.

Learning attitudes from others can be a great advantage, of course, providing they're positive attitudes. A parent who never answers the phone while driving and condemns others that do will help instil similar attitudes in their children. The friend who always wears her seat belt and insists that all her passengers do too will influence her friends' attitudes to wearing a seat belt.

Paying attention to our learner drivers' attitudes

When a learner displays a positive driver attitude, it's helpful to query where they think this approach originates from and then to celebrate it. After all, by reinforcing positive attitudes with your learner, you'll undoubtedly enhance rapport and therefore make it much easier to challenge any negative attitudes when they surface.

Once a negative attitude presents itself, our job is to see if we can guide our learners into a more confident and resourceful approach which will help keep them safe on the roads beyond their time with us. In addition to views relating to learning to drive or taking a driving test, your learners may express negative attitudes relating to:

Speed

- "I like driving fast."
- "I hate driving slowly."
- "Come on, be honest — nobody sticks to speed limits all the time."

Road rage/anger/hostility towards another road user

- "Van drivers really annoy me."
- "It really p****s me off when other drivers cut in."

Using a mobile phone while driving

- "Yeah, I'll answer my phone — if there are no police about!"
- "It's fine to use my phone on handsfree though — you can't get done for that, and it's safer."

Alcohol/drugs

- "I can't imagine going out and not drinking! I guess I'll only have one or two beers if I'm going to be driving."
- "I think I'll feel more relaxed and confident behind the wheel when I've had a spliff."

Distracting passengers

- "I don't see a problem going out driving with my mates; I can concentrate on driving and join in the conversation. I'm an excellent multitasker!"

Over-confidence

- "I have quicker reactions than most other drivers."

Seat belts

- "My mate's an excellent driver; I don't want to insult him by wearing my seat belt!"

Granted, a learner won't always verbalise their attitudes, but that doesn't mean that they don't exist. Looking for body language cues can be one way of "teasing out" their driving attitudes. Imagine you hear a big sigh from your learner while they're driving along a wide clear road with a 30mph limit. Asking, "Why the sigh?" can open a dialogue — "It just feels so slow, this road shouldn't have a 30mph limit!" Sometimes, your learner might appear to "tut" at someone in a situation which you can explore further; "Were you tutting at that cyclist, Carl? Why was that?" At other times, non-verbal cues or micro-expressions can show a learner's thinking: "I noticed that you frowned when that driver didn't give way, Jenny; what was going through your mind?"

Another way to check driver attitude is to occasionally ask your learners their opinions on certain topics. You could either bring these questions up during general conversation or when an event triggers discussion. For example, your learner might spot the driver next to them in a traffic queue chatting away on the phone. Asking your learner, "When do you think you might be tempted to answer your phone when driving?" could trigger a conversation in which their attitude to phone use while driving is highlighted. They may be horrified by your question and say, "What? No way, I'd *never* do that — it's stupid!" to which you could reply, "What about if you're in a traffic queue as we are now? Would it be stupid then?"

Try to see where their boundaries lie, they may say it's acceptable to use a phone while in a traffic queue, after which you can discuss the safety and legalities of doing so. They may reply completely differently, of course, "I don't know what all the fuss is with mobile phones, really. If you keep your eyes on the road, it's no more dangerous than chatting to a passenger." Once we know what our learners' limiting or risky beliefs are, we can start challenging them;

Why is it that some drivers:

- Use a mobile phone even when they know it's dangerous and illegal?
- Drive too close to the vehicle in front even when they know why they should keep a safer distance?
- Drive at 35mph in a 30mph zone even when they know it's illegal and has the potential to kill a child?

You see, it's not what we *know* that's important; it's what we *believe* about that behaviour that's important. Referring back to the ABC model explored in *Chapter 7: Addressing Limiting Beliefs*, you can see how attitudes are reinforced by a chain of events that have no adverse outcome. It's only when the driver experiences a painful, negative result that their belief, behaviour and attitude start to change. Here's an extreme example of how a belief can change because of a negative consequence:

A = Event or situation
B = Belief or thought
C = Outcome or consequence

Dealing With Negative Attitudes

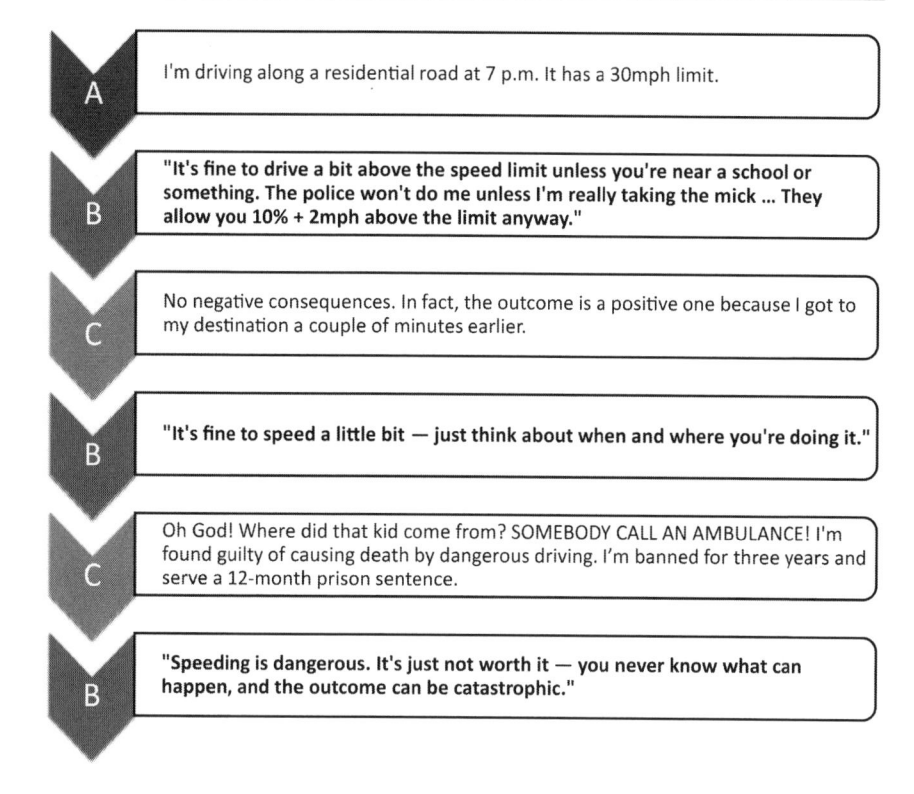

A: I'm driving along a residential road at 7 p.m. It has a 30mph limit.

B: "It's fine to drive a bit above the speed limit unless you're near a school or something. The police won't do me unless I'm really taking the mick ... They allow you 10% + 2mph above the limit anyway."

C: No negative consequences. In fact, the outcome is a positive one because I got to my destination a couple of minutes earlier.

B: "It's fine to speed a little bit — just think about when and where you're doing it."

C: Oh God! Where did that kid come from? SOMEBODY CALL AN AMBULANCE! I'm found guilty of causing death by dangerous driving. I'm banned for three years and serve a 12-month prison sentence.

B: "Speeding is dangerous. It's just not worth it — you never know what can happen, and the outcome can be catastrophic."

These belief changes are common. Although there are a few exceptions to the rule, most rational human beings will have a full belief and attitude shift after experiencing such a drastic consequence. It's not unusual for those who have made a grave mistake to want to spread their message to other people once they've learned the error of their ways, in the hope that others will learn from it. We don't want our learners to have to experience killing a child before their negative beliefs are changed, do we? From experience, we've found some ADIs to have one or both of the following beliefs about beliefs:

- **"It's not my responsibility** to challenge any unhelpful/negative values or beliefs belonging to my learners."
- **"It's impossible** to change the values/beliefs of my learners, particularly within the limited time we have together while they're learning to drive."

We would dispute both of these beliefs.

Firstly, we think *all* ADIs have a responsibility to challenge unhelpful or negative attitudes in the car. In our position as educators of road safety, we shouldn't just sit back and listen to our learner drivers hurling abuse at road users. We shouldn't ignore or laugh off their comments about it being safe to drive after only having one drink. We need to challenge such behaviour; we have a moral duty to do so.

Secondly, invoking belief change, at least on some level, is possible within even the shortest amount of time. Admittedly, it's not easy and can require that we use a variety of different approaches. But it's entirely possible — you just need to know how.

How to deal with negative driver attitudes

Being *aware* of your learner's negative attitudes is easy, what's much more challenging is how to handle these attitudes once they've expressed them. It's easier to stay quiet, laugh, ignore or even agree with the attitude than it is to challenge it. It's also easy to completely flip your lid and tell the learner that you're no longer prepared to work with them anymore. However, as driving instructors, we should start challenging our learners' risky beliefs and negative attitudes right from lesson one. This way, they learn how to work on their own internal dialogue when we're no longer there to challenge it.

A true story ...

I was once teaching a 17-year-old to drive. We'll call her Nicky. Nicky was a pleasant enough girl and, for the most part, reticent during her lessons. During one lesson, however, I saw an entirely different side of her. We were driving through a very busy shopping area in the middle of a town centre. Both driver and passenger side windows were wound down, as it was a hot day (my car didn't have air conditioning).

While we were approaching a traffic queue, a car approached from a junction on our left. He took a quick glance in our direction and pulled out in front of us. Nicky reacted both physically and verbally.

Physically, she stamped on the footbrake and threw her arms up in the air in a rage. The car stalled. Verbally, she screamed racial abuse out of the window at the driver who had pulled out, along with a string of swear words. I was just as dumbstruck as the 30 or so pedestrians who were now staring at my car, shaking their heads and muttering to one another. Her behaviour was shocking and embarrassing. While she was still raging at the other driver, who had by this stage moved on through the junction ahead of us, I instinctively reacted and shouted, "Nicky — stop! That's enough! Right, swap seats with me please ... NOW!"

I was so angry and offended by the way she'd behaved that I drove her home in silence and told her to find another instructor. By the time we reached her road, she was apologising over and over again, but I'd heard enough. Nicky's behaviour had totally caught me off guard. It wasn't the first time she had reacted angrily to another road user's mistake, but I was still new to instructing and hadn't come across anything like this before. I didn't know how to handle it in the heat of the moment. If I'm honest, part of me reacted in the way I did because I was so embarrassed that one of my learners had done this. Many members of the public were staring at my driving school car with my name emblazoned down the side — her racial abuse and road rage,

I felt, reflected negatively on me, and I immediately felt the need to publicly distance myself from her behaviour.

The other part of me just couldn't see how this behaviour was ever acceptable and I didn't want anything to do with it. I wanted to show Nicky that I wasn't going to put up with it. A few days later, Nicky called me on the phone to apologise yet again. She was very upset, sorry and embarrassed by the way she'd behaved and she begged for a second chance. Sure, I could have left it at that and refused to ever work with her again, but having a background in psychology and an interest in why people behave the way they do, I was intrigued as to why she had reacted in such a way. If possible, I also wanted to help her deal with her road rage. But I wasn't sure how.

Nicky was an extreme case, but she wasn't the only learner I had to deal with who had attitude problems. Over the years, I've learned a few strategies to deal with negative attitudes when they arise. I share them here in the hope that they'll help you with your own learners.

React calmly

As challenging as this might be, you mustn't fly into a rage at your learner's attitude. Instead, convey your disapproval or discomfort firmly but calmly. Try not to provoke a defensive reaction.

- **Question why they said what they said or did what they did** — try to accurately gauge their true intent.
- **Convey your feelings** — let them know how what they said or did made you feel.
- **Question how it makes them feel when they react like that** — is it helpful, did it or does it change the situation?

- **Find out how they'd like to feel instead** — what state would be most helpful for them to be in, e.g. calm, relaxed, focused?
- **Create a different story or adopt a "can't change it" mindset** — what's happened has happened, there's nothing they can do to improve the situation now, so just let it go.

Be a role model

To be quite honest, I've met a fair few PDIs and ADIs in my time who could do with working on their own attitudes before they have any hope of helping their learners to solve theirs! Driving instructors are mentors and role models to their learners. If a mentor is regularly criticising the actions of other road users and pointing out everyone's mistakes, their learner will accept that behaviour as the norm.

Don't get me wrong — I suffer from attitude issues from time to time, too — I'm certainly no saint. But any thoughts are internalised when working with other people or when my children are in the car. Externally, I try to show restraint and acceptance of other road users' mistakes. Improving and changing our attitudes isn't a one-time thing, it takes work.

React towards the issue, not the person

In *Chapter 2: Coaching*, we highlighted "experiencing unconditional positive regard for your client" as one of the nine fundamental principles of coaching. Although it's a challenge to have unconditional positive regard for a learner who thinks all cyclists are "w*****s" or who seems intent on trying to break the speed limit, it's vital to remember that behind every behaviour is a positive intention. In our experience, we've found this to be true. People who react angrily when they've been "cut up", or shout and swear at another driver who shakes their head at them do so as a defence mechanism; they feel they've been attacked in some way.

The positive intention behind poor driver behaviour may be a selfish one, too. For example, driving a few miles an hour over the speed limit, or too close to the car in front, may have the positive intention of getting to the destination quicker so that the person at the end of the journey won't be upset, angry or disappointed in us. In having unconditional positive regard for your learner when they're expressing an undesirable attitude or behaviour, our first port of call is to acknowledge their anger or concerns. Only once we've done so can we try to understand the reasons for the outburst or the action. This needs to be in a non-judgemental way so that the learner feels able to express themselves freely:

- "I can see you're upset/angry/frustrated with ..."
- "I can totally understand why you're feeling annoyed by that driver's actions."
- "I sense you have a dislike for cyclists/van drivers/BMW drivers."

Once we've acknowledged the learner's thoughts, feelings or emotions, we can then help them to move forward.

Understand where the belief stems from

From just a few months old, children learn what's right and wrong from their parents and other carers. Shouting, acting aggressively, gesticulating at other road users, getting upset and using bad language all becomes a part of normal driving behaviour. By the time the adolescent reaches the age at which they're eligible to start learning to drive, they've already accumulated more than 17 years of road rage experience. It can be helpful to know where an attitude may have come from so that the learner can recognise that the position isn't necessarily correct. Thought patterns that have been learned from someone else, or formed from one or more negative experiences, can be unlearned, too.

Rationalise the behaviour of the other person

When we see another road user make a mistake or do something silly, we almost always jump to a negative conclusion. This is reflected in what we say:

- "Look at this idiot!"
- "Open your eyes, you moron!"
- "How the hell did you get a licence?"
- "What a prat!"
- "Look at this stupid cyclist … Move over for God's sake! They think they own the road!"

How many of these people are genuinely stupid idiots, morons or prats? Aren't they all just ordinary people, dealing with their own lives and issues, who happen to make mistakes from time to time, just like the rest of us? In *Chapter 6: Learning Styles*, we discussed the concept of using perceptual positions to help our learner drivers see things from other people's perspectives. It's also a great technique for dealing with attitude problems and quelling the early signs of road rage.

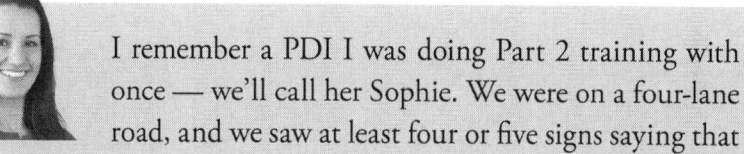

> I remember a PDI I was doing Part 2 training with once — we'll call her Sophie. We were on a four-lane road, and we saw at least four or five signs saying that the right-hand lane was closed ahead. Along with most of the other traffic on the road, Sophie and I were queuing in the left-hand lane and moving very slowly. The lane closure was just before a major set of traffic lights, so it took us about four sequences of light changes before we got closer to the lane closure. As we got to the lane closure, a car came at speed down the right-hand lane. He had his left indicator signal on with an intention to move into the left lane just before the cones at the start of the lane closure. The lights changed to red again, and Sophie was adamant that she wasn't letting the driver in.

She edged within inches of the bumper of the car in front and came to a stop.

Sophie: "I'm not letting him in the cheeky sod!"
Claire: "Sophie, let him in."
Sophie: "No! Why should I?"
Claire: "Imagine you have a call from your daughter's school and she's been rushed to hospital with a bad injury. You jump in your car to get to the hospital as quickly as possible. You arrive at these road works. Do you (a) wait patiently in the left-hand lane for four or five light sequences before getting through these lights, or (b) drive down the clear right-hand lane hoping to God that someone is kind enough to let you into the left-hand lane at the front?"

The result was fantastic. Within seconds, Sophie flipped from an angry, non-compliant and stubborn driver to a vulnerable and compassionate parent. Her shoulders dropped, her facial expression softened, and she looked upset at imagining her poor little girl in the hospital without her. She let him in with a remark that sounded like she was unconvinced of his motives.

Sophie: "Yeah... But he's just pushing in for the sake of it."
Claire: "Maybe he is, Sophie, but you're not him, and you don't know what's going on in his world."
Sophie: "Hmm... I suppose so."

I like to think that whenever Sophie is out with her learners and one of her learners displays the same sort of attitude to someone who has made a poor judgement, a mistake or just seems to be taking liberties, she's transported back to that day and uses the same technique with her learners.

Dealing With Negative Attitudes

The fact is, we have absolutely no idea what's going on in the world of the other person. We have an instinctive tendency to create a negative story in our minds about why they did what they did. We have 100% control over the stories we tell ourselves.

Rationalising behaviour in this way and showing empathy to the other driver can help your learner drivers see different points of view.

Faith: "He should have let me through! The cars were on his side!"

ADI: "Yes, the cars were on his side. Well done for noticing he was coming through first and dealing with the situation."

Faith: "Oh, yeah … Thanks."

ADI: "Why do you think he came through first?"

Faith: "I don't know. I just know he should have given way to me."

ADI: "Yes, if the obstruction is on his side, he could have given way, although we should never assume he'll give way. How long might he have been there already before we got there?"

Faith: "Hmm, well … Maybe a while because he waited for those two cars that were a bit in front of me."

ADI: "Yes, I think so too. And what if he was running late for work? How do you think that would have influenced his decision as to when to go?"

Faith: "Well I suppose he would have gone as soon as he could."

ADI: "Are there any other reasons that you can think of which would make him want to push through first? Or any reasons that would make you push through first in a similar situation?"

Faith: "Well, if I was late picking the kids up from school, I might try and get through first then."

ADI: "Yes, things like that can influence our behaviour at the wheel. Anything else you can think of?"

Faith: "Not really."

ADI: "Okay, I can think of a few things. Maybe he was desperate for the loo? Maybe he's just had some bad news and wasn't concentrating fully and misjudged the gap. Maybe he's unfamiliar with the area and is concentrating more on which road he needs next. Maybe he thought you were going slower than you were because of the L plates."

Faith: "Yeah, I suppose so."

ADI: "So, is it fair to recognise that we can all make misjudgements or mistakes sometimes?"

Faith: "Yeah."

ADI: "How would you like others to respond to you when you make mistakes?"

Faith: "Not get angry with me."

ADI: "So what are your options for dealing with others who make mistakes?"

Faith: "Well I can just allow for them and be patient, I suppose."

ADI: "That's a good choice, yes, it'll certainly keep your blood pressure down!"

Faith: "Yeah, I guess so!"

Encouraging our learners to recognise how their thinking is worsening the situation rather than helping or diffusing it may aid them in re-evaluating their behaviour. We can help our learners by encouraging them to propose solutions, or even suggesting solutions ourselves if they're not able to come up with enough of their own.

Explore the potential consequences of road rage

Sometimes, bad attitudes can end in disaster. Just seeing a few road rage related news articles and videos can help to influence your learner's attitude. Depending on the circumstances, you might decide to keep the discussion light-hearted by showing the road rage video of the driver who forced a minibus to stop in the middle of the road and later got beaten up by Mickey Mouse and SpongeBob SquarePants (yes, seriously!).

Humour can work to help defuse a tense situation — not that watching a guy getting beaten up by cartoon characters is something to laugh about, of course ... Well, maybe just a little! Scan the QR code to watch the video, or visit **http://gedclai.re/spongebob**

However, less lighthearted examples can be more beneficial in helping your learner to fully understand the potential consequences of engaging in aggressive behaviour on the roads. One example is the van driver who cut across the path of an HGV travelling in the centre lane of a free-flowing motorway and repeatedly slammed on his brakes, eventually stopping altogether. His behaviour wasn't without provocation from the HGV driver, as can be seen and heard in the video clip. But his actions, and the video footage which captured it all, resulted in the van driver losing his business and his family having to flee their home for fear of reprisals. Scan this QR code to read the full story and watch the dashcam video of the incident, or visit **http://gedclai.re/m60roadrage**

When charged in court, the van driver was handed an eight-month prison sentence, suspended for 18 months. He was ordered to carry out 200 hours of unpaid work and attend a probation service anger management course. He was also banned from driving for 18 months and should he want to regain his driving licence once his ban has been lifted, he will need to take an extended driving test.

Then there was the driver and the cyclist who exchanged words on a road in West Yorkshire. The driver then deliberately drove at the cyclist in a fit of temper. Tragically, the cyclist fell into the road and suffered severe brain damage; he later died. The driver was sentenced to four years and eight months in prison. Scan the QR code to read the full story, or visit **http://gedclai.re/radford**

We need to help our learners become aware of the potential risks of getting involved in any public altercation. We've no idea who we're dealing with — what if they happen to be an exceptionally nasty character — someone with a weapon, perhaps? What if the other person launched a violent physical attack? Scan the QR code to see how road rage can get you more than you bargained for, or visit **http://gedclai.re/ragefight**

Our learners also need to understand the consequences for the supposed perpetrator. What if their actions resulted in a court case, a driving ban, a prison sentence? What would that mean to them and how would it affect their life from that point? Failure to get into university? A criminal record with no chance of getting the job they really wanted? Their children having a parent serving time in prison?

Don't treat everyone else like they're an idiot

Parents, and some ADIs for that matter, are full of well-meaning advice, but "treat everyone else like they're an idiot" is a damaging prescription. On the face of it, it sounds like quite helpful advice; if you treat everyone else as an idiot, you can expect all manner of things to happen around you. Other drivers will pull out in front of you, people will overtake when it's not safe, pedestrians will step out into the road, etc. But think about the message this piece of advice sends to your learner driver, especially considering what we now know about the Belief Window. If our learners truly believe that "everyone else is an idiot", their Belief Window actively seeks out evidence to support this belief, which in turn reinforces it. This perception only increases the likelihood that our learner will engage in hostility towards other road users.

What would be a better belief for parents to pass on to their children and for ADIs to pass on to their learners? How about, "treat everyone else like they're a human being"? After all, we *all* make mistakes.

Look for positive examples of good driving/riding

The Belief Window is part of our reticular activating system (RAS), something we discussed in more detail in *Chapter 1: Why Drivers Crash*. Our RAS enables us to filter out all the millions of pieces of information available to us at any one time and let through only what we deem to be important. We like to think of it as being like a club bouncer at the door of our mind. Our beliefs and our current focus dictate what's allowed into our mind. The bouncer only lets things in which are "on the list", and everything else gets turned away: "If your name's not down, you're not comin' in!"

Our RAS filter naturally seeks out danger because its primary function is to keep us safe. Therefore, the human brain naturally seeks out negative things, things which could cause us harm. This is an essential feature, but it doesn't exactly help in keeping drivers free from road rage, as it means we'll all have a natural tendency to spot things people are doing wrong. We need to train our RAS to filter *out* examples of poor driving behaviour and instead to allow *in* examples of good driving. It's not as hard as it sounds, though — it just takes a little conscious effort. This is an exercise you can try with your own learner drivers, particularly those ones who tend to notice everyone else's mistakes.

ADI: "I've decided that today is National Positivity Day! We're leaving all negativity behind. Today, we're only allowed to notice and comment on examples of *good* driving, cycling or riding. Let me know when you see someone doing something well — that might be keeping a proper clearance, signalling promptly, driving at a safe speed, checking before they turn, etc. I'll do the same, and we'll see just how many things we notice."

It might sound crazy, but we find it works really well. If you have an instinctive tendency to spot examples of bad driving too, try it yourself today and notice just how much is right with the world. It will certainly change your perception of other road users and make you feel a lot happier. One of the main complaints of driving instructors is having to deal with impatient drivers. But not everyone is impatient, it just seems that way because your "mind bouncer" is only allowing those instances to stick in your mind. Make a conscious choice to change your focus of attention.

Reframe the situation

Often easier said than done, reframing a situation can transform the way we feel and behave. Reframing, in simple terms, involves stepping back from the situation and looking at it from a different perspective. For example, you could reframe a weakness as a strength, a problem as an opportunity or an impossibility as a distant possibility.

A — **A**ctivating Event / Situation → **B** — **B**elief / Thought → **C** — **C**onsequence / Emotion

Remember this ABC model from *Chapter 7: Addressing Limited Beliefs?* The situation or event itself doesn't trigger the consequence or emotion; it's our *interpretation* of that situation or event that does so.

Reframing is all about changing our understanding of the event. B, in this case, is the story we tell ourselves about the other driver and the motives behind their actions.

The overtaking driver

What happened (A): While driving in the left lane of a dual carriageway, an overtaking driver cuts across your path to leave at the next exit, causing you to brake.

What you think (B): "The guy is an inconsiderate idiot and has zero respect for anyone else!"

Consequences (C): You swear, shout, shake your head and sound your horn. You throw your hands up in disgust, and your blood pressure soars. You lose focus on the road ahead and dwell on the actions of the other driver.

The overtaking driver: reframed

What happened (A): While driving in the left lane of a dual carriageway, an overtaking driver cuts across your path to leave at the next exit, causing you to brake.

What you think (B): "Wow, he must be in a rush to get somewhere quickly or was so lost in thought that he didn't realise his exit was coming up. Perhaps he has a lot of negative things going on in his life, and his mind isn't on his driving.

Consequences (C): You feel relieved that you managed to avoid colliding with the other car. You stay alert and can quickly regain your focus on the journey.

We don't have to be a victim of our thoughts — we can choose to believe a different story!

> Reframing isn't always easy to do, but with practice, it does become quite natural. I've had to work on this myself. For example, I regularly attend meetings and training courses in Birmingham and have to deal with the M6; I occasionally get stuck in heavy traffic. In the past, I could easily get very stressed by the thought of being late and having to make my apologies. This thought would get me muttering negative things under my breath, criticising other drivers,

> driving closer to the vehicles in front, and so on. But I've learned to reframe any traffic jams as a great opportunity — an opportunity to listen to an inspiring audiobook or to mentally work through some business plans or problems. Why create emotional pain out of a current situation over which we have no control? It makes no sense.
>
> I've also reframed the way in which I think about late notice cancellations. Getting a text or phone call a few hours, or minutes, before a scheduled lesson happens to us all. We can choose to sit there and get annoyed and irritated by what's happened, or we can accept the situation as something we have no current control over and come up with some ways in which we can use the time productively. I choose the latter. Cancellations are a part of life for us as driving instructors; they're part of the job. Now, I quite look forward to them, as they give me some valuable me time so I can work on the things I need to get done.

Help your learners to reframe any negative situations that crop up during their lessons by encouraging them to think more positively and to transform their negative thoughts, stories and attitudes into positive, helpful ones.

Act "as if"

Acting "as if" might sound a bit crazy, but bear with us. Another great way to transform a negative thought or attitude is to deliberately behave differently than we would normally. This practice is based on the concept that our thoughts, emotions and behaviours are all inextricably linked.

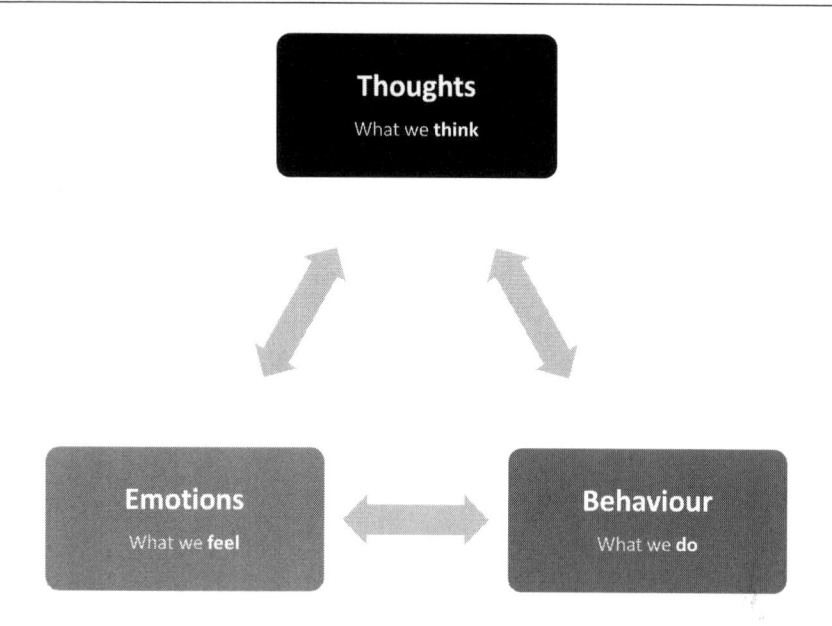

```
┌─────────────────┐
│    Thoughts     │
│  What we think  │
└─────────────────┘
      ↕     ↕
┌──────────┐   ┌──────────┐
│ Emotions │↔  │Behaviour │
│What we feel│ │What we do│
└──────────┘   └──────────┘
```

Change your behaviour, change your attitude

By acting "as if" enough times, our emotional response changes and our attitude will inevitably change, too. In the earlier example where we talk about being cut up on a dual carriageway, we could *choose* a different behaviour without necessarily changing our attitude first. So, when an incident like this happens, regardless of our instinctive thoughts about the other driver, it's a good idea to take a deep breath, be grateful for having responded in time and then consciously focus on the road ahead. By doing so, our emotional response will be different; our blood pressure and heart rate will return to normal quicker, and we'll begin to think a little differently about the other driver, too.

If we do this enough, in such situations where we feel personally aggrieved by another driver's actions, we'll slowly begin to change our attitude towards other road users from annoyance of other people's mistakes to acceptance of them. If you can help your learners try out new behaviours and coping strategies, it's possible, that with enough practice, they can change their attitude too.

It all comes down to choice

It's worthwhile taking some time to ask your learner to consider how their negative attitudes affect them physically and emotionally. If another road user makes a mistake, how does that manifest in them physically? Do they become hot and flushed? Does their heart rate increase? Do their fists clench? Do they grit their teeth? Does their body tense up? How does it make them feel emotionally? Does it make them upset? Does it make them angry?

Would your learner *choose* to feel this way if they believed they had a choice? The fact is, they do have a choice. Your learners can choose their thoughts; their thoughts don't define them, they're the ones in control. Nobody else can make them feel the way they do; they're just choosing to feel that way.

> *"Between stimulus and response there is a space. In that space is our power to choose our response. In our response lies our growth and our freedom."*
> *— Unknown*[100]

Who am I?

We've created a useful and straightforward self-scaling exercise that you can download from our website by visiting **http://gedclai.re/selfscaling** or by scanning this QR code. Asking your learners to complete it with as much honesty as possible will significantly raise their awareness of their driver attitude. Discussing their answers over the course of lessons can help them become aware of how they choose to behave on the road. Making them mindful of the fact that they're in control, and have complete freedom of choice over their thoughts and behaviour, can help them decide whether to keep their current thoughts and actions or to change them.

Points for reflection

- Which negative learner driver attitudes have you come across in your work as a driving instructor? How have you dealt with them in the past? Have you laughed them off, joined in, ignored them or challenged them? Based on what you've learned in this chapter, what might you try differently?
- What unhelpful thoughts or attitudes do you have as a driver and a driving instructor? Where do those beliefs come from? Can you see how these thoughts and attitudes can negatively impact those around you, including your learners and children (if you have any)?
- How would it be more helpful to think? How would this change in thought positively impact your physical, emotional and psychological states?

YOUR NEXT STEPS…

Video Message: Ged & Claire discuss what's next

http://gedclai.re/nextsteps

So, you've reached the end of the book. Well, almost…

In the following pages (Appendix A), we provide you with many useful practical scenarios which you can adapt or replicate with your learners. We appreciate that sometimes the theory can be challenging to put into practice when you're not sure where to start, so we're sure you'll find the Appendix enormously helpful.

When you bought this book, you may have had a range of motivations and expectations, from, "I'm learning to become an ADI, and I need some solid tools and techniques" to, "I've been in the job a while, and I need a fresh perspective." Now that you've reached this point, we hope that you have everything you need. Recognise that you have taken the first steps in your journey to becoming an even better driving instructor. Start using some of the tools and techniques we have given to you. Step beyond the boundaries of your comfort zone to try approaches you've never tried before. You might just surprise yourself.

Sure, a few approaches might not work as well as you'd hoped when you first use them, but don't give up. Accept that you'll never achieve perfection, but never stop striving for it. Reflect on why it didn't work, learn from it and try it again another time.

Rest assured, however, that when you try out some of the suggestions in this book with your learners, you will be *amazed* by some of the results. We both remember being surprised by just how much learners can discover for themselves if we just give them the opportunity. Not only did our work become more insightful, interesting and rewarding, but we found the people we were working with excelled in their training and enjoyed their learning experience much more. Some of your learners will even undergo some significant personal transformations as a result of you helping them develop their levels of self-awareness and responsibility. Helping people to improve their lives is an incredible thing to witness, and it makes you realise that being a driving instructor is about much more than teaching people to control a car.

Being a brilliant driving instructor is an endless journey of new learning opportunities. Take the time to actively listen, be open-minded and have unconditional positive regard for every person you work with, and you'll learn so much — not just about your work, but also about yourself. As we always say, "Never stop learning, because life never stops teaching."

If you ever need any help, guidance or one-to-one development with us, feel free to get in touch through one of the methods on the next page. We're always happy to hear from like-minded ADIs and anyone keen to improve themselves and their businesses.

Enjoyed this book?

If you found this book to be helpful, we would ***massively*** appreciate you taking two minutes out of your day to leave us a book review on Amazon. Would you please do that for us?

To leave your review, simply visit **http://gedclai.re/review** or scan this QR code.

Thank you so much - it really does mean the world to us!

KEEP IN TOUCH!

If you're on Facebook, please join our **"Who's In The Driving Seat?" discussion group**, where you can ask questions, share your feedback and get involved in discussions related to all things client-centred:

http://gedclai.re/bookgroup

It's a really supportive group of like-minded PDIs and ADIs, where there is no such thing as a stupid question. So come along and get involved!

Other ways that you can connect with Ged & Claire are listed below.

The "Who's in the Driving Seat?" resource website:
whosinthedrivingseat.com

Our growing range of online courses for PDIs and ADIs:
thedrivingecademy.com

One-to-one training, assessments and development:
activedrivingsolutions.com

Read our blog:
gedandclaire.com

Email us:
hello@gedandclaire.com

Call us:
0161 410 1080

Facebook - Ged & Claire's business page:
www.facebook.com/gedandclaire

Twitter:
twitter.com/gedandclaire

YouTube:
www.youtube.com/GedWilmot

APPENDIX A

USEFUL COACHING SCENARIOS

> Video Message: Ged & Claire explain the coaching scenarios
>
> http://gedclai.re/appendixa

Passengers

Encouraging your learners to invite Mum or Dad along to observe the lesson from the back of the car can be useful. Not only can Mum and Dad see how their son or daughter is progressing (so you won't keep getting pressured to book them in for their driving test after 10 lessons), but it will also give your learner the valuable experience of carrying passengers or driving under pressure.[§§]

As research has shown though, it's driving with younger passengers that significantly increases risk, so it's even more important for your learners to experience this before they pass their driving test. Having one or two of your learner's friends in the back of the car can be a beneficial experience. Regardless of the age of the passengers you invite in on the lesson(s), it would be wise to ensure that your learner has reached a good level of driving competence first. You don't want to be introducing this experience too early on when your learner is still struggling with basic car control.

Your objective is to create a real-life situation; a sterile environment where the friends sit still and keep silent isn't realistic. Encourage conversation between the driver and passengers; your job is to assess how passenger distraction affects the driver and their concentration.

[§§] This can be particularly useful for a learner you may be thinking of asking along for your Part 3 test or Standards Check lesson as you'll get a good idea of how they react when being observed.

Of course, you may need to control the passengers if they do become a little too rowdy! You can then encourage your learner to discuss how the conversation and their friends' actions affected their ability to concentrate on the driving task. What errors did they make as a result of having passengers on board? If you feel it would be helpful, or even necessary, you could have this discussion at some point during the lesson itself, with the passengers present.

This experience is hugely beneficial for the driver as it enables them to recognise their own limitations and to come up with coping strategies for once they've passed their driving test and are carrying distracting passengers. It also makes the passengers aware of how *their* actions can affect a driver, so when they're out with their friends, they can be much more considerate and passengers, too. Peer pressure, showing off and distractions from conversations all increase the risk to a young driver, so anything you can do to help your learners experience the real dangers while in a safe driving lesson environment can only be a positive thing.

The following are two examples of how you can encourage your learner to assess risks and come up with solutions that reduce them.

Scenario 1: Passengers (practical)

Goal

Give your learner driver the experience of driving with friends. Identify possible risks and suitable solutions that reduce those risks when driving with friends in the car.

Format

Ask your learner to invite a couple of friends in on the lesson. Create lots of conversation with everyone in the car and encourage them to talk to each other like they would when you're not there. You could explain to the friends that the purpose is to let your learner get used to driving and talking at the same time and that they're encouraged to talk as they would normally.

Instructor's role

As the instructor, you need to notice:

- how, in general, your learner responds to being distracted
- how your learner's driving is affected — are there any errors, changes in speed or ability to plan effectively, etc.?
- situations your learner doesn't deal with particularly well
- other road users, situations or events that your learner seems oblivious to because of the passenger distraction
- how your learner's driving style differs when their friends are in the car — do they wind the seat back or drive with an arm on the door, etc.?

Reflective discussion and questions

After (or maybe during) the experience, encourage your learner to reflect on how having their friends in the car affected their driving.

- How aware were they of everything going on around them?
- Are there specific incidents that they can recall?
- How did they respond to those incidents, if they were aware of them in the first place?
- How distracting do they think they are when they're a passenger?
- How could they help the driver concentrate when they're the passenger?
- What type of driver do they aspire to be?
- What type of driver do they want their friends to think they are?

Benefits

Giving this type of experiential learning can provide both you and your learner with a practical example of how risk increases when passengers are in the car. By shifting the perceptual position of your learner from the role of *driver* to *passenger*, you can encourage your learner to become aware of how distracting they could be as a passenger and in turn, what impact this might have on the driver. This will help them to become a safe and responsible passenger, too. Finally, by asking what type of driver they want to be, you'll be able to identify any possible attributes and attitudes that may need further discussion at an appropriate time, for example:

Learner: "I want my mates to think I'm a good driver."
ADI: "Great — so what do you think makes a 'good driver'?"

Scenario 2: Passengers (theoretical)

Although practical experience is best when it comes to making an impact, we appreciate that some instructors may decide not to take that option. The next best thing then would be to deal with the potential issue of distracting passengers in a theoretical context during a normal driving lesson.

Goal

Give your learner driver the experience of driving with friends. Identify possible risks and suitable solutions that reduce risks when driving with friends in the car.

Format

A theoretical discussion with your learner which may or may not be instigated by a comment from them.

Example conversation

In this extended example, we also show you how you could integrate route planning into a natural discussion.

ADI: "Which friends will you be giving lifts to when you pass?"

Charlie: "Well I've already said that I don't mind driving when we go out on a Friday night."

ADI: "Okay, so who will you be giving lifts to and where do you go on a Friday night?"

Charlie: "Just Max and Harry, we normally go to the Red Lion."

ADI: "And do you normally have a drink?"

Charlie: "Yes, but don't worry — I won't if I'm driving!"

ADI: "Why's that?"

Charlie: "Because I know it badly affects your driving, and I don't want to get points on my licence. Even worse, my mum and dad would absolutely kill me!"

ADI: "It's good to know that you're going to be a sensible driver and make the right decisions. So many people think they can get away with it. Do Max and Harry drink?"

Charlie: "Yeah they do, not stupid amounts though."

ADI: "Will they try and get you to have just one drink if you were the one driving them home at the end of the night?"

Charlie: "I doubt it. But if they did I'd just tell them I don't want to. They wouldn't push it."

ADI: "Okay, what do you think they'll be like in the car with you when they've been drinking?"

Charlie: "They'll be okay, although Harry gets really loud when he's had a few beers."

ADI: "Haha, yes. I've got mates like that too! So how do you think that might affect your concentration when you're driving?"

Charlie: "I suppose it'll be quite distracting."

ADI: "So Harry will cause a distraction. What will the road conditions be like when you're driving home from the pub?"

Charlie: "Well, it'll be dark, and the roads are quite bendy from the Red Lion back to where we live."

ADI: "Ah yes, there are quite a few bad bends along there, aren't there? There aren't any street lights, either. What's the speed limit along those roads?"

Charlie: "Hmm, national ... 60mph ... But I wouldn't go that fast with all those bends."

ADI: "Good. So, let's say that Harry is loud, it's night, and you're driving down those national speed limit, unlit, bendy roads in the dark. What are the risks?"

Charlie: "Well, Harry is going to distract me, I won't be able to see that well, and they're quite bad roads."

ADI: "So what might be the outcome?"

Charlie: "I could crash if I'm not concentrating hard, I guess."

ADI: "And what could be the consequences of crashing?"

Charlie: "Well I could kill myself or my mates. Or I could just get hurt, but the car would get trashed!"

ADI: "What options do you have to reduce the risks, so that doesn't happen then?"

Charlie: "Well I could go the long way around on the main 30mph roads, so I don't have to go on those dark bendy roads. Or we could go to the Old Bell instead, it's nearer."

ADI: "Okay, great. What else?"

Charlie: "I suppose I could get Max to sit in the front, he's quieter, and then it'll be easier to shut Harry out."

ADI: "Anything else?"

Charlie: "I might even tell them that I want to have a drink as well and we can share a taxi back like we normally do."

ADI: "Anything else?"

Charlie: "Nah, nothing I can think of."

ADI: "Okay, so your options are to avoid the unlit, bendy roads and go the long way around, go to the Old Bell instead, get Max to sit in the front, or not drive at all and get a taxi. Is that right?"

Charlie: "Yeah."

ADI: "Well it seems you have come up with some great solutions to keep you and your mates safe, Charlie!"

Charlie: "Yeah, I guess so. I never would have thought about all that, but it makes sense."

Appendix A: Appendix A: Useful Coaching Scenarios

Benefits

Summarising your learner's own solutions back to them gives them the opportunity to adjust, or add to them further. When they come up with their own solutions, they're more likely to implement them post-test. Also, by rehearsing mentally, the brain registers the possible solutions as actual events in the unconscious mind, even though the events haven't happened yet. A bit like when you wake up from a dream, and you're convinced it was real until your conscious mind catches up, and even then, you can often question yourself!

Another powerful way to develop your learners' awareness and understanding of the additional risks posed by carrying passengers is to use news articles to highlight how young passengers can increase a driver's risk of crashing. We think the more personal or local the news story is to your learner's geographical area, the greater the impact of this exercise. We hope it's obvious, but please exercise sensitivity when discussing news stories such as this. Our aim here is not to place blame on anyone or scare our learners into never driving with passengers in the car, but to help them to become aware of the risks and to come up with strategies to reduce them. Refer to the bar chart in *Chapter 1: Why Driver's Crash*, which highlighted how having three or more passengers under the age of 21 quadruples the fatality risk significantly.

Visit **http://gedclai.re/holmfirth** or scan the QR code to see a tragic news article from our local area. You could ask your learner to read this article after a lesson and then to reflect on some questions, such as the ones we have listed below. It can then form part of a 5-10 minute chat during the next driving lesson.

Questions for reflection could be:

- "What factors contributed to the crash?"

- "Imagine being in the car driven by Harriet — describe what the atmosphere may have been like in the moments before the crash."
- "How might have Harriet's driving been different if she had been on her own?"
- "How do you think the prison sentence has affected Harriet's life in the short and long-term? How would it change your life if this happened to you?"
- "What could you do differently if you were in this situation as a driver or passenger to reduce the risks of something like this ever happening to you?"

Children

Babies and young children can be a huge distraction for parents and carers. It can also be quite daunting to drive with your new baby or children as passengers for the first time. Crying babies cause a huge distraction, and when they grow, toddlers can be just as challenging with their endless chatter, questions, whining or tantrums. Some of your learners will have children. You may have even been asked if their children can come along on a driving lesson when they've had childcare issues. We know many instructors refuse this for various reasons, but it's such a valuable learning opportunity if done correctly; one which could even save their lives or lives of others if only they'd experienced it within the safety of a driving lesson with a professional ADI.

When your learner reaches a level of competence in their driving with which you both feel sufficiently comfortable and confident, suggest they have experience of driving with their children in the car — even if only for a part of the lesson. On those lessons, take the time to notice your learner's verbal and non-verbal body language which may indicate they're becoming distracted, anxious or stressed. Use these moments as an opportunity for you to discuss their thoughts and feelings. Help them to recognise the extra challenges that this experience brings and to develop strategies to cope with them.

Providing the child is old enough to understand, this is also an excellent opportunity for you to encourage your learner to help their children to understand the risks of distracting Mummy or Daddy while they are driving.

- Check your driving tuition insurance policy for any conditions on carrying passengers — it's unlikely you will find any, but it's best to check.
- If necessary, ensure your learner brings along an appropriate car seat and that they fit it securely.
- Make sure the children concerned have no history of travel sickness. This can affect many young children but can be easily prevented with medication or nausea-relief wristbands. In any case, make sure your learner agrees to foot the cleaning bill in case their darling child decides to "decorate" the inside of your car!

Scenario 3: Children (practical)

Goal

Give your learner the experience of driving with children. Identify possible risks and suitable solutions that reduce risks when driving with children in the car.

Format

When your learner feels comfortable, suggest they have a practice at driving with their children in the car.

Instructor's role

Watch carefully for body language and pay attention to comments that suggest your learner is starting to get distracted, anxious or stressed. Be aware of:

- how your learner responds to being distracted
- situations your learner doesn't deal with particularly well
- other road users and situations your learner seems oblivious to
- how your learner's mood and driving style differs when they have their children in the car — do they seem stressed or anxious, or does their driving become erratic?

Reflective discussion and questions

Watch and listen carefully for body language and/or comments that suggest your learner is getting distracted and use this as a trigger to start a discussion.

- How are they feeling about driving with their children in the car?
- What specifically is causing them to feel their current emotion?
- How will feeling that way affect their driving?
- What could be the possible outcome if their driving is negatively affected by having their children in the car?
- What journeys will they be taking with their children?
- Are there any additional risks with those journeys?
- What could they do to minimise those risks?

Solutions

Using thought-provoking questions, help your learners to come up with some safe strategies for driving with their children in the car. You may be able to suggest others, too.

Appendix A: Appendix A: Useful Coaching Scenarios   267

- "If my baby is crying, I'll focus on my driving until I can pull up somewhere safe to check what she needs."
- "I'll check my baby is properly fed and changed before setting off."
- "I'll allow extra time on my journeys so I can stop to feed the baby, change their nappy, or find their dummy."
- "I'll bring some things to occupy my children in the car. There's 'car bingo' and lots of other games online that I can print off."
- "I'll discuss with the children before setting off that Mummy/Daddy needs to concentrate on their driving to keep us all safe."
- "Me and the kids will agree on a phrase that means 'I can't talk to you just this minute because I need to concentrate. But I'll answer you in a few minutes.'"
- "I'll organise things the night before so that I can leave the house earlier and as stress-free as possible."

Benefits

Giving this type of experiential learning can provide your learners with a real understanding of how risk increases with children in the car. If having read the above, you still don't want to have your learners' children in the back of your car, bear in mind that this could also be dealt with theoretically. You could either begin a discussion during a lesson or ask your learner to read something in between lessons in preparation for discussion next lesson. Scan the QR code, or visit **http://gedclai.re/distracted**, to view a typical article you could ask your learners to read in preparation for the next lesson.

In this article, being distracted, possibly by his child, seems to be the most probable cause of the sad death of this father.

Another news story details the tragic death of a young mother. Visit **http://gedclai.re/mumcrash** or scan the QR code to read the article. Reading the article, there are many risk factors mentioned, one of those being inexperience, having only passed her driving test fifteen days before the crash. Could distraction from her child have been one of the contributory factors of the crash? What could your learners learn from a story such as this?

Questions you could ask after your learner has read the article could be:

- "What reasons contributed to the crash?"
- "What do you think was happening in the car at the time of the crash?"
- "If this happened to you and you could see the aftermath, what would you be telling yourself with the benefit of hindsight?"
- "What will life be like for Rory? What would your child's life be like without you?"

Could gaining experience driving with children, and discussing the above points and stories like this prevent a similar tragedy happening?

We hope it goes without saying that discussion of such tragic events should be done very sensitively, especially if the article relates to something which happened locally, and/or in which people lost their lives.

Music

When we suggest having the radio on during driving lessons, or listening to music, we often get a look of utter disbelief from some driving instructors. "What? Put the car stereo on? Isn't that a bit unprofessional? Surely the learner needs to concentrate on driving?" Our answer to this is, "No, it's not unprofessional at all, if it's done in the correct context and with learner drivers who have achieved a certain degree of independence."

We're not condoning telling your learner that you want to check in on the horse racing results, or that you want to listen to a football match.

Instead, what we're suggesting is that you ask your learner driver what radio station they would normally listen to, for example. Then ask them to find their station, set the volume at their preferred level and, for the next section of the lesson, just notice how it affects their driving. Suggesting that your learner driver plays their favourite music playlist via Bluetooth or bring their favourite CD is also an option. Remember, this is about *them,* not you. Listening to your preferred station won't have the same effect, as they'll just filter it out.

There have been numerous studies carried out to establish how music affects driving. One such study by Warren Brodsky in 2002, conducted in a driving simulator, found that the tempo of the music directly affected the driver's simulated driving speed and speed estimate. Music tempo also consistently affected the frequency of virtual traffic violations. The faster the tempo, the greater the impact.[101] Bearing in mind many young people enjoy listening to fast-paced dance music, this is well worth knowing and discussing with your learners.

Another study, by Warren Brodsky and Zack Slor, explored the effects of driver-preferred music on driver behaviour. They found that:

> *"While there were elevated positive moods and enjoyment for trips with driver-preferred music, this background also produced the most frequent severe driver miscalculations and inaccuracies, violations, and aggressive driving. However, trips with music structurally designed to generate moderate levels of perceptual complexity, improved driver behaviour and increased driver safety."*[102]

Many drivers, particularly younger ones, listen to music quite loudly in their own cars. Some even wear sound-cancelling earphones when driving. This can affect their ability to hear other vehicles, emergency sirens and horns.

Experiencing the effects of music genre, tempo and volume within the safe, controlled, driving lesson environment enables you and your learner to discuss these risks and potential consequences fully, so they don't have to experience them for real when out on the road for the first time on their own.

Learner drivers that we, and other ADIs, have tried this with have said things like:

- "I just zoned out of my driving and started singing when my favourite song came on. It was fun, but I'm not sure my driving was as good as without music."
- "I started to go over the speed limit!"
- "I found the talking bits really distracting, as I was trying to listen to them more than focus on my driving. Perhaps the music channels might be less distracting."
- "I needed to turn the sound down when I had to follow the signs as I couldn't think properly."
- "It really helped me to relax! Can I have the radio on during my driving test?"[1]

Scenario 4: Music (practical)

Goal

Give your learner the experience of driving while listening to music. Explore the effects of listening to music on the driving task.

Format

Ask your learner to bring their music to their lesson and set the volume control to their usual level.

---

[1] The answer to this is "yes", by the way. As long as the volume is at a reasonably low level, it can be a great tool to help your anxious learners to relax.

Instructor's role

Watch carefully for body language and pay attention to comments that suggest your learner is starting to get distracted. Be aware of:

- how your learner responds to being distracted
- situations your learner doesn't deal with particularly well
- other road users and situations your learner seems oblivious to
- your learner's body language cues — do they seem confused or lacking focus, or are they totally relaxed?

Reflective discussion and questions

Reflecting back, ask your learner what they noticed about their driving.

- How do they feel their driving was affected?
- How aware were they of their surroundings?
- How would having their music on with their friends in the car affect their driving?
- What are the possible risks of listening to music at a high volume?
- How would it affect them if they had music on and they were in an unfamiliar area?
- How could they minimise risks?

Solutions

Your learner may realise how distracting their music is and be able to ignore it when they need to concentrate fully. They may even turn the volume down themselves. It may even be an idea to suggest to your learner, whenever they're coming up to a complex situation, "Would you like to turn the volume down while you concentrate here?" If repeated enough, it will become a natural reaction for them to turn the volume down whenever the driving task becomes more demanding.

Benefits

This exercise allows your learner to assess the effect their music has on their driving. They'll be able to identify times when music will be more of a distraction and decide on what to do when the risks increase.

Mobile devices

Social media can be addictive to some; you only need to take a walk down any high street to see how many people are attached to their smartphones. As we explored in *Chapter 1: Why Drivers Crash*, we live in a world of instant communication where immediate replies are expected. To some, ignoring messages is the same as ignoring someone face-to-face.

Drivers speaking on mobile phones are up to four times more likely to crash; remember, it doesn't matter if they're on a handheld mobile phone or using a hands-free setting. It's not the action of holding a phone which increases risk, it's the distraction of the conversation itself.[18]

When talking on the phone, drivers have slower reactions and have difficulty controlling speed and lane position.

Scenario 5: Mobile phone (practical)

Goal

Give your learner the experience of a distraction like that of a phone call.

Format

Once you feel that your learner has reached a sufficient skill level and can keep the car safe, talk to them about something irrelevant whilst they are dealing with some complex situations and junctions. Avoid explaining the purpose of you asking such questions until after the learning experience is over. Ask the questions when they're concentrating on driving tasks, "What did they do at the weekend? Where was their most recent holiday? What was it like?"

Instructor's role

Watch carefully for body language and pay attention to comments that suggest your learner is starting to get distracted, anxious or stressed. Be aware of:

- how your learner responds to being distracted
- situations your learner doesn't deal with particularly well
- other road users and situations your learner seems oblivious to
- your learner's body language cues — do they seem uncomfortable, frustrated or annoyed?

Reflective discussion and questions

Reflecting back, you can use this experience to draw parallels to when your learner may be talking on the phone when driving.

- How did they feel about you going on and on when they were trying to concentrate?
- How would they deal with someone talking on the phone/over Bluetooth when they're trying to concentrate in a complex situation?
- How likely are they to use the phone when driving, and under what circumstances?
- What could they do before a journey to reduce the chances of using the phone while driving?
- If they must use the phone, what could they do to reduce the risks associated with the distraction it causes?

Solutions

Your learner may come up with some great strategies for reducing the temptation of using their phone while driving. You could suggest other solutions once they have exhausted their own list.

- "If I need to answer a call, I could ignore what's being said if I'm in a complicated situation, then ask them to repeat what they said when I'm in a safer environment."
- "I could say 'Just a minute, I need to concentrate' when I'm dealing with complex situations."
- "I could be straight to the point and just say 'I'm driving, I'll call you back.'"
- "Set my phone to 'driving mode' or use an app that blocks calls or answers them with an 'I'm driving right now' message."
- "Switch off my phone."
- "Don't activate my Bluetooth, so I can't answer or make calls."
- "Put my Bluetooth on so I know when I can ignore an unimportant call."
- "Make necessary calls before getting into my car."
- "Put my phone out of sight."
- "Pull up safely to answer calls."
- "Let my friends and family know that I won't answer calls when I'm driving."
- "Set up a code with family members in case of an emergency. For example, three successive calls mean that the call is urgent and I have to answer."

Benefits

Allowing your learner to experience a distraction that's like a phone call can really open their eyes as to how difficult it is to concentrate on the driving task. Hopefully, this will help them realise just how dangerous it can be to use a phone while driving. Even if your learner chooses to use their phone while driving once they have passed their driving test, they may just limit the calls that they make and accept. Being aware of the consequences may help them balance the importance of the call and the demand of the driving task at that moment in time.

Scenario 6: Text and social media messaging (practical/theoretical)

Research has found that texting behind the wheel can result in the driver taking their eyes off the road for an average of 4.6 seconds.[103]

Goal

Give your learner the experience of a distraction like that of reading a text message or social media message.

Format

While your learner is driving, ask them if they'd be willing to close their eyes for five seconds. Hopefully, most will say something like "No way! Are you mad?!" If they're okay with closing their eyes, it's best to tell them you don't really want them to, but you would like them to work out how far they travel along the road in five seconds.

Instructor's role

Help your learner work out how far the car will travel in five seconds. Try it at different speed limits: 20mph, 30mph and 40mph. Inform your learner that 4.6 seconds is the average time a driver has their eyes off the road while texting.

Reflective discussion and questions

Encourage your learner to discuss the complications of texting and driving.

- Under what circumstances are they likely to text while driving?
- When they receive a message notification, what's the average time they take between receiving the message and reading it?
- What type of message would they consider to be important?
- How often do they get important messages?
- How did/would it make them feel taking their eyes off the road for five seconds?
- What did they think about the distance travelled in five seconds?
- What are the risks of them taking their eyes off the road for five seconds?
- What would be the likely consequences to their life when they crashed after taking their eyes off the road for five seconds?
- What would be the consequences if they killed someone — criminal record, imprisonment, lifelong crippling guilt?
- How will they deal with texts and other notifications when driving so that risks are minimised?
- How will they deal with a driver wanting to use their phone if they're a passenger?

Solutions

Your learner may come up with some great strategies for reducing the temptation of using their phone while driving. You could suggest others when they have exhausted their own list.

- "Use a drive agent app, so my messages and alerts are blocked or answered with an 'I'm driving right now' message."
- "Switch off my phone."
- "Send and read necessary texts before getting in my car."
- "Put my phone out of sight."
- "Pull up safely to check my messages and alerts."
- "Let my friends and family know that I won't message back when I'm driving."

Benefits

Allowing your learner to experience the distance travelled in the time it takes to read a message can help them realise the enormity of the risk associated with taking their eyes off the road, even for just a few moments. It might just help them decide that it's not worth it.

It's also important that you help your learners recognise their personality traits when they use messaging apps. Do they need to know straight away who sent the message and what it said? Do they need instant gratification or are they impatient? Is there a way in which they can recognise when messages may be urgent and deal with them differently to the non-urgent ones? They may even become a more responsible passenger — recognising friends' tendencies to use their phones while driving, and offer to read their messages and reply on their behalf.

Route planning

Reading a satnav while driving is as potentially dangerous as using a mobile phone while at the wheel. Irrespective of this fact, we need to have realistic expectations; satnav systems are legal to use and socially accepted as "safe" by most. They are also an integral part of the UK driving test. It's highly likely that your learners will be using their satnav to navigate to new places after they pass, so it's essential to give them the *safe* experience of doing so during their driving lessons. That way, they can experience how best to use one and, more importantly, they can become familiar with the limitations and risks of satnav systems.

Using your own satnav unit is one option, but it's preferable for your learners to become familiar with the one they'll be using after they pass their driving test. If your learner has their own satnav — which might even be an app-based system on their mobile phone — ask them to bring it along to a few lessons.

Scenario 7: Planning the journey in advance (practical)

Goal

Help your learner program and use satnav systems effectively and safely.

Format

Ask your learner to choose a destination to navigate to, using their satnav, or have a few addresses ready for them. See if they can work out how to program the satnav, but give help where needed. Ask your learner what the estimated time of arrival is and how long the journey will take, according to the satnav.

Instructor's role

Observe your learner's temperament while programming the satnav. Do they find it easy or difficult? During the drive, how comfortable are they responding to the satnav? How accurate are they at following the satnav directions? What was the actual journey time? Also, pay attention to:

- how your learner responds to being distracted by the satnav
- situations your learner doesn't deal with particularly well
- other road users and situations your learner seems oblivious to
- your learner's body language cues — do they seem uncomfortable, frustrated or annoyed?

Reflective discussion and questions

Once at the destination, reflect on the journey with your learner.

- How difficult did they find it to follow the satnav, on a scale of 1–10?
- What did they like or not like about the satnav?
- How distracted did they feel when concentrating on the satnav?

- How aware were they of everything going on around them?
- Are there specific incidents that they can recall?
- Were there any specific incidents that they were unaware of that you can mention?
- How did they respond to those incidents?
- What do they perceive as the risks of using a satnav?
- What happened when they took the wrong turn?
- How long did the actual journey take, and for which journeys will they need to factor in additional time, regardless of what the satnav says?
- Were there any challenges in understanding the style of language or direction used by the satnav?

Benefits

Allowing your learner to experience using a satnav will help them become more proficient at using them. Now that they're not reliant on your directions, you can identify any undesirable traits, such as getting close to cars in front or signalling late and discuss these further with them.

Although most of your learners will rely on route planning with a satnav once they've passed their test, there may be times where they don't have access to one, or it stops working. Therefore, we'd also encourage you to help your learners to develop the skills of route planning *without* access to a satnav, using road signs and maps, for example. This method of route planning presents a whole new set of interesting challenges.

Different road types

Taking your learners beyond the geographical boundaries of the driving test routes is *so* important, as it will give them experience driving on roads that they're likely to encounter after they have passed their test. As an example, when we used to work in the Oldham and Tameside areas (a few miles outside Manchester), all our learners also experienced driving through the most challenging areas of Manchester City Centre. We wanted to be satisfied that they could handle even the busiest, most complicated areas of the city. Most of our learners at an advanced stage of learning also had experience driving along Woodhead Pass and Snake Pass towards Sheffield (sometimes in the dark during the winter months), which even experienced drivers can find challenging.

Scenario 8: Different road types (practical)

Goal

Help your learner experience different road types.

Format

Take your learner on all types of roads, including city streets, country lanes, single-track roads, dual carriageways and, from 4th June 2018, motorways.

Instructor's role

Help your learner to identify the risks associated with the roads they're driving on, and ask them how they feel. Pay attention to:

- how easy or difficult your learner finds dealing with a different type of road or environment
- how your learner responds to hazards
- situations your learner doesn't deal with particularly well
- other road users and situations your learner seems oblivious to
- your learner's body language cues — do they seem uncomfortable, frustrated, annoyed, stressed, anxious or nervous?

Reflective discussion and questions

Encourage your learner to reflect on potential risks they experienced or encountered.

- How did they feel driving on a specific type of road?
- How did that affect their ability to plan and deal effectively with hazards and risks?
- What did they find most challenging about driving on that type of road?
- What would increase the risks even further?
- What additional risks could they identify if they used that type of road at different times of the day/week/year?
- How could they reduce the risks they experienced?

Solutions

Your learner may come up with some great strategies for reducing their risk on roads that they're not familiar with. You could suggest others when they have exhausted their own list.

- "I could pull up in lay-bys on faster country lanes to let faster traffic pass."
- "Stay in the left-hand lane of the dual carriageway/motorway until I get used to the higher speed."
- "Make sure that I stay focused on looking and planning ahead."
- "Use those limit points you showed me to help plan better for bends."
- "Reduce the distractions in my car, like the radio, phone calls or conversation with my passengers."
- "Look for alternative routes on roads I prefer to drive on."
- "Use Google Street View to check out routes and junctions before I drive them for the first time."
- "Use commentary driving as a way to keep myself focused."

Benefits

Allowing your learner to experience different road types, especially ones that aren't local to them, will help them to become a well-rounded driver. It also gives you the opportunity to discuss possible risks and solutions before they drive on those types of roads, instead of them having to do it for themselves once they pass their test.

Time of day

Varying the time of day at which your learner has their lesson is important, too. The occasional experience of driving at rush hour is very beneficial; this can sometimes be a challenge for learners who only have specific times of availability, but it's important for them to experience as much variety as possible. Use your powers of persuasion to encourage them to schedule at least one or two lessons outside their "normal" time.

During the winter months, learners should schedule daytime and evening lessons, allowing them to gain valuable experience of driving in darkness.

Scenario 9: Time of day (practical)

Goal

Give your learner the experience of driving in a variety of traffic conditions.

Format

Change the lesson time so that your learner gets to experience both light and heavy traffic.

Instructor's role

Help your learner to identify risks associated with different times of the day. Ask them how they feel driving in heavy traffic. Be aware of:

- how your learner finds dealing with a different traffic volume
- how your learner responds to hazards
- situations your learner doesn't deal with particularly well
- other road users and situations your learner seems oblivious to
- your learner's body language cues — do they seem uncomfortable, frustrated, annoyed, stressed, anxious or nervous?

Reflective discussion and questions

Encourage your learner to reflect on potential risks they experienced or encountered.

- How did they feel driving in heavy traffic?
- How did that affect their ability to plan and deal effectively with hazards and risks?
- What did they find most challenging about driving in heavy traffic?
- What would increase the risks even further? Bad weather? Feeling unwell, angry, upset or tired? Running late?
- What additional risks could they identify if they were driving in an unfamiliar city?
- How can they reduce the risks they experienced?

Solutions

Your learner may come up with some great strategies for reducing their risks in busy traffic for when they have passed. You could suggest others when they have exhausted their own list.

- "I could stop off at a McDonald's until the traffic's quietened down."
- "Make sure I stay focused on looking and planning ahead."
- "Allow a greater distance in front to give me more time to deal with hazards and lane changes."
- "Reduce the distractions in my car, like the radio, phone calls or conversation with my passengers."
- "Look for alternative routes that avoid main roads."
- "Use Google Street View to check out routes and junctions before my journey, as well as potential alternative routes."
- "Use commentary driving as a way to keep myself focused."

Benefits

Allowing your learner to experience driving in rush hour traffic and in busy city centres will help them become a well-rounded driver. It also gives you the opportunity to discuss the possible risks and solutions of driving in such traffic conditions, instead of them having to work it out for themselves once they've passed their test.

All-weather driving

It's not always possible to time lessons so that every learner has a lesson in heavy rain, wind, snow or bright sunlight, but it's important to give your learners the opportunity to explore what risks they would associate with various weather conditions, and what they could do to minimise these risks. You may include tyre and vehicle safety features in these lessons too.

Scenario 10: All-weather driving (practical/theoretical)

Goal

Give your learner the experience of driving in various weather conditions.

Format

Practical experience (if safe to do so) or theoretical discussion.

Instructor's role

Help your learner to identify the risks associated with varying weather conditions. Include discussions on:

- safety margins
- vehicle control and handling
- vehicle speed, reaction times and stopping distances
- visibility, themselves and others, and planning for hazards
- how your learner will react when driving in adverse weather conditions — will they feel uncomfortable, frustrated, stressed, anxious, nervous or scared?

Reflective discussion and questions

Encourage your learner to reflect on potential risks they could experience or encounter.

- What are the risks they can think of when driving in heavy rain/wind/snow/bright sunlight?
- How would it affect their ability to plan and deal effectively with hazards?
- What would they find most challenging about driving in heavy rain/wind/snow/bright sunlight?
- What would increase the risks even further? Feeling unwell, angry, upset or tired? Running late or driving on unfamiliar roads?
- How would the condition of their car affect their risks? Worn brakes? Incorrectly inflated tyres? Dirty headlights or windows? Faulty ABS?

- How can they reduce the risks when driving in heavy rain/wind/snow/bright sunlight?

Solutions

The learner may come up with some great strategies for reducing their risk when driving in adverse weather conditions. You could suggest others when they have exhausted their own list.

- "I could pull up somewhere to see if the weather calms down."
- "I could get a lift or use public transport instead."
- "Make sure I'm focused on looking and planning ahead."
- "Increase my distance."
- "Check the condition of my car and my tyres before I set off."
- "Reduce the distractions in my car, like the radio, phone calls or conversation with my passengers."
- "Look for alternative routes, avoiding roads which may be affected worse, such as steep gradients in snow."
- "Use commentary driving to keep myself focused."
- "I could get a set of winter tyres fitted to my car."

Benefits

Allowing your learner to experience different weather conditions, or to talk about them hypothetically, will give them greater confidence for when they need to drive in adverse conditions. It also gives you the opportunity to discuss the possible risks and solutions ahead of time.

Emotional and physical state

It's essential that your learners develop a full understanding of how their emotional and physical state can affect their driving, such as in their ability to remain fully focussed on the driving task and to drive safely. As human beings, our emotional and physical states are changing all the time. You should get at least one or two good opportunities during a course of driving lessons to help your learners to become aware of how they are feeling, both emotionally and physically, and to develop safe coping strategies for the future.

Scenario 11: Emotional and physical states (practical)

Goal

Help your learner understand how their emotional and physical state affects their driving.

Format

A great question to ask at the beginning of every driving lesson is, "How are you feeling today?" Notice if your learner expresses worry about their exams, sadness after a relationship breakdown, anger after an argument with a friend, and so on. You should also pick up if they're feeling overly tired or sick. If you're made aware of the emotional and/or physical state at the start of the lesson, take some time to explore this important topic before moving off. In some situations, the outcome of the discussion might be to not continue with the lesson — this might be the best outcome for both the learner and the instructor.

Instructor's role

Help your learner become aware of their emotional and physical state and discuss how this might affect their driving. Decide together if the planned lesson goals need adapting or changing, or if the lesson should be discontinued altogether.

Reflective discussion and questions

Assuming the lesson continues, encourage your learner to discuss the effects of their emotional or physical state on their driving.

- How was their planning affected and how well did they respond to hazards?
- How patient were they with other road users?
- What did they notice about their speed choices?
- How often did they make mistakes?
- How were their concentration levels affected?

Solutions

Your learner may come up with some great ideas for reducing the negative consequences of their emotional or physical state. You could suggest others too, once they have exhausted their own list.

- "Make sure I get enough sleep so I'm not tired the next day."
- "Cut out my caffeine intake in the evenings."
- "Only take absolutely necessary journeys when I'm feeling ill."
- "Listen to music to calm down if I'm feeling angry."
- "Use commentary driving to help with my concentration or to disconnect from whatever's happened prior to me getting behind the wheel."
- "Open the window to get some fresh air or to keep the car cool."
- "Take a stretch break."
- "Ask someone else to drive or rearrange my commitments."

Benefits

Allowing your learner to experience the way in which their emotional or physical state affects their driving increases their awareness of the issues it creates. When they are mindful of the effects, they can make more responsible choices, which might include not driving at all.

Extra skills

If you've been an ADI for a while now, you probably already incorporate some of the following in your lessons, but read through and see if there any ideas you can develop further.

Choice of manoeuvre locations

The decision of where to practise manoeuvres is so often the choice of the instructor, but who will need to choose the place to turn around once the learner passes? Choosing a place to manoeuvre is as much a skill the learner needs to develop as the manoeuvre itself.[***]

You could either encourage your learner to take complete responsibility for the choice of location or you could work together to find one.

- "What about this road? How suitable would you say it is on a scale of 1 to 10, where 1 is dangerous, illegal and inconvenient and 10 is 100% safe, legal and convenient?"
- "What do you think makes it unsuitable?"
- "What potential risks does that *[point out a danger that the learner appears to have missed]* pose?"
- "How happy are you to carry out the exercise here?"

Ideally, your role here is to develop your learner's skill at making their *own* decisions; making it for them will only take responsibility away from them. If your learner doesn't choose somewhere suitable this lesson, consider encouraging them to make it a goal for the next lesson. When they realise that it's *their* responsibility to find somewhere, they'll come to their next lesson more determined to find a suitable road.

[***] Being able to turn the car around safely is still a skill all your learners need to develop, even though the turn in the road and left/right reverse exercises are no longer assessed on the practical driving test.

Freestyle manoeuvring

We find this skill fantastically beneficial and if you don't already practise this, we're sure you will too. Once you and your learner have worked on developing their manoeuvring skills, begin to encourage them to work out how to turn the car around independently. The idea here is to get your learner to choose the safest, most efficient way of turning to go back the other way, simulating what they'll need to do many times post-test.

You could take them into a tight cul-de-sac or country lane and ask them to turn around to go back the other way using the safest means possible. Alternatively, as they're driving along a main road, you could ask them to imagine they've just driven past a junction which they intended to turn into, so they need to find a way back within the next couple of minutes. Once they've learned the skills of reversing around corners, turning in the road, doing U-turns and taxi turns, they need to be able to choose the method most appropriate for the situation. They could even go all the way around a roundabout if they wanted to. Remember, it's all about giving your learner choice and responsibility.

Multi-storey car parks

An old friend of ours once bounced off the wall several times on the spiral ramp coming out of one of the multi-storey car parks in Manchester. He was a bit tight with money and decided to turn his engine off to save fuel. Yes, you've guessed it, the steering lock came on and he couldn't steer!

Most car parks give you around ten minutes from taking the ticket to drive out again without having to pay.[†††] Ten minutes to save

---

[†††] While most multi-storey car parks have this facility, in case you cannot find a parking space and need to park elsewhere, we cannot guarantee that your local multi-storey offers this as standard.

embarrassment and damage to the learner's car once they pass is a good use of ten minutes during a lesson, don't you think?

Practice negotiating the tight corners and ramps, discussing the importance of using headlights and anticipating dangers and, of course, stopping close enough to the machine at the exit to avoid having to get out of the car to insert the ticket!

Filling up with fuel

Encourage your learner to have a go at filling up with fuel. Maybe knowing how to fill up correctly won't prevent a crash, but it may certainly prevent them from making an expensive mistake by filling up with the wrong fuel.

- How do they find out which side the fuel cap is?
- What are the different types of fuel available?
- What are the consequences of filling up with the wrong type of fuel?
- What are the rules about not using mobile phones on the forecourt?
- How does the pay-at-pump facility work?
- Why should they lock their car if they go to the kiosk to pay?
- What happens if they can't pay or don't pay?

For some interesting facts on petrol stations that you can discuss with your learner drivers, visit **http://gedclai.re/petrolstation** or scan this QR code.

Visiting the drive-through

There once was an instructor we knew who used to get her learners to drive through McDonald's so she could get a cup of coffee. She also used to eat her lunch during lessons. She even delivered parcels during her lessons, with her paying learners being the delivery driver! Even though we feel that most of her behaviour was highly unprofessional, she taught her learners some valuable skills. How many scrapes happen at the McDonald's drive-through? You just need to look at the crooked, dented and multicoloured bollards to guess. If your learner plans on using the drive-through, let them practice, they'll thank you for it, and they'll feel much more confident when they drive through with their friends. A bonus is that they'll get more confident dealing with other situations where they may have limited space.

APPENDIX B

GOALS FOR DRIVER EDUCATION (GDE) MATRIX

Our version of the 5-level GDE Matrix can be found on the next page.

Due to the page size in this book, you might find it quite challenging to read it clearly. You can download a larger, printable version at **http://gedclai.re/GDE** or by scanning this QR code.

Also on the same resource page is a document we have written which breaks down each level of the GDE Matrix into more detail. Download and read it to help you better understand each section of the Matrix.

Essential elements of driver training

	Knowledge and skills to master	Awareness of risk-increasing factors	Self-evaluation
Level 5 Social environment	*Knowledge of and control over:* • cultural and sub-cultural issues • work-related issues • group goals, values and motives • social environment and position	*Risks related to:* • cultural or work issues impacting on driving • context of journey such as work or pleasure • passengers	*Self-evaluation and awareness of:* • how culture or work issues impact on driving decisions and judgements • how placement within social group or work environment influences choices
Level 4 Personal goals for life and skills for living	*Knowledge of and control over:* • how life goals and personal tendencies affect driving behaviour • personal motives and competencies • lifestyle/life situation • age-related issues • personal values and ambitions	*Risks related to:* • acceptance of risk • self-enhancement through driving • high sensation seeking • susceptibility to social pressure • use of alcohol or drugs • personal values and attitudes to society	*Self-evaluation and awareness of:* • personal skills for impulse control • attitude towards risk • introspective competence • risky tendencies and habits • safety-negative motives
Level 3 Goals and context of driving	*Knowledge and skills concerning:* • purpose of the journey • route planning • evaluation of required driving time • evaluation of necessity of journey • safety and control of passengers	*Risks connected with:* • driver's physiological condition • purpose of the journey • driving environment such as rural/urban or day/night • social context and in-vehicle company	*Self-evaluation and awareness of:* • own physiological condition • journey planning skills • typical journey goals or expectations • typical risky driving motives • self-critical thinking skills
Level 2 Mastery of traffic situations	*Knowledge and skills concerning:* • traffic rules • observation • signals • anticipation • speed adjustment • safety margins	*Risks caused by:* • wrong expectations/assumptions • vulnerable road users • disobeying rules • unpredictable behaviour • information overload • difficult conditions such as darkness	*Self-evaluation and awareness of:* • ability to deal with a variety of traffic situations • observational skills • planning and anticipation • personal driving style • personal safety margins
Level 1 Vehicle control and manoeuvring	*Knowledge and skills concerning:* • control of direction and position • tyre grip and friction • technical aspects of vehicle • physical handling when cornering, accelerating and braking	*Risks associated with:* • insufficient skills • poor speed adjustment • difficult road conditions • improper use of seat belt, head restraint, etc. • under-inflated or worn tyres	*Self-evaluation and awareness of:* • understanding of essential knowledge and skills • strengths and weaknesses of basic vehicle control • ability to control the vehicle in challenging conditions

Hierarchical levels of driver behaviour
(Higher levels directly influence lower levels)

ABOUT THE AUTHORS

Ged Wilmot

After leaving college I was unsure which career path to follow, but my interest in how humans learn, develop and interact led to me taking a degree in Psychology & Health Psychology at the University of Wales. Like many students after graduation, I found it difficult to land my perfect job. It seemed everyone else *also* had a degree in Psychology!

For years and years, my mum and dad had badgered me to become a teacher, telling me how great I would be at it. I quite liked the idea of teaching, but after a year's voluntary work at my former primary school, I began to realise that working with big classes of noisy, young kids wasn't my thing. As for secondary school, well, there was absolutely *no* way I would have had the patience to deal with a class of hormonal teenagers!

An advert in the local newspaper was the spark that ignited my career as a driving instructor. It claimed I could work my own hours, be my own boss and earn around £30,000 per year. Best of all, I'd be teaching adults who *wanted* to be there. I went along to a national training company for a chat, took out a Career Development Loan to pay for the course fees and signed on the dotted line.

Sadly, the training for the Part 3 test was woefully inadequate, resulting in me seeking outside help from an independent trainer. Within two years of qualifying as an ADI, I'd gained some more advanced driving qualifications, taken a Train the Trainer course and even started teaching my first few PDIs — I loved it. Everything I'd learned during my degree began to come to fruition, as now I had the opportunity to pass on my knowledge and experience of how people learn, how to communicate effectively and establish and adapt to different learning styles. My new passion was training the trainers, and I knew that this was how I wanted to spend my time.

I've now been training ADIs on a full-time basis since 2002. Claire and I joined forces in 2005 when we set up our business, Active Driving Solutions. Our company has gone from strength to strength, and we're privileged to work with some of the most dedicated professionals in the industry. We're thrilled with the fact that people will travel from all corners of the UK to train with us, even flying in from the south of England, Northern Ireland, the Isle of Man and the Orkney Islands. We pride ourselves on doing a great job, and the buzz we get from being able to help people is off the scale!

Claire Wilmot

I have my Mum to thank for loving what I do; she decided to train as a driving instructor, and when I turned 17, I became her first learner when she started working on a trainee licence. I'd love to say that we got on great, that I took everything on board that she taught me and that we had a fabulous teacher-student relationship. But in reality, I argued with her and questioned everything she told me. I was probably the learner from hell. I like to think that my mum's challenging experience teaching me was a huge learning curve for her, and that it contributed to her becoming a fantastic instructor!

Thankfully, I didn't put her off too much as she asked if I wanted to become a driving instructor and offered to train me when I turned 21. It wasn't easy balancing a full-time job and a part-time job with studying until midnight, but once I start something, I've just *got* to succeed.

In 1996, I became a fully qualified driving instructor. At 22 I set up my own driving school and became my own boss. I'm a firm believer that everything happens for a reason and knowing how much I had struggled to pass my Part 3 test inspired me to set out on a journey of professional development. Gaining knowledge, experience and qualifications has helped me to become better and better at doing what I love.

I started training PDIs in 2000, and a year later I set up a new driving school, Latics Driving Training, with my business partner, and fellow ADI, Glyn. Latics now has a fantastic team of over 30 instructors, and I'm so proud of all their hard work and commitment. After being introduced to Ged by our mutual friend, Kathy, in 2004, we went into partnership in life and business. Together, we love helping others achieve their potential, their goals and their dreams. It's not just a job, it's part of our life, and the pleasure it brings us to help others reach their goals is what keeps us going. I always aim to learn more, and if you're reading this, I guess you do too; thank you for allowing us to be a part of your journey.

REFERENCES

1. Williams, D. (2011). *The Problem of Insuring Young Drivers*. The Telegraph. [online] Available at: http://www.telegraph.co.uk/motoring/road-safety/8437307/The-problem-of-insuring-young-drivers.html [Accessed 18 Mar. 2018].
2. GOV.UK (2017). *History of Road Safety, the Highway Code and the Driving Test*. [online] Driver & Vehicle Standards Agency. Available at: https://www.gov.uk/government/publications/history-of-road-safety-and-the-driving-test/history-of-road-safety-the-highway-code-and-the-driving-test [Accessed 18 Mar. 2018].
3. GOV.UK (2017). *Vehicle Licensing Statistics: Annual 2016*. [online] Department for Transport. Available at: https://www.gov.uk/government/uploads/system/uploads/attachment_data/file/608374/vehicle-licensing-statistics-2016.pdf [Accessed 18 Mar. 2018].
4. GOV.UK (2017). *Reported Road Casualties in Great Britain: 2016 Annual Report*. [online] Department for Transport. Available at: https://www.gov.uk/government/uploads/system/uploads/attachment_data/file/648081/rrcgb2016-01.pdf [Accessed 18 Mar. 2018].
5. Safe Driving for Life. (2018). *Safe Driving for Life*. [online] Available at: https://www.safedrivingforlife.info [Accessed 18 Mar. 2018].
6. GOV.UK (2017). *Reported Road Casualties in Great Britain: 2016 Annual Report*. [online] Department for Transport. Available at: https://www.gov.uk/government/uploads/system/uploads/attachment_data/file/648081/rrcgb2016-01.pdf [Accessed 18 Mar. 2018].
7. GOV.UK (2015). *Facts on Young Car Drivers*. [online] p.5. Available at: https://www.gov.uk/government/uploads/system/uploads/attachment_data/file/448039/young-car-drivers-2013-data.pdf [Accessed 18 Mar. 2018].
8. GOV.UK (2017). *Table RAS50002*. Contributory Factors for Reported Road Accidents (RAS50). [online] Available at: https://www.gov.uk/government/statistical-data-sets/ras50-contributory-factors#table-ras50002 [Accessed 18 Mar. 2018].
9. TED (2012). *The Optimism Bias*. [video] Available at: https://www.ted.com/talks/tali_sharot_the_optimism_bias?language=en [Accessed 18 Mar. 2018].
10. Mulkana, S. and Hailey, B. (2001). The Role of Optimism in Health-Enhancing Behaviour. *American Journal of Health Behaviour*, 25(4), pp.388-395. Available at: http://www.ingentaconnect.com/content/png/ajhb/2001/00000025/00000004/art00004 [Accessed 18 Mar. 2018].
11. Harbluk, J., Noy, Y. and Eizenman, M. (2000). The Impact of Internal Distraction on Driver Visual Behaviour. [online] Available at: https://www-nrd.

nhtsa.dot.gov/departments/Human%20Factors/driver-distraction/PDF/1.PDF [Accessed 18 Mar. 2018].

12 AAA Foundation for Traffic Safety (2015). *Using Naturalistic Driving Data to Assess the Prevalence of Environmental Factors and Driver Behaviours in Teen Driver Crashes.* [online] Washington, DC, p.4. Available at: http://newsroom.aaa.com/wp-content/uploads/2015/03/TeenCrashCausation_2015_FINALREPORT.pdf [Accessed 18 Mar. 2018].

13 Levitin, D. (2015). *Why the Modern World Is Bad for Your Brain.* [online] The Guardian. Available at: https://www.theguardian.com/science/2015/jan/18/modern-world-bad-for-brain-daniel-j-levitin-organized-mind-information-overload [Accessed 18 Mar. 2018].

14 Koppel, S., Charlton, J., Kopinathan, C. and Taranto, D. (2011). Are Child Occupants a Significant Source of Driver Distraction? *Accident Analysis & Prevention*, 43(3), pp.1236-1244. Available at: http://www.sciencedirect.com/science/article/pii/S0001457511000066 [Accessed 18 Mar. 2018].

15 AAA Foundation for Traffic Safety (2012). *Teen Driver Risk in Relation to Age and Number of Passengers.* [online] Washington, DC, p.9. Available at: https://aaafoundation.org/wp-content/uploads/2018/01/TeenDriverRiskAgePassengersReport.pdf [Accessed 18 Mar. 2018].

16 Deloitte LLP (2017). *State of the smart. Consumer and business usage patterns. Global Mobile Consumer Survey 2017: The UK cut.* [online] London, p.4. Available at: https://www.deloitte.co.uk/mobileuk/assets/img/download/global-mobile-consumer-survey-2017_uk-cut.pdf [Accessed 18 Mar. 2018].

17 AAA Foundation for Traffic Safety (2015). *Using Naturalistic Driving Data to Assess the Prevalence of Environmental Factors and Driver Behaviours in Teen Driver Crashes.* [online] Washington, DC, p.34. Available at: http://newsroom.aaa.com/wp-content/uploads/2015/03/TeenCrashCausation_2015_FINALREPORT.pdf [Accessed 18 Mar. 2018].

18 McEvoy, S. (2005). Role of Mobile Phones in Motor Vehicle Crashes Resulting in Hospital Attendance: A Case-Crossover Study. *BMJ*, 331(7514), pp.428-0. Available at: http://www.bmj.com/content/331/7514/428.short [Accessed 18 Mar. 2018].

19 Burns, P., Parkes, A., Burton, S., Smith, R. and Burch, D. (2002). *How Dangerous Is Driving with a Mobile Phone? Benchmarking the Impairment to Alcohol.* [online] TRL. Available at: https://trl.co.uk/reports/TRL547 [Accessed 18 Mar. 2018].

20 European Agency for Safety and Health at Work (2010). *A Review of Accidents and Injuries to Road Transport Drivers.* Luxembourg: Publications Office of the European Union, p.44. Available at: https://www.narcis.nl/publication/RecordID/oai:tudelft.nl:uuid%3Ae9a20676-31e7-48c1-9b3c-439bb62a99dd [Accessed 18 Mar. 2018].

References

21. The Telegraph. (2016). *How Do Emotions Affect Your Driving?* [online] Available at: http://www.telegraph.co.uk/cars/road-safety/how-emotions-affect-driving/ [Accessed 18 Mar. 2018].

22. Dingus, T., Guo, F., Lee, S., Antin, J., Perez, M., Buchanan-King, M. and Hankey, J. (2016). Driver Crash Risk Factors and Prevalence Evaluation Using Naturalistic Driving Data. *Proceedings of the National Academy of Sciences*, [online] 113(10), pp.2636-2641. Available at: http://www.pnas.org/content/113/10/2636.abstract [Accessed 18 Mar. 2018].

23. RAC Foundation (2013). *Young Driver Safety: Solutions to an Age-Old Problem*. [online] London, p.10. Available at: http://www.racfoundation.org/assets/rac_foundation/content/downloadables/young_driver_safety-box_wengraf-july2013.pdf [Accessed 18 Mar. 2018].

24. Sowell, E., Thompson, P., Holmes, C., Jernigan, T. and Toga, A. (1999). In Vivo Evidence for Post-Adolescent Brain Maturation in Frontal and Striatal Regions. *Nature Neuroscience*, 2(10), pp.859-861. Available at: http://www.nature.com/neuro/journal/v2/n10/abs/nn1099_859.html [Accessed 18 Mar. 2018].

25. Isler, R. and Starkey, N. (2008). The 'Frontal Lobe' Project: A Double-Blind, Randomized Controlled Study of the Effectiveness of Higher Level Driving Skills Training to Improve Frontal Lobe (Executive) Function Related Driving Performance in Young Drivers.

26. Horne, J. and Reyner, L. (1995). Sleep Related Vehicle Accidents. *BMJ*, 310(6979), pp.565-567. Available at: https://www.ncbi.nlm.nih.gov/pubmed/7888930 [Accessed 18 Mar. 2018].

27a. Åkerstedt T, Bassetti C, Cirignotta F, et al. (2013) White paper "Sleepiness at the Wheel": French Motorway Companies (ASFA) and the National Institute of Sleep and Vigilance (INSV).

27b. Owens, J. (2014). Insufficient Sleep in Adolescents and Young Adults: An Update on Causes and Consequences. *American Academy of Pediatrics*, [online] 134(3), pp.e921-e932. Available at: http://pediatrics.aappublications.org/content/pediatrics/early/2014/08/19/peds.2014-1696.full.pdf [Accessed 18 Mar. 2018].

28. Hill, S. (2016). *Is Blue Light Keeping You up at Night? We Ask the Experts*. [online] Digital Trends. Available at: http://www.digitaltrends.com/mobile/does-blue-light-ruin-sleep-we-ask-an-expert/ [Accessed 18 Mar. 2018].

29. Vohs, K., Glass, B., Maddox, W. and Markman, A. (2010). Ego Depletion Is Not Just Fatigue: Evidence from a Total Sleep Deprivation Experiment. *Social Psychological and Personality Science*, [online] 2(2), pp.166-173. Available at: http://liberalarts.utexas.edu/_files/markman/SPPS11.pdf [Accessed 18 Mar. 2018].

30   Direct Line and Brake (2014). *Reports on Safe Driving 2012-2014 Report 2*. [online] Available at: http://www.brake.org.uk/assets/docs/dl_reports/DLFittoDriveReport_2013sec2.pdf [Accessed 18 Mar. 2018].

31   Watson, P., Whale, A., Mears, S., Reyner, L. and Maughan, R. (2015). Mild Hypohydration Increases the Frequency of Driver Errors During a Prolonged, Monotonous Driving Task. *Physiology & Behaviour*, 147, pp.313-318. Available at: http://www.sciencedirect.com/science/article/pii/S0031938415002358 [Accessed 18 Mar. 2018].

32   James, W. (1950). *The Principles of Psychology*. [New York]: Dover Publications.

33   Rock, I., Linnett, C., Grant, P. and Mack, A. (1992). Perception Without Attention: Results of a New Method. *Cognitive Psychology*, 24(4), pp.502-534.

34   Simons, D. and Chabris, C. (1999). Gorillas in Our Midst: Sustained Inattentional Blindness for Dynamic Events. *Perception*, [online] 28(9), pp.1059-1074. Available at: http://www.chabris.com/Simons1999.pdf [Accessed 18 Mar. 2018].

35   Levin, D. and Angelone, B. (2008). The Visual Metacognition Questionnaire: A Measure of Intuitions about Vision. *The American Journal of Psychology*, 121(3), p.451. Available at: https://www.researchgate.net/profile/Daniel_Levin8/publication/23258962_The_Visual_Metacognition_Questionnaire_A_Measure_of_Intuitions_about_Vision/links/54f8d0380cf28d6deca2c0f7/The-Visual-Metacognition-Questionnaire-A-Measure-of-Intuitions-about-Vision.pdf [Accessed 18 Mar. 2018].

36a   Forsyth, E. (1992). *Cohort Study of Learner and Novice Drivers*. 1st ed. Crowthorne, Berkshire: Road User Safety Division, Road User Group, Transport Research Laboratory.

36b   Brake.org.uk. (2016). *Driver rehabilitation*. [online] Available at: http://www.brake.org.uk/facts-resources/15-facts/502-traffic-offender-education [Accessed 12 Feb 2018].

37   Whitmore, J. (2002). *Coaching for Performance*. 1st ed. London: Nicholas Brealey.

38   Hatakka, M., Keskinen, E., Gregersen, N., Glad, A. and Hernetkoski, K. (2002). From Control of the Vehicle to Personal Self-Control; Broadening the Perspectives to Driver Education. *Transportation Research Part F: Traffic Psychology and Behaviour*, 5(3), pp.201-215. Available at: https://www.cambsdriveiq.co.uk/Control_of_the_vehicle_to_self-control.pdf [Accessed 18 Mar. 2018].

39   Keskinen, E. (2014). Education for Older Drivers in the Future. *IATSS Research*, [online] 38(1), pp.14-21. Available at: http://www.sciencedirect.com/science/article/pii/S0386111214000090#bb0255 [Accessed 18 Mar. 2018].

40   Gallwey, W. (1974). *The Inner Game of Tennis*. New York: Random House.

References

41. Whitmore, J. (2002). *Coaching for Performance.* 1st ed. London: Nicholas Brealey.
42. Bartl, G., et al. (2010). High Impact Approach for Enhancing Road Safety Through More Effective Communication Skills in the Context of Category B Driver Training. EU HERMES Project Final Report.
43. Teachingcommons.stanford.edu. (n.d.). *Promoting Active Learning | Teaching Commons.* [online] Available at: https://teachingcommons.stanford.edu/resources/learning-resources/promoting-active-learning [Accessed 18 Mar. 2018].
44. Kolb, D. (2014). Experiential Learning: Experience as the Source of Learning and Development. FT press.
45. Pickles, T. (2017). *Experiential Learning Articles and Critiques of David Kolb's Theory.* [online] Reviewing.co.uk. Available at: http://reviewing.co.uk/research/experiential.learning.htm#axzz55reznT5x [Accessed 18 Mar. 2018].
46. Kimsey-House, H., Kimsey-House, K., Sandahl, P. and Whitworth, L. (2011). *Co-Active Coaching: Changing Business, Transforming Lives.* Nicholas Brealey Publishing.
47. Economy, P. (2015). *37 Earl Nightingale Quotes That Will Empower You to Soar High.* [online] Inc.com. Available at: http://www.inc.com/peter-economy/37-earl-nightingale-quotes-that-will-empower-you-to-soar-high.html [Accessed 18 Mar. 2018].
48. Whitmore, J. (2002). *Coaching for Performance.* 1st ed. London: Nicholas Brealey.
49. Rogers, C. and Dorfman, E. (1951). *Client-Centred: Its Current Practice, Implications, and Theory.* ICON Group International.
50. McPherson, S. (2016). *Meet the Woman Driving Sustainability and Corporate Responsibility at Tiffany & Co.* [online] Forbes.com. Available at: https://www.forbes.com/sites/susanmcpherson/2016/01/25/meet-the-woman-driving-sustainability-and-corporate-responsibility-at-tiffany-co/ [Accessed 18 Mar. 2018].
51. Whitmore, J. (2002). *Coaching for Performance.* 1st ed. London: Nicholas Brealey.
52. Gordontraining.com. (2016). *Learning a New Skill Is Easier Said Than Done — Gordon Training International.* [online] Available at: http://www.gordontraining.com/free-workplace-articles/learning-a-new-skill-is-easier-said-than-done/ [Accessed 18 Mar. 2018]. www.gordontraining.com, info@gordontraining.com
53. Oxford Dictionaries | English. (2018). Complacency — Definition of Complacency in English | Oxford Dictionaries. [online] Available at: https://en.oxforddictionaries.com/definition/complacency [Accessed 18 Mar. 2018].

54. Elephant.co.uk. (2009). *Driving Comfort Zone Leads to Danger Close to Home*. [online] Available at: https://www.elephant.co.uk/pressReleases/75/Driving-comfort-zone-leads-to-danger-close-to-home [Accessed 24 Oct. 2017].

55. Whitmore, J. (2002). *Coaching for Performance*. 1st ed. London: Nicholas Brealey.

56. EU HERMES (2010). *EU HERMES Project Final Report*. [online] Vienna: European Commission DG TREN, p.8. Available at: http://www.cieca.eu/sites/default/files/documents/projects_and_studies/HERMES2.pdf [Accessed 18 Mar. 2018].

57. Blakey, J. and Day, I. (2012). *Challenging Coaching*. 1st ed. London: Nicholas Brealey Publishing.

58. Blakey, J. and Day, I. (2012). *Challenging Coaching*. 1st ed. London: Nicholas Brealey Publishing.

59. Hayward, F. (1979). *The Educational Ideas of Pestalozzi and Fröbel*. 1st ed. Westport, Conn.: Greenwood Press.

60. Henson, K.T. (2003). Foundations for Learner-Centred Education: A Knowledge Base. *Education*, 124(1), pp.5-17. Available at: http://go.galegroup.com/ps/anonymous?id=GALE%7CA108911198&sid=googleScholar&v=2.1&it=r&linkaccess=fulltext&issn=00131172&p=AONE&sw=w&authCount=1&isAnonymousEntry=true [Accessed 01 Feb. 2018].

61. Dewey, J. (1959). *The Child and the Curriculum* (No. 5). Chicago: University of Chicago Press.

62. Rogers, C. and Dorfman, E. (1951). *Client-Centred: Its Current Practice, Implications, and Theory*. ICON Group International.

63. GOV.UK (2017). *DVSA ADI1 Standard Operating Procedure*. [online] Driver and Vehicle Standards Agency. Available at: https://www.gov.uk/government/publications/guidance-for-driving-examiners-carrying-out-instructor-tests-adi1 [Accessed 1 Feb. 2018].

64. GOV.UK (2014). *National Standard for Driver and Rider Training*. [online] Driver and Vehicle Standards Agency. Available at: https://www.gov.uk/government/uploads/system/uploads/attachment_data/file/377667/national-standard-for-driver-and-rider-training.pdf [Accessed 18 Mar. 2018].

65. Wilmot, G. (2013). *Motivating the Unmotivated Learner Drivers — Ged & Claire*. [online] Ged & Claire. Available at: https://www.gedandclaire.com/coaching/motivating-the-unmotivated/ [Accessed 18 Mar. 2018].

66. Whitmore, J. (2002). *Coaching for Performance*. 1st ed. London: Nicholas Brealey.

67. Rogers, C. (1980). *A Way of Being*. 1st ed. Boston: Houghton Mifflin.

68. Oxford Dictionaries | English. (2018). *Rapport — Definition of Rapport in English | Oxford Dictionaries*. [online] Available at: https://en.oxforddictionaries.com/definition/rapport [Accessed 18 Mar. 2018].

References

69. O'Connor, L. and Seymour, J. (1993). *Introducing Neuro-Linguistic Programming*. 1st ed. London: Aquarian/Thorsons.
70. Vecsey, G. (1989). *Sports of The Tims; Make Way for the Other Pros*. [online] Nytimes.com. Available at: http://www.nytimes.com/1989/01/08/sports/sports-of-the-tims-make-way-for-the-other-pros.html [Accessed 18 Mar. 2018].
71. BBC News. (2014). *The Unstoppable March of the Upward Inflection?* — BBC News. [online] Available at: http://www.bbc.com/news/magazine-28708526 [Accessed 18 Mar. 2018].
72. Wells, S. and Clague, T. (1998). *Choosing the Future: The Power of Strategic Thinking*. 1st ed. Butterworth-Heinemann.
73. Allvectors.com. (2018). *Burger Vector*. [online] Available at: http://www.allvectors.com/burger-vector/ [Accessed 18 Mar. 2018].
74. Oxford Dictionaries | English. (2018). *Intuition - Definition of Intuition in English | Oxford Dictionaries*. [online] Available at: https://en.oxforddictionaries.com/definition/intuition [Accessed 18 Mar. 2018].
75. Starr, J. (2008). *The Coaching Manual*. 1st ed. Harlow, England: Pearson Prentice Hall.
76. Kohn, A. (2011). Feel-Bad Education: And Other Contrarian Essays on Children and Schooling. Boston, Mass.: Beacon.
77. GOV.UK (2017). *DVSA ADI1 Standard Operating Procedure*. [online] Driver and Vehicle Standards Agency. Available at: https://www.gov.uk/government/publications/guidance-for-driving-examiners-carrying-out-instructor-tests-adi1 [Accessed 1 Feb. 2018].
78. Robosoul.co.uk. (2018). *Robosoul Apps for Driving Instructors by Neil Beaver*. [online] Available at: http://www.robosoul.co.uk/reflective.html [Accessed 18 Mar. 2018].
79. GOV.UK (2017). *DVSA ADI1 Standard Operating Procedure*. [online] Driver and Vehicle Standards Agency. Available at: https://www.gov.uk/government/publications/guidance-for-driving-examiners-carrying-out-instructor-tests-adi1 [Accessed 1 Feb. 2018].
80. Apple.com. (2017). *Apple (UK) — Education — Real Stories — Jeanne Halderson*. [online] Available at: https://www.apple.com/uk/education/real-stories/jeanne-halderson/ [Accessed 18 Mar. 2018].
81. Honey, P. and Mumford, A. (1989). *Learning Styles Questionnaire*. Organization Design and Development, Incorporated.
82. Vark-learn.com. (2018). *VARK | A Guide to Learning Preferences*. [online] Available at: http://vark-learn.com/ [Accessed 18 Mar. 2018].
83. Advanceddrivingtraining.co.uk. (2018). *Advanced Driving Days with Chris Gilbert*. [online] Available at: http://www.advanceddrivingtraining.co.uk/ [Accessed 18 Mar. 2018].

84. Whitmore, J. (2002). *Coaching for Performance*. 1st ed. London: Nicholas Brealey.
85. Gibbs, G. (1988). *Learning by Doing*. 1st ed. [London]: FEU.
86. Pransky, J. (2011). *Somebody Should Have Told Us!* 1st ed. Terrace, B.C.: CCB Pub., p.9.
87. Oxford Dictionaries | English. (2018). *Belief — Definition of Belief in English | Oxford Dictionaries*. [online] Available at: https://en.oxforddictionaries.com/definition/belief [Accessed 18 Mar. 2018].
88. Hamilton, D. (2014). *David R Hamilton PhD | Does Your Brain Distinguish Real from Imaginary?* [online] David R Hamilton PhD. Available at: http://drdavidhamilton.com/does-your-brain-distinguish-real-from-imaginary/ [Accessed 18 Mar. 2018].
89. Beck, A. (1976). *Cognitive Therapy and the Emotional Disorders*. 1st ed. New York: International Universities Press.
90. Ellis, A. (1957). Rational Psychotherapy and Individual Psychology. *Journal of Individual Psychology*, 13(1), p.38. Available at: https://search.proquest.com/openview/3daf7b0bbaf357bfc538a15d736f25b3/1?pq-origsite=gscholar&cbl=1816607 [Accessed 18 Mar. 2018].
91. Smith, H. (2000). *What Matters Most*. 1st ed. New York: Simon & Schuster.
92. Jonathanpassmore.com. (2018). *Jonathan Passmore, Professor, Leading Psychologist, Author, International Speaker*. [online] Available at: http://www.jonathanpassmore.com/ [Accessed 18 Mar. 2018].
93. Urban Dictionary. (2018). *Mood Hoover*. [online] Available at: https://www.urbandictionary.com/define.php?term=mood%20hoover [Accessed 18 Mar. 2018].
94. Beck, A. (1976). *Cognitive Therapy and the Emotional Disorders*. 1st ed. New York: International Universities Press.
95. Ellis, A. (1962). *Reason and Emotion in Psychotherapy*. 1st ed. New York: Stuart.
96. Whitten, H. (2011). *Cognitive Behavioural Coaching Techniques for Dummies*. 1st ed. Hoboken: John Wiley & Sons.
97. YouTube. (2018). *Wayne Dyer — When You Change the Way You Look at Things*. [online] Available at: https://youtu.be/urQPraeeY0w [Accessed 18 Mar. 2018].
98. YouTube. (2018). *George Carlin — Idiot and Maniac*. [online] Available at: https://youtu.be/XWPCE2tTLZQ [Accessed 18 Mar. 2018].
99. Hogg, M. and Vaughan, G. (2005). *Social Psychology*. 1st ed. New York: Prentice Hall.
100. Pattakos, A. and Dundon, E. (2010). Prisoners of Our Thoughts: Viktor Frankl's Principles for Discovering Meaning in Life and Work. 3rd ed. Berrett-Koehler.
101. Brodsky, W. (2002). The effects of music tempo on simulated driving performance and vehicular control. *Transportation Research, Part F: Traffic Psychology and Behaviour*, 4, 219–241.

References

[102] Brodsky, W., & Slor, Z. (2013). Background music as a risk factor for distraction among young-novice drivers. *Accident Analysis & Prevention, 59,* 382-393.

[103] Olson, R., Bocanegra, J., Hanowski, J. and Hickman, J. (2009). *Driver Distraction in Commercial Vehicle Operations.* [online] U.S. Department of Transportation, p.99. Available at: https://www.fmcsa.dot.gov/sites/fmcsa.dot.gov/files/docs/DriverDistractionStudy.pdf [Accessed 18 Mar. 2018].

Printed in Great Britain
by Amazon